Food, Culture & History

Food

Culture & History

VOLUME I

EDITED BY

Gerald Mars & Valerie Mars

THE LONDON FOOD SEMINAR

1993

BOSPHORUS BOOKS
Publishers & Booksellers
Ⓖ
Box 3452 ♦ 3 Ridge Road
Groton Long Point, CT 06340 ♦ USA
Tel & Fax: 203♦536♦2540

For
Alan Davidson
with gratitude

ISBN 0 9521746 0 X

ISSN 1350–4800

Published in July 1993 by The London Food Seminar
53 Nassington Road, London NW3 2TY, United Kingdom
Telephone 071 794 4442
Fax 071 431 6339

Printed and bound in Great Britain by Hartnolls Limited
Set in Galliard by Tony Kitzinger
Designed by Gillian Riley
Copy-edited by Chloe Chard, with Cathy Dean

Contents

Contents

Contributors

CHLOE CHARD, PhD is a freelance writer and lecturer. Much of her academic work is concerned with travel writing and the representation of the foreign: she is currently writing a book entitled *Pleasure and Guilt on the Grand Tour*. Among her publications is a critical edition of Ann Radcliffe's Gothic novel *The Romance of the Forest* (1791), published by Oxford University Press in the series 'The World's Classics' (1986).

ANDREW DALBY, PhD, a lapsed classicist, came back to ancient history (and to a special interest in Greek food) through observing the similarities between classical Mediterranean and modern South-East Asian culinary cultures. He was a founder member of the London Food Seminar and is working with Sally Grainger on a wide-ranging book on the food of early Greece and Rome.

NICOLA HUDSON, PhD, wrote a thesis entitled 'Food: a suitable subject for Roman verse satire.' She has published a chapter in *Exeter Studies in History: satire* and is currently working as a video producer/director and freelance writer.

ALISON JAMES, PhD, is Lecturer in Applied Anthropology at the University of Hull. She has written on children's food preferences and practices, representations of chocolate in the British diet and the ideologies associated with organic food.

VALERIE MARS is a founder member of the London Food Seminar and has written numerous papers on food in its social context. At present she is writing up a PhD in social history at Leicester University, a study that uses methods and concepts from social anthropology to study Victorian Domestic Dining.

GERALD MARS, PhD, a founder member of The London Food Seminar, is an anthropologist. He has published a number of books and a variety of papers on different aspects of food and drink and he is currently Visiting Professor at the Universities of Cranfield and Brunel.

SRI OWEN was born in West Sumatra and has a degree in English from Gajah Mada University, where she also lectured. She came to London with her English husband, worked for many years as a broadcaster with the BBC Indonesian Section, and has published 6 cookery books, with at least two more on the way.

She is particularly interested in contemporary developments in Indonesian food habits and culture.

GILLIAN RILEY read history at Cambridge and is now a free-lance book designer and food historian, with a particular interest in Italian food.

JANE ROWLANDSON, PhD, is a Lecturer in Ancient History at Kings College London, with research interests in Greek and Egyptian social history. This article results from the cross-fertilization of her academic pursuits with her favourite leisure activity.

MALCOLM THICK is an agricultural historian who has written mainly on market gardening in England in early modern times. He has now widened his interest in vegetables to study their use as food in this period. He is also a tax inspector.

SORAYA TREMAYNE, PhD, is an anthropologist. She has carried out fieldwork in Europe and the Middle and Far East and has published for and currently researches at: The Centre For Cross-Cultural Research, Queen Elizabeth House, Oxford .

JOHN WILKINS, PhD, a Lecturer in Classics at Exeter University, has published on Greek drama and food in antiquity. He recently completed a commentary (with Shaun Hill) on Europe's earliest-surviving recipe book, *The Life of Luxury* by Archestratus, and is currently completing a book on food in ancient Greek comedy.

8

Preface
a note on the London Food Seminar

THE London Food Seminar owes its origins to The Second International Food Congress held at Istanbul in 1988, where concern was expressed at the lack of any regular forum in Britain that brought together scholars from different backgrounds and disciplines who were actively researching on the cultural and historical contexts of food. The Seminar was established that same year and has met six times a year since then. Though it meets in London, its members are widely dispersed.

Not all Seminar members are represented in this collection, but all members have given papers and commented on each other's work. This is essentially, therefore, a collective offering, as indeed is its production and distribution. Gillian Riley designed the volume, Chloe Chard copy-edited most of the papers, while Andrew Dalby assisted with the editing. In addition to the contributors, other members of the Seminar are: Joan Alcock, Maggie Black, Elizabeth Gabay, Emily Gowers, Sally Grainger, Abed Jaber, Peter Mitchell, Anne Williams and David Woodman.

Introduction
Food in culture and history

CHOICES are rarely random, and particularly so with food. The power of food arises not only because ideas about food are shared ideas, and therefore reflect their social contexts, but because they also help to construct them.

These shared variations – and the cultures in which they are set – are the subjects of this collection. Each contribution offers new insights into a different culture's unique use of its food, and in doing so illumines key aspects of its social organisation and values: power, authority, and coercion; competitive prestige and its drive to fad, fashion and display, satirical views of the other, attitudes to time, place and gender are all highlighted through food.

Though the ways in which food can be used are varied, they are also uniquely adaptable, and their impact delicately adjustable. Food is used to separate one group from another, often through satire or taboo, but food also bonds people; it maintains both sides of a boundary whilst variations in obtaining, preparing and serving food can subtly emphasise differences and distinctions within cultures, just as it can within households. And of course, food is a major and universal influence in the training and socialising of children. It is for these reasons that the study of food is so important. In understanding how a culture uses its food we have a unique key to understanding aspects of that culture[1] that are obtainable in no other way. These are big claims to make for the study of food but we hope to justify them.

Humans share the need for food with the rest of the animal world but this kinship is a limited one. As it has been pertinently put, 'food is not

1. Mary Douglas covers many of these points in 'Standard Social Uses of Food', in *Food in the Social Order, Studies of Food and Festivities in Three American Communities*, Russell Sage Foundation, (New York, 1984), pp. 1–39. See also Stephen Mennell, Anne Murcot and Anneke H. van Otterloo, *The Sociology of Food*, Sage Publications, (London, 1992).

feed' Though the biological drive to repetitive eating is the basis of its social potency, this alone is not enough: human cultures, unlike animal groupings, have everywhere loaded, encrusted and elaborated upon the biological need to eat with socially derived and culturally validated rituals and symbolic repertoires. It is this mixture of nature and culture that gives food such power.

Breakfast, lunch, dinner and snacking,[2] to choose our own culture's food-taking, are never just food events, they are also social events (and for some people antisocial events!) that mark out the day, every day, and determine how and with whom we spend it and the degree of formality considered appropriate to it. And it is not just the reiterative daily food cycle that uses food to add form to people's lives. Food also operates at weekly, seasonal and calendrical levels, so that not only the week and the season but the year itself is divided up through food. Thus eating, in dividing the year and marking the calendar, gives form to otherwise amorphous time. Using food to mark out time is indeed one of the few cultural universals. But food is also used to mark out significant lifetime events. Rites of passage, such as christenings, comings of age, wedding feasts and funeral wakes, which convert and impose stages of individual development onto the social scene, invariably do so through the giving and accepting of food[3] – through the creation of obligations and the binding needs of reciprocity that these involve.

It is this recursive feature of human food-taking then, together with its socially determined symbolic embellishments, its inclusions and exclusions, and its bonding through gift-giving and receiving, that gives food its power to emphasise the key aspects of a culture. As these papers demonstrate, for instance, in serving to mark out hierarchical and gender differences, food does not just mark them in a routine and stereotypical form but possesses the power to adjust the degrees of emphasis that particular situations demand. Food use is not just a passive reflector of what is going on: it is a potent way of asserting change in a culture as that culture moves through time.

2. Mary Douglas and Michael Nicod, 'Taking the Biscuit, the structure of British Meals', *New Society*, 30 (1974), pp. 744–7.

3. A. van Gennep, *Rites of Passage*, (Routledge and Kegan Paul, London, 1960).

Some problems in the use of historical ethnography

If the study of eating is so important in understanding society, why then should it have been so long neglected? Why should there have been a comparative silence about ordinary domestic routines that have caused them to be regarded as unworthy of serious scholarship? Here we have a paradox: it is easier to ignore the most basic and routine in everyday existence than to observe and value their opposites. It is the very repetitive nature of food-taking that makes it invisible; after a time one stops noticing the repetitious by virtue of its very repetition: bread and butter concerns are more readily negated than banquets.

Understanding the social role of food in earlier times presents further problems: not only is eating ephemeral but present scholars' sources, the contemporary recorders of previous foodways, were in their turn just as likely to have ignored the routine aspects of their eating. And further, what emerges from the past is essentially arbitrary, fragmentary and, therefore, not wholly representative. Nonetheless we have to make do, not with ideal evidence but with the best evidence obtainable. As several of our contributors show, even small fragments can prove highly illuminating.

Despite the ubiquity of food, the study of food in its different contexts has not received the attention it justifies. And if this is in part because its concerns are not readily captured within any one academic discipline, this collection need make no apology for its diversity.

GERALD MARS
VALERIE MARS
London 1993

13

I

Food in contemporary cultures

Food and the Fellwalker
the symbolism of eating in wild places

JANE ROWLANDSON

Introduction: the problem of mountain food in life and literature

Those who walk and climb mountains have an immediate interest in the subject of food, because of the practical difficulties involved in its provision and preparation. At precisely the time they are engaged in extra physical effort, and need to eat well to replace the energy expended, the availability of food is seriously limited by what can be carried and cooked in remote conditions. The ideal qualities of food in these circumstances are easily listed: it should weigh little before cooking, be highly nourishing in both energy and vitamins, require minimal preparation and cooking time, leave no organic waste; and, perhaps most important, it must be good to eat, capable of restoring the spirits on pitching one's tent on a sodden hillside in a gale. Of course, no food has all these qualities, so it becomes a game of cunning for walkers to find the nearest approximation to their ideal. In such straitened circumstances, the approaches and solutions they adopt to this problem gain a wider, anthropological interest, revealing much about attitudes to food, both those shared by the culture as a whole, and those which mark individual preference.[1]

Since the beginnings of mountain walking as a recreation, food has been subject to the same tendency manifested in all mountain equip-

1. This paper is based on personal experience and reading for pleasure over many years, and I cannot claim to be aware of all the relevant academic or mountaineering literature. I have, however, documented statements to the best of my knowledge. I wish to thank in particular Gerald Mars for his persistence in persuading me to write the paper up; Andrew Dalby for the reference to Schuchat, and for first alerting me to the insights food offers to observers of human behaviour; and Michael Roberts for criticism and references.

ment, that of increasing specialisation. Early mountaineers could draw on the foods used for centuries by all long-distance travellers (dried biscuits, salted meat, pemmican),[2] as well as on tins, a more recent innovation.[3] After the Second World War, army surplus gear and army ration packs were adopted by mountain walkers, despite their weight. But the growth of consumerism and prosperity since the nineteen-sixties has led to the development of special foods, parallel to the special materials like Goretex for waterproofs. Both food and clothing are bought at specialist outdoor shops, mostly located in cities, which charge premium prices.

As with other equipment, the paradigm of food for mountain walkers is provided by the provisioning of expeditions to the Himalayas, the Polar regions and similarly inhospitable areas, an association proudly commemorated on packets of Kendal Mint Cake. The written accounts of Everest expeditions by Chris Bonington and others devote considerable attention to food provision, partly because manufacturers have to be thanked for donating their products but primarily because tolerable cuisine undoubtedly plays a crucial part in maintaining morale, and thus in enabling an expedition to succeed. A sixteen-page Appendix on food to *Annapurna South Face* makes its centrality clear:

It was only the thought of the Crunchie bar you were going to consume at the top of the next fixed rope, and of the elaborate five-course meal that you would prepare when you returned to the tent, that kept you going. Food was the consuming passion and obsession of the expedition, and if members were not actually engaged in eating it or getting rid of it, from one end or the other, they would be talking of it or dreaming of it.[4]

Food thus also plays a prominent role in W.E. Bowman's clever parody of mountaineering literature, *The Ascent of Rum Doodle*:

Pong was crouched over a large stewpan, from which emerged indescribable odours. The ground in front of the tent was littered with empty food tins, and Constant had ascertained that their contents had been those special delicacies which we had chosen to attract the high altitude palate. And when it appeared,

2. Tannahill, *Food in History*[2], Chapter 16, 224–9; Schuchat, 'Camping food in America', 159–60.

3. Tannahill, 310–1.

4. Chris Bonington, *Annapurna South Face*, Appendix D (pp. 260–76: written by Mike Thompson), at p. 260.

the loathsome mess confirmed his forebodings. All our choicest tit-bits had gone into Pong's awful pot; our luscious breast of chicken, the tinned apricots and cream which we had so often tasted in anticipation, the sardines, the caviar, the lobster, the lovely gruyère cheese, the pickled walnuts, the curry, the salmon, even the coffee and the chocolate biscuits: all were reduced to a nauseating brew which might have sent Macbeth's witches shrieking from the place.[5]

However exaggerated, this passage perfectly encapsulates the distaste with which both mountaineers and hillwalkers frequently regard their own (or their companions') culinary efforts.

A case study: the Scottish Highlands

My personal experience of mountain walking is confined to the British Isles. But the Scottish Highlands provide an apt example of the problems of eating in the mountains, because for a number of reasons food can be surprisingly difficult to obtain there. Firstly, habitation throughout the mountainous interior of northern Scotland is extremely sparse; there are very few significant villages and even single shops are often over fifty miles apart. Thus those on foot can easily get into difficulties over supplies unless they know exactly what is available and where.

Secondly, the highland population traditionally subsisted on a restricted diet and limited range of foodstuffs, the result of poor agricultural productivity combined with inaccessibility, especially to land transport. Until recently, the west coast and islands obtained most of their supply of items which could not be produced locally by sea, from Glasgow. In contrast to southern Scotland, the western Highlands had no tradition of baking bread; sliced bread from Glasgow was the normal fare. The local population had little surplus produce to sell to incomers; nor, until the spread of camping and caravanning in the nineteen-sixties, would there have been a significant demand for such produce.[6]

5. p. 82. Compare the seven-course dinner enjoyed by the Annapurna expedition at Camp III: 'Olives and smoked Austrian cheese; Tukte's bread (baked at Base Camp) and pâté de foie gras; Thick onion soup and croûtons ...; Fried pork, fried new potatoes and surprise peas; Fruit salad and cream; Christmas pudding Boysen flambé; Coffee with whisky and cream.' (*Annapurna South Face*, p. 273).

6. The more positive treatment of the traditional Highland diet in Annette Hope's excellent book, *A Caledonian Feast*, includes the food of the aristocracy and the

Thus the cyclists and walkers who explored the Highlands in the nineteen-thirties were reliant upon whatever foods they brought with them, or could manage to obtain, with little regard to variety or balance in the diet. Tom Weir writes of his youthful excursions with a friend who worked in a Glasgow butcher's shop: 'we travelled light, no spare clothes except socks; no tent, no tins, only tea and sugar and lots of butcher meat, steak, chops and special beef sausages.'[7] My father in the nineteen-thirties subsisted for a week at a Youth Hostel on Loch Torridon almost entirely on eggs, tinned pineapple and tea. Even to-day, milk can be surprisingly scarce and expensive (locals, if they keep a cow, barely supply their own needs). In the various general stores, and even in villages such as Mallaig and Kyle of Lochalsh, the shrivelled appearance of fruit bears testimony to the distance it has travelled, while 'exotic' foods, including green peppers, would probably be un-obtainable.[8]

The final reason why food provision on Scottish mountains poses a particular problem lies in the traditionally individualistic and unorgan-ised character of British mountain walking. In contrast, the Alpine routes are scattered with mountain huts, which in many parts provide food as well as accommodation, while in the U.S.A., walking tends to be focused on trails, fixed routes through totally uninhabited territory. On such routes, walkers are obliged to rely primarily on dried foods; they need to carry supplies for up to a fortnight.[9] The organised routes which are becoming more popular in Britain pose no such problem in provisioning; even the West Highland Way (from Glasgow to Fort William) regularly intersects with roads, allowing daily access to shops, cafes or hotels.

But a significant proportion of the campers who frequent the High-

---

produce of the more fertile eastern counties. Even so, the predominant ingredients of her recipes are game, fish, oatmeal, and potatoes. On the history of the Scottish diet, see also Gibson and Smout, 'Scottish food and Scottish history, 1500–1800'.

7. *Tom Weir's Scotland*, p. 12.

8. These comments are not intended to reflect on the quality of food served in hotels in the highlands, where proprietors often go to considerable lengths to supplement good local produce with supplies regularly obtained from Inverness or by mail order.

9. See for instance the letter by Mike Gelder in *The Great Outdoors*, July 1987, 68–9, referring to provisioning on the John Muir Trail.

lands resist 'official' routes, and make their own plans, whether walking over distances, or staying in one area to climb its mountains. In either case, it is necessary to carry at least three or four days' food, plus extra for emergencies. One organised annual event, the Great Outdoors Challenge,[10] leaves participants free to plan their own route across the Highlands from the west to the east coast. Responsibility for all other aspects of planning, including of course food supply, also lies with the individual participants, although novices may receive advice (including warnings about the infrequency of shops) from the organisers.

Another common ambition is to climb all the 'Munros', mountains over 3000 feet high, many of which are situated miles from any public road. While this can be achieved entirely by single-day routes, it is certainly more economical of time and effort, and for many people more satisfying generally, to tackle groups of nearby mountains on multi-day expeditions. An early attempt to climb all in a single continuous walk failed partly because of dietary deficiencies; the first person successfully to accomplish the feat, Hamish Brown, was justifiably proud of his meticulous arrangements for maintaining a healthy and appetising diet for four strenuous months.[11] Martin Moran's subsequent completion of the 'Munros' within a single winter was equally dependent on careful planning of menus, a strategy particularly necessary because he eats no meat.[12]

These prolonged walks represent in the most extreme form the problems of food supply posed by the Scottish mountains; but even fellwalkers of more modest ambition still need to plan their food provision

10. Formerly the Ultimate Challenge. Participants' accounts of their experiences are published annually in the November issue of *TGO*.

11. *Hamish's Mountain Walk*, passim, but especially Appendix II, 342–3. The earlier failure by Brian and Alan Ripley is discussed on pp. 25–6.

12. *The Munros in Winter*, especially 211–3; here Moran mentions a further case of Munro malnutrition: 'Rick Ansell was so plagued by hunger on his non-stop walk of the mainland Munros that he was driven to searching for discarded "half-eaten butties" around the summit cairns. Coming off Beinn Sgulaird, Rick was convinced of suffering hallucinations from hunger when an apple, a cake and three Opal Fruits appeared on the side of the track with a sign "Please Eat" attached, but amazingly the wayside offering proved genuine'! (p. 212). Craig Caldwell's constant diet of dehydrated food and chocolate on his successful year-long completion of both 'Munros' and 'Corbetts' (mountains over 2500 feet) seems to have led to delayed viral syndrome; *Climb Every Mountain*, 359–60.

according to their own individual routes, and cannot rely on easy access to shops for replenishing their supplies. How do they resolve these problems?

Moral discourses: the confusion of nature and culture

Almost inevitably one is faced with a choice between 'real food' and packets of lightweight dehydrated meals. This dilemma is not new; one vintage mountaineering handbook warns:

> The choice of unappetizing foods, those concentrated and vitaminous concoctions which are often offensive to the stomach and nose alike, is not an indication of human toughness but of indescrimination. At huts and in camps the nearer the diet gets to epicurism the better ..... Good food-consciousness is an important attribute of the happy mountaineer. Let those who love *hard-tack* devour the awful stuff; in the presence of bacon and eggs, steak and chips or macaroni cheese any hut pemmican is psychologically disastrous.[13]

Yet even so, the handbook sanctions the use of concentrated foods in bivouacs.

Packeted dehydrated food is undoubtedly useful for mountain walkers who wish to carry more than a couple of days' food supply. But even here, there is no ideal product; brands devised especially for mountaineering use (Raven Brand, for example) are more calorific but also heavier and much more expensive than brands like 'Beanfeast' sold in the supermarket. It is also advisable to experiment a little before setting off for the mountains; a wild night in a remote part of Skye is not the best place to discover that the reconstituted omelette, with which one hopes to restore mind and body, cannot by any means whatever be prised away from the cooking pot. On the other hand, one must not be too fussy; a meal which tastes utterly inedible in the comfort of one's kitchen may become a highlight of gourmet experience after its ingredients have been carried in a rucksack over several mountains. Thus cookery writing for campers needs to be a highly specialised branch of the genre.

13. J.E.B.Wright, *The Technique of Mountaineering*, (3rd ed., 1964), 179–80; the first edition was published in 1955, and Wright's practical guiding experience stretched back to 1924.

There are books which cater for this need,[14] but advice on food is also regularly found in the various magazines devoted to hillwalking, such as *The Great Outdoors*, already mentioned. A consideration of the way food has been treated in these magazines over the last decade offers interesting parallels to more general trends in attitudes to food. Often much more is being conveyed to the reader than mere practical advice. Food can be a fruitful source of amusing anecdotes, such as the caution-ary tale of an inexperienced group who carried five pounds of potatoes for a week around Dartmoor, but never found the energy to peel and cook them.[15] Food as a symbol or demonstration of general hillwalking competence occurs in practice as well as in the literature, as we shall see later.

Even the articles which explicitly offer advice are frequently imbued with strong moral overtones. Underlying much undoubtedly useful advice is the assumption that we are all overweight; and too often the nutritional nostrums of the nineteen-eighties were simply repeated, without considering how far they needed modification in the context of hillwalking. 'Three major enemies include fat, sugar and salt'[16] is hardly specifically relevant to the problems of eating in the mountains; indeed this might be one context where a relatively high intake of all three would be appropriate. Equally the advice to beginners, 'The method of cooking is important; it is preferable to grill, boil or bake rather than to fry',[17] and the suggestion to try a foil-wrapped baked potato, may be useful for day walkers preparing food in the kitchen before setting out; but it unhelpful for the novice camper who really has little choice of cooking method: place all ingredients together in a single pan and add enough water to prevent it congealing on the bot-tom. In my experience, frying food in the wild is undesirable less for medical reasons (with their moral overtones of self-indulgence), than because it is tiresome to clean the pan afterwards without detergent and plentiful hot water.

Much of the advice given in the articles during the nineteen-eighties apparently reflected the discovery by their authors (all experienced walkers and climbers, and predominantly male) of the latest nutritional

14. For instance, Kevin Walker, *Wild Country Camping*, 109–21 (no actual recipes); Frederick Tingey, *The Open Air Cookbook*.

15. *TGO*, May 1987, p. 70.   16. *TGO*, August 1985, p. 54.   17. *TGO*, July 1989, p. 58.

theory, rather than an appreciation of the specific kinds of advice a novice walker might find helpful. After all, an aspiring hillwalker may already possess a highly developed knowledge of nutrition, but may need to be warned that wholemeal quiche requires very careful wrapping if it is to survive even half a day in a rucksack. It is interesting to see that, more recently, a greater realism seems to have emerged; survey articles on food seem largely to have ceased, while *The Great Outdoors* has started a regular monthly section of recipes sent in by readers. These place a firm emphasis on practicality: witness the 'Almost Indestructible Biscuits' recommended as an accompaniment to Duke of Edinburgh Award expeditions.[18]

Another feature of walking magazines in the nineteen-eighties which has now apparently been overtaken by changing sensibilities is the advertisement of 'instant' dishes like Pot Noodle, or the more specialist Hotcan ('Everything you need to prepare a delicious hot meal ... anytime, anywhere ... the ultimate convenience meal').[19] Quite apart from what one might think about the taste or nutritional value of such food, it also leaves a singularly inconvenient amount of inorganic waste material which must be carried around until one reaches 'civilization' again. The advertisers presumably became aware of the inappropriateness of their product to a market increasingly sensitive to the problem of waste in 'wilderness' areas. It is rapidly becoming thought unacceptable for walkers to leave any waste at all behind them, even deeply buried tin cans, or items which are degradable in the long term, such as paper and fruit peel.

But in the heyday of its promotion as the solution to the fellwalker's dilemma, Pot Noodle was responsible to rousing the doyen of Scottish mountain walking, Hamish Brown, to heights of literary indignation far exceeding the remarks of J.E.B. Wright on pemmican quoted earlier. Brown castigates the additives in dehydrated food as detrimental to health; but the core of his objection is to the unnatural character of these foods: 'Outdoor enthusiasts of all people one would expect to be keen on uncontaminated foods. Why not build plastic peaks, line the West Highland Way with synthetic heather and add blue dye to Wind-

18. *TGO*, May 1992, p. 27.
19. Advertised, for example, in *TGO*, January 1986, p. 56.

ermere?'[20] Why not indeed? After all, we already build bridges across streams, and keep footpaths through the mountains in repair – and men did so for centuries before hillwalking became a leisure pursuit.

Thus the moral vehemence of this objection to dehydrated foods for walkers goes far beyond what one would expect from the undoubted practical limitations of these foods. Rather it seems to stem from an insecurity about where the boundaries between the natural and the synthetic are to be drawn; a reluctance to acknowledge that in Britain particularly, no landscape is wholly unadulterated by man, just as there is no completely 'natural' food; food is a cultural artefact. The desire to escape from civilization lies at the heart of many people's love of hillwalking; it is therefore profoundly unsettling to be reminded, as we tip our evening meal from its packet, that precisely those elements of civilization we most despise have accompanied us, polluting the wild places both physically and symbolically.

Of course we cannot escape from our culture simply by walking into the mountains. 'Natural landscapes' are themselves products of cultural definition, and their preservation involves constant human intervention.[21] Nevertheless, in the seclusion of the mountains, our cultural norms can be modified or manipulated in certain ways, and here again food offers a perspective on, and insights into, human behaviour patterns in general.

Solutions to the problem: ingenuity, competence and competitiveness

The kind of individualistic fellwalking under consideration here is ostensibly non-competitive; even in the Great Outdoors Challenge, entrants set their own targets (which differ widely in character and difficulty), and are free to depart from them, so long as they fulfil the minimum requirement of going entirely on foot from one coast of Scotland within the allotted sixteen days. The emphasis is on individual enjoyment, not on quantifying achievement.

20. *TGO*, April 1987, p. 79.

21. Compare Schuchat's conclusions, 166–7; but she does not appear to find anything problematical in this erosion of the boundary between 'nature' and 'culture'.

Walking is also a relatively classless activity. Although items of equipment such as tents and cagoules are by no means cheap, the scale of expenditure better reflects a person's commitment to walking as a hobby than his or her overall wealth. House, address, car, job, have all been left far behind; in a chance encounter on the hill, walkers' identities are signified only by the few items of clothing and equipment they are actually carrying with them. And these items, superficially at least, tend to present a remarkably homogeneous appearance. Even accent, in other contexts often a give-away, has different connotations for practitioners of a recreation which can be enjoyed only in regions of Britain remote from the heartland of Received Pronunciation. In the mountains, all are equal.

But beneath the surface ethos of friendly egalitarianism, subtle forms of competitiveness subsist. The member of a party who, having completed the day's walk, arrives back first at the tent, and has a brew of tea waiting for the others as they straggle in, has earned more than mere gratitude.

When strangers meet on the hill, sociable enquiries about the day's route may conceal an unspoken desire to emerge the tougher hillwalker. Meanwhile, each person silently assesses all visible signs of the other's experience and competence; boots can be particularly informative. More prolonged conversation is likely to turn to explicit discussion of the relative merits of items of equipment. Anyone who dares to admit that his cagoule leaks, that his rucksack has become impregnated with cooking fuel, and that his sleeping bag is soaking wet and is anyway quite inadequate for the weather conditions, will be the object of much derision once he has passed out of hearing distance.

The experience of camping in proximity to others offers much more scope for unexpressed competition, and here food plays a prominent role. The contents of other parties' cooking pots are scrutinised with intense, even overt, interest; nor is it wholly unacceptable to ask directly what someone is cooking. Camping etiquette does not demand that food should be shared in normal circumstances; each person remains entirely responsible for his or her own meal unless explicitly and spontaneously invited to partake of an unexpected surplus.[22] Advice

22. As in the example cited above in note 12.

and expertise, on the other hand, are shared freely; they weigh nothing, and the distribution of a good idea enhances the giver's prestige.

Hardiness and competence are not the only goals, however. The person who climbs Munro after Munro while eating only uncooked food is generally admired, but not so regularly emulated. Most respected of all is the combination of competence with ingenuity in reducing the pervasive discomforts of camping conditions; any fantasies about escaping from civilization to the purity of nature soon recede in face of the reality of downpours, midges, mud and stony ground. Some hillwalkers take the challenge of maintaining a civilized existence in such circumstances to great lengths, even pressing their clothes daily with stones heated on the cooking stove.

Given the very real problem of maintaining any kind of appetising diet when every ingredient has to be carried on one's back, the scope for ingenuity is unlimited, as is the range of individual preference. Some walkers aspire to reproduce French cuisine (accompanied by wine) on mountain summits; others prefer to descend to the valley to dine more traditionally on soup, meat and two vegetables, and pudding and custard (several packets a day for this!). Hamish Brown is noted for recommending Moroccan dishes;[23] indeed cous-cous is very suitable for adaptation to the hillwalker's menu. My own advice would be to take a supply of garlic and dried herbs to the mountains of Scotland's fjord-like west coast, where mussels are the one food a hillwalker can realistically hope to gather from the wild. What could be more civilized than a dish of freshly-gathered mussels after a hard day on the hill, watching the sun sink slowly to the horizon – at least until the midges too come out for their evening meal?

Bibliography

Chris Bonington, *Annapurna South Face* (London: Cassell, 1971)

W.E.Bowman, *The Ascent of Rum Doodle* (London: Arrow Books, 1983; first published Max Parrish, 1956)

Hamish Brown, *Hamish's Mountain Walk* (London: Victor Gollancz, 1978)

Craig Caldwell, *Climb Every Mountain* (London: Sphere Books, 1991)

A. Gibson and T.C.Smout, 'Scottish food and Scottish history, 1500–1800', in

23. e.g. *TGO*, April 1987, p. 75; August 1989, pp. 21–2.

Scottish Society 1500–1800, edited by R.A. Houston and I.D. Whyte (Cambridge, Cambridge University Press, 1989), pp. 59–84
Annette Hope, *A Caledonian Feast* (London: Grafton Books, 1989)
Martin Moran, *The Munros in Winter* (Newton Abbot: David and Charles, 1986)
Molly G. Schuchat, 'Camping food in America: finding nature in food?', in *Food Conservation: Ethnological Studies*, edited by Astri Riddervold and Andreas Ropeid (London: Prospect, 1988), pp. 158–68
Reay Tannahill, *Food in History*, second, revised edition (Harmondsworth: Penguin Books, 1988)
Frederick Tingey, *The Open Air Cookbook* (London: Mirador Books, 1987)
Kevin Walker, *Wild Country Camping* (London: Constable, 1989)
Tom Weir, *Tom Weir's Scotland* (Harmondsworth: Penguin Books, 1982)
J.E.B.Wright, *The Technique of Mountaineering*, third edition (London: Nicholas Kaye, 1964)

Piggy in the middle
food symbolism and social relations

ALLISON JAMES

Introduction

CHARLES Dickens wrote in *Great Expectations*: 'Look at pork. There's a subject. If you want a subject, look at pork'.[1] This article rather belatedly takes up his suggestion. It argues that the pig occupies a peculiar and perhaps unique position in cultural attitudes towards animals classed as edible. It allows us to satisfy physiological needs for food, but also to conceptualize particular sets of social relations in British culture. A primary aim, therefore, is to explore in detail some historical and contemporary attitudes towards the pig as a source of meat; a second line of approach is to ask how this relationship between pigs and humans is culturally conceived. That is to say, following Charles and Kerr, this article will show that 'the food we eat and the form that we eat it in... meet many needs that are socially, rather than biologically determined'.[2] What follows, then, is an anthropological, rather than simply gastronomical, account of pigs and pork.

The main substance concerns the historical role of the 'house pig' or 'cottager's pig' in rural communities in Britain. This interest was stimulated by reading some oral history accounts gathered for a research project on rural life, carried out in Northumberland during 1979–80.[3]

Versions of this article have been variously given as talks and lectures over the last ten years. To all those who have listened and offered me their comments and extra source material I am most grateful. I am especially indebted to Jennifer Hockey, Nigel Rapport and Malcolm Young for their perceptive comments and criticisms of the draft versions of this article.

1. Cited in J. Reekie, *British Charcuterie*.

2. N. Charles and M. Kerr, *Women, Food and Families*, p.239.

3. This article draws on oral history material gathered during the Northumberland Village Project, directed by Brendan Quayle, in which research was carried out in six

Amongst the data collected were some vivid and detailed accounts of the importance of the house pig and the drama of pig-killing day in rural communities from about the nineteen-twenties through to the Second World War. Later, stumbling across Kitteringham's account of changing attitudes to the countryside, interest in the topic was rekindled.[4] Kitteringham suggests that attitudes towards killing animals are one index of social change in rural communities and, by way of illustration, cites the accounts of pig-killing in Thomas Hardy's novel *Jude the Obscure*[5] and Flora Thompson's autobiographical narrative *Larkrise to Candleford*.[6] Samuel's later observation that in traditional rural communities 'there was a whole nexus of economic and cultural relationships built around the cottager's pig which no-one has thought it worth paying research attention to'[7] encouraged my interest further and led me to ask others to remember back to times when the house-pig was common.[8] Three more published accounts added to the mounting data about pigs: Walter Rose's recollections of an English village, *Good Neighbours*,[9] John Berger's narrative, *Pig Earth*[10] and Frazer Harrison's *Strange Land*[11] which all have the pig and its demise as central motifs.

The material upon which the analysis is based is drawn, then, from secondary sources, from oral history accounts, a nineteenth-century novel, an autobiography, a narrative, and historical and contemporary commentaries. These constitute a set of accounts, built upon recollections and interpretations of a past event; as such they are both partial

---

local settings during 1979–80. The project focused on the collection of oral traditions, histories and biographies and on exploring change in rural communities. I am indebted to all those who worked on the project as researchers and informants and am particularly beholden to Brendan Quayle for allowing me access to the field material.

4. J. Kitteringham, 'Country girls in 19th century England',in *History Workshop Pamphlets*,11.

5. T. Hardy, *Jude the Obscure*, first published in 1896.

6. F. Thompson, *Larkrise to Candleford*.

7. R. Samuel, 'Village Labour' in *Village Life and Labour*, edited by R. Samuel, p.6.

8. I am grateful to the members of an adult education evening class, held in Northamptonshire, for this oral history account and their many other contributions.

9. W. Rose, *Good Neighbours*.

10. J. Berger, *Pig Earth*.

11. F. Harrison, *Strange Land: the countryside: myth and reality*.

and highly structured. In stressing a particular viewpoint or perspective on the world, however, they are extremely revealing: in the particularity of each rendering nestle the images and motifs and conceptual schemes through which the world was and is perceived. My questioning of these varied accounts begins, therefore, from an interpretative perspective: 'to draw large conclusions from small, but very densely textured facts: to support broad assertions about the role of culture in the construction of collective life by engaging with them exactly as complex specifics'.[12] There is an undoubted duplicity towards the pig in European cultures: one which, as this article will suggest, rests on a conceptualisation of the pig as a mediator between the human and the animal world. Pigs are not known as 'horizontal humans' without reason and, as Mary Douglas has shown, there is something powerful and potentially dangerous about such boundary transgressors.[13] Of these texts, then, I ask: what do they reveal about the historical role of the pig as a source of meat in rural communities and, conversely, what do attitudes towards the pig reveal about social relations in rural European cultures during the past hundred years?

This little pig...

This porcine portrait begins with a brief historical synopsis of the role of the pig as a source of meat, for this was the house pig's primary role in rural European communities in the late nineteenth and early twentieth centuries.

While the pig was to undergo its conversion to a domestic animal relatively late, – records show that this did not occur until the late Neolithic/early Bronze age – it was certainly highly successful, leading Jane Grigson to remark that 'European civilisation – and Chinese civilisation too – has been founded on the pig'.[14] Pork was common in European peasant communities up until the Industrial Revolution, and may have been the only source of meat other than a chicken or rabbit.[15] But what accounts for its popularity?

12. C. Geertz, *The Interpretation of Cultures*, p.28.   13. M. Douglas, *Purity and Danger*.
14. J. Grigson, *Charcuterie and French Pork Cookery, p.7.*
15. R. Tannahill, *Food in History.* J. Reekie, op.cit.

One reason, undoubtedly, is that the pig is not a choosy animal. Amenable to being kept in a variety of conditions and eating almost anything, the pig, as Tannahill notes, is an ideal meat source. For the Chinese, for example, the pig was considered 'small enough to be kept in the house, could be fed on scraps at no cost to its owner, matured at the age of a year, and produced two bountiful litters annually from then on, each consisting of up to a dozen piglets'.[16] Given this perspective on the pig, it is not surprising that 'for the Chinese, the words 'meat' and 'pork' became, and remain synonymous'.[17]

In Europe, the pig was no less popular. The Romans were particularly partial to suckling pig – three to four weeks old – which was served whole at any celebration or banquet. The stuffed intestines would be made to resemble a bed of straw, on which the roasted pig would lie, a practice which, as Reekie notes, bequeathed to the Ancient Britons the 'invaluable art of sausage making'.[18]

The pig's insatiable and fairly indiscriminate appetite meant that pigs could even be kept in towns, as Tannahill notes. In twelfth century Paris pigs roamed the street quite freely, in fifteenth century Frankfurt an edict, which endeavoured to forbid the building of pig sties in towns, proved totally ineffective, and 'even in 19th century New York the wandering hog was still a familiar sight'.[19] As she goes on to remark, 'the urban pig in fact performed a useful function in the days before city cleansing departments, clearing the highways of a good deal of refuse that would otherwise have lain there and rotted'.[20] Having cleaned the streets, the pig could then usefully fill people's stomachs.

The pig's ability to interbreed successfully may also have contributed to its popularity as an animal destined for the table. The first domesticated pig was more like its wild cousin, the boar, having long legs and being quite thin. Later it was bred to grow quite plump, although it was not until Robert Bakewell crossed the Chinese with the British pig in about 1760 that the enormously fat pigs, with lop rather than prick ears, became a late nineteenth century commonplace. At that time fat bacon and meat was particularly appreciated, as William Cobbett noted in 1822:

16. R. Tannahill, ibid., pp.40–1.   17. R. Tannahill, ibid., p.41.

18. J. Reekie, op. cit., p.13.   19. R. Tannahill, op. cit., p.159.   20. R. Tannahill, ibid., p.159.

if a hog be more than a year old he is better for it. Make him fat by all means. If he can walk two or three hundred yards at a time, he is not well fatted. Lean bacon is the most wasteful thing that a family can use. In short it is uneatable except by drunkards who want something to stimulate their sickly appetites.[21]

The contemporary pig has again changed shape. Slimmed down, it has become less fat than the old breeds in order to meet public demand for leaner meat.

The popularity of the pig as a source of meat for the poor lies largely, then, in its biological flexibility:

the animal's prolific fertility, its uniquely economical capacity to convert minimal rations into substantial quantities of meat, the richness of its dung, and the usefulness of every part of its carcase – hide, bristles, bones etc. – had all established it as the animal most capable of being profitably raised by the poorest peasantry.[22]

However, this is not, as Harrison concurs, a sufficient explanation for both past and contemporary European attitudes towards the pig. Why was the pig, as Flora Thompson describes in her memories of an Oxfordshire childhood, 'everybody's pride and everybody's business'[23] when, at the same time, it could serve as a symbol of abuse and a source of disgust? To begin to answer these questions I turn to the various accounts of pig-rearing and killing in rural communities. These suggest that, in its role as a highly economic and necessary source of food, the pig also served to symbolise and facilitate other aspects of the social world in four important ways. In traditional rural communities in Europe, the pig was a symbolic vehicle for a) expressing and affirming the different roles of men and women in the division of labour; b) articulating relationships between an individual family and the wider community; c) expressing social status d) symbolising the nature/culture divide.

This little pig stayed at home

Primarily, of course, the pig's significance for the rural poor of the late nineteenth and early twentieth centuries in Europe lay in its economic

21. Cited in J. Reekie, op.cit., p.17.　22. F. Harrison, op.cit., p.50.
23. F. Thompson, op.cit., p.24.

role. As Flora Thompson remarks, in Oxfordshire during the 1880s, the smell of the pig for the villagers 'was in a sense a healthy smell for them; for a good pig fattening in the sty promised a good winter'.[24] In the Northumbrian villages too, often cut off from the outside world for many months during the winter, the pig provided an invaluable source of meat for the ordinary villager. Later, during the rationing of the Second World War, owning a pig was similarly of great economic value. But this critical nourishing role which the pig played, was elaborated symbolically within traditional rural culture. The pig became what Marshal Sahlins has termed a vehicle of 'practical reason'.[25] In the expressed attitudes and descriptions of actions towards the pig can be seen displayed some of the 'structures of signification' which informed people's lives at that time.[26] Pigs were kept primarily to be eaten but they were thought about, cared for, killed and eaten in particular and culturally significant ways as can be seen in the following description, which draws on accounts from Northumberland, Buckinghamshire, Cambridgeshire, Berkshire and rural France.[27] There seems to have been very little variation.

In rural Northumberland in the early part of the century it was common practice for each labouring family to keep a 'house pig'. A single piglet was purchased in the spring and then kept in a sty at the end of the garden. It would be fed on a mixture of household scraps and waste products such as 'tattie peelings' which were occasionally eked out with extra grain. This meant that even the poorest family could afford to sustain a pig on left-over food and household waste. The house pig was indeed a viable economic proposition. Even when, at lean times of the year, food had to be purchased for the pig, its future as a source of meat outweighed this disadvantage. This view was common as Rose recalls:

Hidden away under the glossy black hair, lay prospective hams, gammons, chines, haseletts, and rearings, not to mention the two flitches of streaky bacon that, later on, would grace the wall of his living room. His heart warmed with genial tolerance; it was good policy to be generous and kind.[28]

24. F. Thompson, ibid., p.24.

25. M. Sahlins, *Culture and Practical Reason.*   26. C. Geertz, op.cit.

27. Thomas Hardy (1839–1928) centred his novels in an imaginary Wessex which corresponds with the counties of Dorset, Berkshire and Wiltshire. *Jude the Obscure* is set in Berkshire.   28. W. Rose, op.cit., p.62.

Throughout the summer months, the pig would be fattened up in preparation for its slaughter at the back-end of the year when winter began to set in. In Northumberland, as one account relates, 'you waited till the flies had passed before you killed your pig' for any 'jumper flies' would spoil the meat. The fatter the pig, the more proud its owners for, at this time, fat bacon was still very much liked. One memorable Northumbrian pig was said to have been six foot long. In Flora Thompson's account, Queenie relishes the size of her pig which she offers sour milk lovingly and remarks: 'can't hardly see out of his eyes, bless him'.[29] A Northumbrian woman talked of the value of keeping pigs during the war when the bacon ration was two ounces a week. Whilst those that kept a pig lost their ration, as she wryly commented, it was 'a poor pig that only weighed 104 ounces'. In Berger's biographical narrative, set in rural France, the size of the pig is similarly something to be admired: it is described as being 'as long as a pew'.[30]

A common saying about the pig, which appears in many of the accounts, is that 'nothing but the squeak was wasted' when a pig was killed. If that could have been found it would also have been used. This lore is substantiated in the following account of pig-killing, described by one Northumbrian woman. It details how every part of the pig was put to some use. First, the pig had to be 'hungered' the day before its slaughter by the local specialist. In Northumberland a man might get a reputation for 'felling' a pig and he would be called in by the family; 'putting a pig down' was a skilful business for, if care was not taken, there was a risk that the meat would not be fit to eat. Indeed, in Hardy's novel it is the late arrival of the pig-killer which drives Jude to attempt the process himself, for he cannot bear the poor creature's crying for food. Traditionally, the pig was 'felled' with a 'mell' – a mallet or a large heavy hammer. When the animal had been stunned in this way, its throat was slit and a bowl placed under to catch the blood. Great care was taken to ensure that every drop of blood was squeezed out. As one Northumbrian informant remarked, 'you've got to be very particular about getting those veins out, that's full o' blood, otherwise they would cake and be more or less apt to go bad'. In Hardy's novel, Arabella urges Jude to let the pig bleed slowly: 'The meat must be well bled, and to do

29. F. Thompson, op.cit., p.39.   30. J. Berger, op.cit., p.36.

that he must die slowly. We shall lose a shilling a score if the meat is red and bloody'.[31] During the second world war, when the rifle or human killer replaced the 'mell' and the pig was shot before its blood was let, it was said that the meat did not taste so good with this method of killing.

The bloodless corpse was then scalded with boiling water and its skin scraped to remove the bristles. Next, it was scalded again until 'a lovely clear white skin' was achieved. Afterwards the pig was hung up to cool all day. At night the carcase was taken down and jointed, the liver, heart and other offal removed. A man who killed many of the pigs in North-umberland describes the process of jointing the meat:

I always cut the pig down and dressed it, the flicks and the hams. It's split down the middle and you have a head-leg and fore-leg on one side and a head-leg and foreleg on the other. And of course you've got to take the head-quarters off, that's what they call the ham... you dress them up. You've got to square your flick up the side of bacon and you can either hang it up to dry just as it is or you can have it rolled.

Each of the joints of meat was rubbed with salt and cured by placing salt petre in the bone joints. The pieces of meat were 'salted away' for about three weeks, although the flitches (the sides) could be removed from the larder slab after a fortnight. In rural Buckinghamshire during the nine-teen-thirties these joints were laid in lead trays, – known as 'the leads' – which were supported on wooden trestles in the larder. The salted pieces of meat would then be washed in cold water and wrapped in clean white sheets to keep off the flies and dust during the rest of the year. These were then hung from the rafters of the kitchen or pantry. As one Northum-brian woman describes them, 'they were our oil paintings'.

Besides the main joints of meat, other pieces of meat were obtained from the pig. These were for more immediate consumption. The pig's feet were sawn off and steeped in water, as one Northumbrian inform-ant describes, for the purpose of getting 'all the smell of the pig' off them.' Only then were they considered clean: 'you just took a big fork and took the cluts off' (the nails). The trotters were then put into cold salt water until ready to be boiled. As one lady remarked, there 'were quite a bit of pickings on them'. The spare ribs were also removed at the time of jointing and would be eaten the next day, either roasted or

31. T. Hardy, op.cit., p.110.

made into spare-rib stovies. Occasionally, bits of liver would be fried for immediate consumption.

The innards of the pig provided further produce. The fat was boiled and rendered down until it turned liquid. It was then strained to remove the 'little crispy bits' (the scratchings). The bladder, which had previously been washed out and steeped in salt water, was then filled with the liquid fat and hung from the ceiling. This lard from the pig lasted well through the winter. Some of the little crispy bits from the lard were saved and put into the black pudding, made from the blood in the bowl. This had to be placed in a pot by the fire and stirred to prevent it curdling. A bit of liver, some pearl barley and about two pints of milk, mint, salt and pepper constituted the other ingredients and it was all boiled together and then cooked in a pie-dish. In Northumberland, grey pudding and white pudding were also made, which 'had everything that was good' in – the heart, the liver and the kidneys, mixed with barley and seasoning and cooked in a similar manner.

However, sausages were made from raw meat. All the bits of meat which could be picked off the bone, the lean bits and the pickings were put through the mincer and mixed with breadcrumbs and sage. The intestines of the pig provided the 'pudding skins'. They were cleaned by steeping in salt water and then scraped to remove the fat. Often this was done with a wine glass; a knife would have been too sharp and may have cut the intestines. When the outside was done, the intestines were turned inside out and the process repeated until the skins were clean and looked like a 'thin type of slinky plastic'. The skins were then attached to a funnel on the end of the mincer, the sausage-filler, and the meat was squashed in. Links were made by twisting the sausages as they fell from the mincer. Finally, the pig's head was used for potted meat. The tongue was removed, scraped and skinned, and also used for potted meat. As one lady remarked, the house-pig 'made a lot of nice food'. Even the bones were thrown out for the hens to pick over. In Buckinghamshire 'bone pie' was made: 'the small bones, on which there was some rather tasty, sweet meat were put into a large pie-dish, seasoned, and covered with a pie-crust made with the fresh lard'. Rose describes a similar practice:

He who has not tasted backbone pie has missed a minor delight. Who can describe the delicious compound of jelly and sweet flesh that lay beneath that homely roof of crust? We always ate them cold, and folk today, who long ago dined with us by chance at such times, still declare that never before nor since have they known such enjoyment.[32]

Pig-killing day was a 'very exciting time' and the whole process – killing, curing, preserving and making sausages – took two days. As one woman commented, 'we never went to bed the night we killed the pig.'

This little pig is a symbol

As the foregoing account suggests, pig-killing was an extremely busy time; it is described in many of the accounts as a ritualised killing. Its prescribed and ordered form was traditional, the precise details of killing, butchering and cooking passed down through the generations. In Hardy's novel, for example, Jude chooses to scald the carcase, rather than singe it, saying that 'I like the way of my own country best'.[33] For Thompson, 'the whole scene, with its mud and blood, flaring lights and dark shadows, was as savage as anything to be seen in an African jungle'.[34] As she goes on to describe, after the killing came the ritual feast: 'at the pig feast there would be no sweet pudding, for that could be had any day, and who wanted sweet things when there was plenty of meat to be had'. The day the pig was killed was special, its ritualised nature underscored by the high degree of consistency between the various accounts.

But rituals are not just about tradition; rather, from an anthropological perspective, what is important about rituals is that they highlight many of the key conceptual structures which inform everyday activities. In ritual, the everyday is writ large and, as Leach depicts it, 'we engage in rituals in order to transmit collective messages to ourselves'.[35] If, as Mary Douglas has shown, deciphering a meal can reveal a set of implicit meanings about social intimacy and the boundaries which order social events,[36] what collective messages do these various accounts of pig-rearing and killing offer us about the nature of social life in traditional rural communities?

32. W. Rose, op.cit., p.67.   33. T. Hardy, op.cit., p.108.
34. F. Thompson, op.cit., p.26.   35. E. Leach, *Culture and Communication*, p.45.
36. M. Douglas, 'Deciphering a Meal' in *Implicit Meanings*, edited by M. Douglas.

One immediate and obvious theme running through the accounts is the emphasis placed upon the gendered division of labour in rural communities. In this sense, the ritualised killing of the pig highlighted traditional distinctions between work done by men and women. The actual killing of the pig was a strictly male domain, carried out by the head of the household or, more usually, by a known 'pig killer' or 'pig sticker'. Although women and children may have looked on, they took no part in the killing. Hardy underlines this in his novel through Jude and Challow's disapproval of Arabella's part in the killing of the pig. The jointing and curing of the pig was also a male task. A Northumbrian man remembers:

I had it all to myself... and of course the womenfolk were waiting of the offals... that's all the dressing that you take off that goes into sausage, potted meat, black pudding or whatever the case may be. That was for woman folk... they attended to that end. They reckoned that it wasn't for a woman to do, not to put a pig away... and she can go with the offals, you know making all that ready.

Men passed the skill of pig-killing from father to son or from man to man. It was a skill much prized:

I used to lay pigs away for different people. They would ask us to go along. Would I come and lay them a pig away? There's a lot of people, you know, they wouldn't tackle that job, You see it's a funny job, laying a pig away. I mean you can lay a dozen pigs away and they can come alright and you might lay one away and the bacon could be spoilt. Now that's a serious thing, if you're laying a pig away for any other body.

Women's skill, on the other hand, lay in the preparation of sausages and puddings, an art also passed down through the generations. Although knowing in principle what was involved in the different activities involved at each stage of killing and preparing the pig, men and women maintained their own spheres of knowledge. It is therefore female informants who provide the most detailed descriptions of making potted meat and puddings; men merely comment that they were made. By contrast, it is men who describe in detail the killing of the pig and the jointing of the meat. In Berger's account, for example, there is a sketch to illustrate the way in which the joints of meat are laid out by the men on the trestle table, 'like a flower bed of pink delphiniums'.[37] While the

37. J.Berger, op.cit., p.57.

male narrator remembers seeing some of the cooking processes during his childhood, he later became estranged from this activity. Describing the making of traditional stuffed cabbage at pig-killing time he remarks: 'when I was younger I had watched her do it. Now I was drinking last year's cider like a man'.[38]

This division of labour was reinforced during the pig-killing ritual through the belief that women could contaminate the raw meat through touch. One Buckinghamshire informant remarked that 'only the men were allowed to do the curing and touch the meat. It was thought that, because women menstruate, the meat would not remain in good condition if any woman came in contact with it before it was pickled'. This is supported in Kitteringham's summary of an old Dorset belief: 'the females of the family would do the cooking and preserving but on no account was a female allowed to touch the meat whilst she had a period as this would have given it a peculiar taste, a taste which was easily discernible.[39]

In the ritual of pig killing, therefore, a number of social divisions are writ large: the separation between men and women, and between the raw and the cooked, are maintained during the ritual by proscriptive taboo. They constitute a set of binary oppositions which is conceptually mapped onto a pair of spatial oppositions, between outside and inside activities. This reinforces their symbolic power. The pig was killed and jointed outside in the barn or shed in the company of men; the offal was cooked by women in the kitchen inside the house, where small children would also look on.[40] The men also dealt exclusively with the outside of the pig, the women with its innards, and a strict spatial separation was again maintained, for it was said that any blood left inside the pig would contaminate the meat. Although this undoubtedly has a factual basis, this proscriptive taboo also served a symbolic role in maintaining the sets of binary oppositions. For example, the inner/outer distinction is heavily marked in the accounts, as women speak of continually cleaning the pig meat, to wash away its smell, to wash away

38. J.Berger, ibid., p.55.   39. J.Kitteringham, op.cit., p.39.

40. Contemporarily it may be remarked that such spatial divisions are perpetuated in a late twentieth century food ritual: the barbecue. It is men who usually cook the prestigious raw meat outside, while the women are inside preparing the accompaniments to it, such as sauces, salads and breads.

– as it were – its raw animality. As one Northumbrian woman remarked, 'everything had to be thoroughly cleaned, as the pig's a dirty
thing, but it has some lovely meat when it is worked down'. The outside
natural form, the animal, is thus conceptually distanced from its edible
form – pork – through cultural acts of cleansing and cooking, performed by women.

In this way, pig-killing time served to reflect and reaffirm the social
divisions and boundaries operative in everyday rural life in the late
nineteenth and early twentieth centuries. In Northumberland, for example, it was traditional for men to work mainly outside the home, at
shepherding or quarrying or as labourers on the farms. They would
have their 'gardens' or allotments, sometimes distant from the house,
where family vegetables would be grown and where the men would
meet to talk. Here, often, the pig too would reside. In Oxfordshire, as
Thompson notes,

men callers on Sunday afternoons came, not to see the family, but the pig, and
would lounge with its owner against the pigsty door for an hour, scratching
piggy's back and praising his points or turning up their noses in criticism.[41]

Rose, too, notes that 'to call on a neighbour without asking, "How's
the pig a-doing?" was a plain breach of courtesy, not to be lightly
excused'.[42] Women, on the other hand, were largely confined to the
home, entertaining and working inside the domestic sphere, growing
flowers rather than vegetables in their gardens. Therefore, just as
women transformed the raw vegetables grown by their menfolk in the
gardens into food for the family, so the raw meat of the pig was cooked
and transformed by them into food during the pig-killing ritual.

There was however a differential prestige given to the different parts
of the pig: the joints and hams were prestigious, the offal and puddings
less so. That hams should be described as 'oil paintings' or pictures
(as instanced in accounts from Northumberland and in Walter Rose's
recollections is particularly evocative. In poor rural cottages, where
decoration would be minimal, the 'hams' took the place of pictures in
being skilful works of culinary art, for a badly cured ham would not last.
In this way, then, the hams symbolised wider community relationships, between landlord and labourer or rich and poor. The ancestral

41. F. Thompson, op.cit., p.24.   42. W. Rose, op.cit., p.60.

paintings adorning the walls of the big house in Northumberland represented, for the landlord, the family's heritage, registering continuity between the past and future. As figurative 'oil paintings' the hams were, similarly, an investment against the future lean months of winter when food was scarce, a source of pride which, when well cured, would literally mediate between the past and the future. The black pudding and sausages, by contrast, were soon eaten. Although no less skill went into their preparation, they did not hang from the rafters as prestigious reminders. In this sense, the making of sausages reflected other forms of women's labour in the domestic sphere: cleaning, cooking and washing pass unremarked, only noticed in their absence. Thus, further oppositions, central to traditional rural life, were made explicit at pig-killing time: visible and invisible work, prestigious status and low status, investment in the future as opposed to consumption in the present, and men's position vis à vis that of women.

However, women's significant role in traditional rural communities of facilitating and furthering social relationships between the family and the community was also highlighted at pig-killing time.[43] The meat that men dealt with was meat for the family alone, whereas the food the women prepared was often shared with those who had assisted at the kill. A bit of liver or some sausage would be given by way of thanks. Only if there was debt to be paid off would other kinds of meat be used.[44] Berger, writing of rural France, describes how 'every year when the pig was killed, all the neighbours and Monsieur le Curé and the schoolmaster were invited to eat'. Stories would be recounted as the women served the food:

Whenever a plate was empty, my mother piled more stuffed cabbage on to it... The faces shone in the heat and, the table become more and more untidy. My mother brought on an apple tart the size of a small cart-wheel.[45]

In this example, as in other accounts, it is women's cooked food which sustains wider social relationships. In this way, the pig symbolically mediates not just the relations between men and women, but also those between the family and the community.

43. Flora Thompson, op.cit. illustrates well women's role in facilitating village social networks.

44. J. Kitteringham. op.cit.   45. J. Berger, op. cit., p.56.

A further subtle symbolic relationship between 'pigs' and 'women' can be detected running through the various accounts. It is the sow, the female pig, who through her fecundity ensures the physical continuity of the rural poor by providing her babies as a source of meat. In the human world this is paralleled by women who, as shown above, whilst also replenishing the social world through giving birth establish social continuity in another way as well: through the distribution and sharing of the pig's cooked meat. Given these conceptual links, the existence of the menstrual taboos described earlier comes as no surprise: if menstruation is a sign of failed reproduction then menstruating women could well have been thought to have the potential to disrupt the supply of meat in the future. The fact that for poor rural women – subject to impoverished diets, frequent childbearing and breastfeeding – menstruation may have been rare could have served to underscore its symbolic significance.[46]

The pig also served to reinforce traditional class relations in one Northumbrian estate village as one man remembers:

We once sent some meat to the hall... The aristocracy has no idea how ordinary folk lived. We once sent some sausages to the Hall with some black puddings. We received a letter of thanks from them and I asked the lad who brought the note if they had enjoyed the meat. He said that they had enjoyed the sausages but that he (the hall owner) had given (the servants) the black pudding.

This example is particularly interesting for it was customary for the estate landlord to give meat to his workers at Christmas, another ritual time. Joints of meat, the prestigious food, would be ceremonially distributed amongst the villagers, thereby demonstrating the landlord's largesse. In this instance, it could be argued that, through sending sausages and black pudding – less prestigious meat – to the Hall, this villager signalled her acceptance of the class system. As a symbolic inversion it throws into stark relief the patterning of class relations. It is surely not without significance that the sausages (made of raw meat and therefore more prestigious) were eaten by the landlord, but the

46. Keith Thomas notes that sixteenth-century gynaecologists described pregnant women as breeding and that 'one pre-Civil way clergyman in the pulpit compared women to sows. Puritan opponents of the churching ceremony sometimes did the same, referring to the mother as a sow with her piglets following', *Man and the Natural World: changing attitudes in England 1500–1800*, p.43.

black pudding (made from the cooked innards and therefore less prestigious) was given to the servants to eat. As Kitteringham notes, 'to
many of those in other social classes [pig-killing] was held to epitomise
the degradation and low character of those within the labouring
class'.[47] As she points out, Hardy clearly shows that 'Jude is repelled by
what he considers Arabella's coarseness and lack of feeling over the
slaughter of the pig'. This can perhaps be seen in one oral history
account from Northumberland. The lady, who had been a head servant
to the landlord and worked in the Hall, denied that she had ever kept a
pig. When her husband contradicted this statement, saying that of
course they had kept a pig, she replied that that was only during the war
because of the rationing.[48] Was having to raise, rather than buy, one's
meat, seen by this woman as stigmatising, as a sign which would affirm
her low social status?

This little piggy is human

The discussion so far has suggested that in the rearing and killing of the
house-pig can be seen reflected the implicit structures of signification
around which traditional rural communities were conceptually ordered. In this the pig may not be unique for, undoubtedly, the cow, the
horse or the village pub might serve equally well. Thus, although not
claiming that the pig had this role uniquely, it is clear that the pig did
have a role which was uniquely its own. This can be seen reflected in the
wider symbolic meanings attached to the 'pig', which have meant that
the pig has come to occupy a particular position with respect to the
human world. In traditional rural communities the pig was, quite literally, in an ambiguous position, being both part and not part of the
family. In Oxfordshire it lived in its own little house which was a lean-

47. J. Kitteringham, op.cit., p.11.

48. In the film, *A Private Function,* many of this article's themes are expressed. Set
during food rationing after the war a pig is fattened for a town feast. The pig comes to
mediate many sets of social relationships, particularly those of social class and gender.
Ironically, it is the pig who fouls the home of those who would be upwardly socially
mobile. Of significance, too, is the way that, through the course of the film, the pig
gradually turns from animal to metaphoric human, coming to share not only the
human's food and affections but also their care and home. In the end, however, it is
the pig who is finally sacrificed and eaten.

to attached to the side of the family's house. Living close by the family, it was almost part of the family. Hardy describes the pig as having 'a voice which could be continually heard from the corner of the garden'.[49] For Thompson, 'piggy' was pampered by the whole family; the children gathering snails and dandelions for the pig on their way home from school, mother boiling up 'little taturs' and father even going 'without his nightly half-pint' when towards the end other food was scarce and the pig had to be fed on barley meal.[50] But the pig was also clearly not human; it lived off the family's refuse, food which was not fit for humans to eat. Moreover, it was conceptually a 'dirty thing' and the muck heap, as Thompson describes it in Oxfordshire, was 'a nasty, smelly eyesore to have within a few feet of the windows'.[51] And yet, on the other hand, the pig transformed this rubbish into an important and prestigious food; its own muck provided valuable manure for the vegetable gardens and allotments. 'Pigs for health' is an Oxfordshire saying which acknowledges the debt of humans to the pig. The pig, then, was a friend but a friend who had to be sacrificed so that others could continue to live. One woman described for me this cyclical dilemma:

Being a land girl on a Buckinghamshire farm during the Second World War I had to learn that the ritual of killing the pig every year was something I had to endure. The first time it happened I wept, as I found the whole procedure most upsetting, after feeding it with household scraps, potatoes and barley meal every day for months. I must confess though I enjoyed most of the produce from the pig.

Ambivalence indeed – a response which is echoed in other accounts. Jude says, 'Upon my soul I would sooner have gone without the pig than have had this to do!... A creature I have fed with my own hands.'[52] For Thompson, the killing of the pig was when 'months of hard-work and self-denial were brought on that night to a successful conclusion'.[53]

In Berger's account the pig is portrayed as having human qualities, as being intelligent and itself sensitive to this ambiguity:

He fitted a noose around the pig's snout, being careful not to let it tighten. The pig followed him obediently, past the five cows and the mare, through the

49. T. Hardy, op.cit., p.108.   50. F. Thompson, op.cit., pp.24–5.
51. F. Thompson, ibid., p.24.   52. T. Hardy, op.cit., p.109.
53. F. Thompson, op.cit., p.56.

stable door and into the sudden harsh light of the snow. There the pig hestitated. All his life the pig had complied. Meme had fed him as if he were a family member. He, for his part, had put on his kilo per day. One hundred and forty kilos. One hundred and forty-one. One hundred and forty-two. Now, for the first time, he hesitated.[54]

In this role of provider of meat, the pig is forced into an ambivalent position: piggy in the middle, it sits on the threshold of life and death, mediating between hunger and full stomachs, between nature and culture.

Does this position mean therefore that the pig might have some of the power invested in other symbolic boundary crossers? Oral history accounts from the Alnwick coast suggest this may be so. Fishermen, who daily confront nature through fishing trips in the North sea, were traditionally held to be particularly cautious about pigs. Although not minding seeing a pig and indeed often rearing pigs at home, hearing the word ' pig' spoken was regarded as a potent of disaster and a fisherman would not set sail that day. Pigs were therefore referred to by other terms : as 'caldie', 'minister', 'grunters' and 'guffies'. Legend describes how a fishermen on his way to work once fell over a pig in the village street and that night the entire crew of the boat he was on were drowned. Here the pig created havoc with conceptual orders.

Such cultural attitudes are not, however, specific to those who have had to participate in pig-killing or a quaint feature of oral history accounts. The ambiguity and ambivalence which surrounds the pig finds expression in a much wider context. If as Lévi-Strauss suggested, 'animals are good to think with' then it seems that the British have a considerable cognitive debt to the pig .[55] Porcine metaphors and references abound in the English language. Many of these are derogatory – to make a pig's ear of something, to buy a pig in a poke, to pig oneself, to eat like a pig, to be pig sick or pig headed, to be like pigs in shit and to pig it, that is to be slovenly. The term 'pig' is also a form of abuse – applied to policemen as well as to the general public – and the term swine is far from an endearment. 'If pigs could fly', we say, then all would be well, for 'you can't make a silk purse out of a sow's ear'. The phrase 'a nice bit of crackling' is used by men in the North as a chauvinistic description of a sexually attractive woman. On the other hand, the

54. J. Berger, op.cit., p.48.   55. C. Lévi-Strauss, *Totemism*.

pig is also depicted as having a more positive metaphoric role: we speak approvingly of 'bringing home the bacon' or 'saving someone's bacon', and insist our children place their money in 'piggy banks'. Thus, whatever the sentiment, the pig is portrayed as mediating between the animal and the human world, a vehicle for our thoughts and often for our baser feelings.[56]

For Harrison, the pig is so rich a source of metaphors because of its 'ultimately abominable quality: its manifold resemblance to the human being'.[57] Not only did the house-pig live with humans, it literally embodied them through its pink and hairless skin. Referring to Leach's suggestion that the proximity of dogs and cats to the domestic environment ensures their inedibility[58] – eating them would be like eating a member of the family – Harrison compares the role of the pig. In his view, because the pig occupies such a position, 'in order to render the animal eligible for its heinous treatment [being eaten] exceptional efforts have to made, which involve ascribing to it an atrocious character'.[59] Harrison goes further, suggesting that our common conceptual association of pigs with dirt and squalor rests ultimately on shame and guilt for, left to their own devices, pigs are clean animals:

The pig is nothing but food in the making and, in that the ultimate destiny of all food is to become excrement, we might be said to keep it for this additional purpose . Though the same applies to the turkey, the pig is uniquely identified with excrement and we feel ourselves to be uniquely identified with the pig.[60]

For Harrison,

the shaved and dressed carcase of a pig, which can often be seen hanging in butcher's shops, does have a macabre similarity to the human body because of

56. Once alerted to their presence we become aware that pigs crop up frequently in human metaphoric form in many literary contexts, such as William Golding's *Lord of the Flies*, the baby who is a pig in Lewis Caroll's *Alice in Wonderland*. The most obvious example is George Orwell's *Animal Farm*. The pigs lead the revolution at the farm and, towards the end of the book, have taken on human qualities, strutting about on their hind legs. The book's last paragraph is most revealing; ' the creatures outside looked from pig to man, and from man to pig, and from pig to man again; but already it was impossible to say which was which',p.120.

57. F. Thompson, op.cit., p.64

58. E. Leach, Anthropological aspects of language: animal categories and verbal abuse, in *New Directions in the Study of Language,* edited by E.H. Lennenberg.

59. F.Harrison, op.cit., p.62.   60. F.Harrison, ibid., p.66.

the whiteness and 'cleaness' of the skin and the not inhuman proportions of its torso. When the carcase is suspended from its rear trotters, its spine and rear legs lie along the same plane; this creates the alarming illusion of an erect posture which is, after all, the human anatomy's distinctive feature.[61]

Berger's account of pig-killing makes this correspondence explicit. It is intertwined with an account of the marriage and death of a man and, it is the pig's severed head which alone witnesses the man's lonely death in the farm courtyard.

Conclusion

There is no doubt that much more could be said about the symbolic elaboration of the pig in its role as a meat producer. For example, in other cultures, where the pig is also placed in a special category, pork is a forbidden, rather than prized, food. This is often contemporarily explained in terms of clean and unclean meat and related to concepts of food hygiene. Mary Douglas however offers an alternative explanation in terms of ritual cleanliness and taboo. This again devolves on the ambiguity of the pig, which gives it a unique classificatory position. For the Israelites, she argues, it was because the pig is a cloven hoofed but non-cud-chewing animal that there was a prohibition against eating pork. The pig was matter out of place, ritually rather than organically unclean: 'failure to conform to the two necessary criteria for defining cattle is the only reason given in the Old Testament for avoiding the pig; nothing whatever is said about its dirty scavenging habits'.[62]

This article has stressed the pig's role as a symbolic mediator of social relations. Not only did the house-pig and its meat provide the focus for everyday sets of social distinctions in nineteenth- and twentieth-century rural communities, they also literally mediated in times of hardship, between life itself and death. Unlike sheep, goats, chicken and cows, the pig has no by-products such as eggs or wool or milk: its supreme quality lies in its own death. Raised only that he might die, the pig represents the ultimate in self sacrifice. Through this act was gained not only meat for the poor but pig-skin leather and hogs hair bristles for the rich. As a metaphoric human, the pig displays altruism of an exceptional kind.

61. F.Harrison, ibid., p.65.   62. M. Douglas, *Purity and Danger,* op.cit., p.55.

Two contrasting dining styles
suburban conformity
and urban individualism[1]

GERALD MARS AND VALERIE MARS

EVERYONE knows that there are different eating styles and that the way people entertain varies widely. But to date food writers have not related entertaining styles to the working life of householders nor to how they relate to the communities in which they live. Instead, dinner parties are condemned as exercises in indulgent, conspicuous consumption, as commentators from Petronius to Veblen have asserted, or are dismissed as mere expressions of group identity and good fellowship.

It was with these considerations in mind that we began a study of household consumption in London in the late eighties/early nineties, in which dinner-giving was one area of inquiry. The principal method used was the intensive participant observation of households. The sample was all of the same social class and income, with both method and sample being deliberately selected in an attempt to refute market researchers' approaches to consumption. These use standardized questionnaires and social-class categories – regardless of the specific circumstances of each household – often in association with a 'Life Styles' approach to consumption based on the discredited Maslovian idea of a 'hierarchy of needs' which treats values and attitudes as free-floating and independent of social context.[2]

1. This paper is derived from a wider study of household consumption and organisation which covered thirty six households. The theoretical orientation is informed by Mary Douglas's and colleagues' work on cultural theory, and also by Pierre Bourdieu's *Distinction*. Particular thanks are due to the 'Browns' and the 'Joneses' who generously welcomed us into their homes and who accepted the imposition of fieldwork with a cheerful and surprising tolerance. We are also most grateful to Mary Douglas for her comments on an earlier draft of this paper.

2. Maslow argues that human needs can be divided into basic (physiological) needs and derived (more sophisticated social/psychological) needs; and that there is a

This study's theoretical underpinning is based upon the Cultural Theory model that originated with the anthropologist Mary Douglas and which has had extensive empirical testing, though not, until this study, in households. Cultural theory links the values and attitudes of people, their 'world view', to the types of social relationships in which they are involved. Its argument is that since people need to make some sense and order of their worlds, their values and attitudes are used to justify and interpret their social relationships. Values and attitudes, in this approach, are not therefore free-floating but are rooted to, and act in mutual alignment with, social relationships in a continuous process of mutual adaption. World views on the one hand, and social relationships on the other, therefore, act together to produce a coherent way of life. It is when misalignment develops between world view and social relationships that change occurs.[3]

This paper first discusses typical home entertaining among the 'Browns' and their friends, a group of middle-aged residents who all live in the same south London suburb and who demonstrate how they use food and its setting to consolidate a tightly bounded and exclusive group, and in doing so, confirm a shared, ordered, highly structured and conformist lifestyle. A contrast is then drawn with dinner-giving among the 'Joneses' and their friends who are all of the same social class and income as the Browns but who are all non-conforming urbanites, who use home entertaining quite differently: to break down boundaries in order to extend their range of contacts and to maintain, and if possible further, their position in a competitive world. What we find when looking at the dinner parties of our two representative households, therefore, are not just two very different ways of organising a social event but key indicators of two very different ways of life.

Mr Brown is a departmental manager in a fruit and vegetable merchant's in London's New Covent Garden where he has worked since he left school and his wife is a locally employed part-time secretary.

---

regular and graded progression through these so that when one need is satisfied, motivation is then applied to satisfying the next. The argument falls, of course, when it is realised that members of different cultures and classes rate their needs differently, a point discussed in Thompson *et al*, *Cultural Theory* p.55.

3. A comprehensive account of cultural theory is to be found in Thompson.

Their friends share similar status jobs with the men's workplaces being dispersed throughout London and with their wives typically being locally employed. They and their friends share a world view that emphasises ordered hierarchy as a natural state of things; that values tradition and the past as validating the present; that sees human nature as needing rules, constraints and structure to be able to operate effectively; that takes a long view of affairs; and that values ritual and precedent.

All of these values are reinforced at each dinner party the Browns give and attend, not only in the nature of the food served and in the choice of guests, but in the settings in which they are offered. This world view is in conformity with the bounded and hierarchic social relationships which dominate life in their suburb and which is typically experienced and reinforced in their day-to-day working lives as it is in the lives of their guests.

The Joneses, on the other hand, though formally of the same social class and income level, are involved in very different social relationships to those of the Browns. Mr Jones is a graphic designer, his wife acts as his agent, both are in their forties and their guests are overwhelmingly linked to the design world, mostly as illustrators but including agents, contractors and their partners. Their social relationships largely derive from the nature of their work as independent entrepreneurs in what is an extremely competitive occupation. It is a world that owes nothing to the very different and bounded world of hierarchic organisations. Nor is it limited to the physical neighbourhood in which they happen to have their home. For the Joneses, social relationships operate in the open field of networking with all the freedom from group-based constraints that this offers. Their world view values the importance of a freedom to transact with minimum interference; an intolerance for preset categories that leads to impatience with rules and conventions; and that relishes the short-term and the fashionable. All these values are similarly evident, as we shall see, in their choice of menus, in the way their meals are prepared, in the choice of guests invited to share them, and in the settings in which they occur.

The physical setting

An early intimation of differences in the two ways of life is evident on approaching each house. With its emphasis on order and control, the Browns' suburban garden offers a public declaration of their values: a painted wrought-iron gate leads to a well-kept garden containing neatly defined borders and carefully clipped hedges. Their sitting room is readily visible from the street and on its window ledge a number of ornaments are displayed facing outwards. The Joneses, on the other hand, who relate only minimally to their neighbours, have an unkempt urban garden, and their house windows are effectively blocked from the street by blinds. Once past the two front doors the contrasts mount.

Guests entering the Browns' have their coats taken and hung in a coat cupboard in the hall. They see on their right a staircase, down which is hung a series of nineteenth-century prints of aristocratic country houses. At the bottom of the staircase hangs a watercolour by a local artist – a birthday present to Mr Brown from his family – which shows the Browns' semi as a detached house surrounded by trees that do not exist in reality and seem to give it a wooded 'estate-like' aspect.

The Browns' entertaining rooms, and those of their friends and neighbours, are decorated and furnished within a range of taste designed not to surprise, so that colours and fabrics coordinate within tight conventions. Sitting-room upholstery is in rich dark colours and carpets are invariably neutral or coordinate with upholstery. The Browns have a royal blue three piece suite – their carpets are a matching blue. The choice of pictures follows similar conformist conventions: formulaic mass-produced reproductions of landscapes and urban scenes are popular and the Browns' favourite is of Old Covent Garden vegetable market where Mr Brown has worked since he left school. Family photographs are prominently displayed.

The contrast between the decor of the Browns' and the Joneses' could not be more stark. For the Joneses, conformist order is negated and autonomous individualism is given freer rein. Once through the Joneses' unkempt garden, guests enter a relatively shabby hall where coats are taken and hung unceremoniously over a banister. Inside the Joneses' entertainment room the impact is, however, dramatic. This is a multi-purpose room demonstrating function and contrasts and it is boldly decorated and effectively insulated from the street by a painted blind that covers the street window. Doubling as gallery and conference room, it exhibits framed examples of Mr Jones's work and is divided into sitting and dining areas. Along one wall are revealed a dishwasher, a boiler and hand-crafted cabinets, and then, mounted over a large black leather settee, a startling, full-size, six-foot, fibreglass, Blue Marlin. And at the room's far end, in a conscious parody of suburban taste, is a flight of silver flying ducks set against a black wall. The overall effect is bold and individualistic. The Browns too have a domestic boiler in their traditional dining room. It is however, made to match the rest of the decor by being concealed in a false mahogany casing.

Clothes, Crockery and Cutlery

For the Browns, their Saturday night dinners are occasions when they not only bring out their best crockery and cutlery but also the clothes that are specific to these times. As Mrs Brown says, 'I wear a nice blouse – nothing sparkley, a velvet skirt, either straight or full, pearls and my silver jewellery and always dark-coloured high heels with dark stockings – but not black – and never trousers – none of us wear trousers for dinners. The men wear a blazer or jumper, usually with a tie but if it's warm they take off their jackets or jumpers since they're among friends.' It is evident that the Browns' choices in clothes, crockery and cutlery, also echo their choices in decor: they range only within extremely limited fields and in doing so emphasise the conformity and the shared tastes that negate competition.

The Joneses reject constraints. When they and their guests give dinner parties, they do not use special crockery or cutlery and they wear their everyday clothes. But these are all carefully chosen on individualistic grounds which, like their decor, can range widely and which is enhanced by ornament. Mrs Jones, for instance is noted for her choice of unusual and personalised earrings.

Dinner at the Browns'

Who attends?

The Browns are both in their late fifties and their income, though it has now stabilised, has steadily increased with Mr Brown's promotions. They entertain, and are in turn entertained, by similar-status friends in rotation about once every six weeks. With their friends they form a grouping of four to five couples that is both long-standing and remarkably homogeneous. Their dining arrangements reflect this consistency. The Browns always entertain their friends as couples and select them from a limited field, most of whom have known each other for much of their married lives. They have been attending each other's dinners for the past fifteen years, but have socialised together for considerably longer than this. As well as being approximately of the same age, all have grown-up children and all are of the same social class (C1/2 – lower middle/upper working class). In addition, they all live in the same neighbourhood as owner-occupiers of the same kind of three-bedroomed semis, what in North America are called 'duplexes', and which they typically bought in the early years of marriage.

The preliminaries
The essence of suburban entertaining is its consistency and its carefully maintained structure, with different stages of the meal being marked by different kinds of alcohol. Guests always arrive close to the same time on Saturday evenings and they enter the better of two sitting rooms used only for such special occasions. Each couple bring two gifts – the men wine, the women chocolates, flowers, some small decorative item or a book. Mrs Brown has on occasion given light, humorous writings such as those by Maureen Lipman. On arrival, guests are offered a range of proprietary 'nibbles' – crisps and nuts – and drinks, with the drinks always referred to by their brand names: sherry is 'Crofts'; gin 'High & Dry'; and whisky 'Whyte & Mackay'. Women do not usually drink spirits.

After some half-an-hour of chat about events since their last dinner, the party enter the dining room. This too is a special preserve, its use also limited to celebratory occasions. Crockery and cutlery are likewise those not used during the normal domestic week. The table, prelaid by Mrs Brown, has men and women seated alternately. On it are bottles of white and red wine ready opened and both set in acrylic coolers. Women drink white wine only, though men drink both.

The food

A favourite starter of Mrs Brown is deep-fried mushrooms that are stuffed with *Matteson's*, a proprietary paté she serves with mayonnaise. Her main course (which is never fish: 'Jim is not a fish man') is most commonly a lamb, beef or pork joint, though she sometimes serves *Beef Wellington* and occasionally poultry, most commonly chicken. If the joint is unboned it is always carved at the table by Mr Brown, and if boned is carved by him in the kitchen. All meat at the Browns' is served with gravy made with cornflour and Bisto (a proprietary gravy powder). 'It's always Bisto – I'm a creature of habit – and sometimes on meat or chicken I use an Oxo cube too – it depends on what I serve.'

Vegetables at the Browns' tend to be more exotic than those usually served in their circle since Mr Brown gets them from his workplace. They are always cooked ahead of time and then placed in a heated hostess trolley to await dinner; fashionable notions of *al dente* have no place in this milieu. Two of Mrs Brown's friends use similar trolleys but, like her, they use them only for entertaining since ordinary daily dinners are always served ready plated from the kitchen.

Mrs Brown and her friends usually serve three puddings, and although consistency and conformity prevail, this is one area where limited innovation is found: two puddings tend to be established and familiar to their circle but occasionally the third might be new to them.

The meal concludes with cheese and biscuits, followed by coffee and liqueurs or sometimes port, which are again offered by name. After the table has been cleared, the diners then play popular board games, not as couples but as two opposing gender-based teams.

Dinner at the Joneses'

Who attends?

The Joneses' dinner-giving serves very different functions when compared with the Browns', and the form and organisation differ also. Firstly, the Joneses' dinners are given irregularly – though their larger dinners are scheduled several weeks ahead – and their guests come not from the same neighbourhood but from the same occupational base, which is within the same social class category as the Browns and their friends. And whereas the Browns' guests are repetitively invited as symmetrical couples and a careful balancing of numbers is always achieved, the Joneses are more flexible: their numbers often vary, usually from eight to ten and the constituency of their parties is likely to differ from one party to another. Gender is not important to the Joneses as a criterion in their selection of guests or in their seating nor is marital status, age or place of residence. To be included in one of the Joneses' dinners, guests have to be part of the world of graphic design and be able to participate at an appropriate level in the network of their occupational group – a group noted for its erratic and uncertain earnings. As such they are called upon to offer vital gossip, keep each other abreast of the latest developments in their field, offer mutual reassurance in what is a shifting and competitive milieu and preferably be stimulating and amusing.

The Joneses positively relish the opportunities that their friends' shifting alliances give to further extend their network: 'When our friends split they still come round to dinner with their new partners, and their old ones come too – with *their* new ones. It all makes for interest.' The Browns, on the other hand, recount examples of people who have 'gone off the rails' with partners not their legal spouses and who, as a result, have been banished from suburban social life and the dinners which are integral to it. As Mr Brown put it when joking about wife-swapping and the throwing of car keys in a circle: 'No – we respect ourselves too much for that.'

The food

Just as there is wide variance in the physical setting of these two very different kinds of dinner party as well as in who attends them, so too there are marked differences in what is eaten and drunk. Mrs Jones places much less emphasis on the ordered planning of her meals and indulges in greater spontaneity in their preparation and purchasing than does Mrs Brown. Her menus are essentially eclectic and derive from an infinite range of sources. She often buys party food on impulse, but only if it is a good buy, and she stores such party items as fresh sardines and tuna in her freezer ahead of her needs. She regularly chats to the Greek working in her local deli, and from him often gets ideas of what to serve. But she might well adapt his advice to her own idiosyncratic interests and experience or mix dishes or constituents of different cuisines from various parts of the world. Since, for instance, Mrs Jones comes from Ireland, one of her favourite offerings is *Champ*, a traditional Irish dish of potatoes, spring onions and melted butter. But she periodically varies the accompaniments, usually serving it with sausages: 'It's nice served with game sausages or Greek sausages or a German ring sausage or chops.'

In the same way the serving of drinks at the Joneses' is also unstructured when compared with the Browns. They liberally serve the same basic wine throughout the evening instead of structuring the meal with different kinds of alcohol, as do the Browns. And there are no gender differences in what is drunk at the Joneses.

Since Mrs Jones, unlike Mrs Brown, is keen to add variety and individuality to her food and seeks to make most impact from least expenditure, she maximises originality by finding inexpensive but nonetheless relatively exotic items: by choosing, for instance, a variety of fancy bread, from different Continental bakers, or, as she puts it, by 'cheating', especially in preparing her desserts. 'I love cheats', she says. 'Cheats' involve either making a dish look more expensive than it is, or making it appear as if much more effort has been spent to produce it than it has. One of her 'cheat' dishes, for instance, is Morello Cherry Jelly, which is unusual enough to be exotic, looks expensive and yet is cheap and quick to prepare – merely requiring a jar of East European cherries from the deli which she prepares with gelatine and garnishes with cream. Another individualist gambit of Mrs Jones is her provision of what she calls ' 'nearly cuisine' – nearly Chinese, nearly Mexican', which brings even more flexibility to her menus.

Mrs Brown, on the other hand, never claims individuality for her dishes – quite the reverse. All the meals she serves are set within a bounded range of tastes. There is nothing here to startle her guests, and indeed this would be the last thing she would wish to do. To this end her dinners are an exercise in controlled and conformist expenditure, with both upper and lower levels set by the group. As Mrs Brown herself says, 'We don't try to keep up with the Joneses.'

While Mrs Jones strives for the esoteric, the fashionable and the new, Mrs Brown's recipes derive from limited sources known to all her guests. They mostly come from friends and from the middle-range tabloids (the Daily and Sunday Express, and the Daily and Sunday Mail are prominent) and these she systematically files in loose-leaf folders. The cookery books she uses are also well accepted within her group. They include Delia Smith's various publications, *Perfect Cookery* by Marguerite Patten and a contemporary *Mrs Beeton*.[4] These conventional books are the three best sellers in their field.[5]

Whereas Mrs Jones loves to 'cheat', the meals served by Mrs Brown require no subterfuge. She would, for instance, consider it quite inappropriate at a dinner party to serve what she calls 'cheapo mousse', a dish she readily serves to her family and which is simply made of evaporated milk, coffee essence and gelatine.

The role of time and tradition

To Mrs Brown, ideas of tradition are important in justifying her present situation. Although in culinary matters there is no link between what she serves now and what was served in her mother's time, she is able to build effective traditions by regular, shared and ritualised repetition. Mrs Jones, however, does not look to a past to justify her present culinary practices: instead she continuously and creatively exploits time, place and fashion to adapt her essentially innovative cuisine.

Mrs Brown's recipes offer obeisance to a past that for her never really existed.[6] She and members of her circle, in common with most of their generation have never been as prosperous as they are now. Plain roasts represent one common thread with their past but their frequency was much rarer then than now. Bisto and Oxo are probably the most consistent elements to have survived over time, both products having entered the market in 1910.

Because of their relatively long history, such products as Bisto and

4. Mrs Beeton is a pseudonym used for a recipe book which has been continually rewritten since the author's death in 1865. Modern versions bear no relationship to the original, thus turning the work into a branded product.

5. Michael Bateman, 'Who's the Greatest Cook of all?', p. 56, gives some sales figures: *Mrs Beeton* has sold over 3 million, Marguerite Patten, whose first book was published in 1960, and who has written 175 cookery books in total, has sold 2 million copies of *Cookery in Colour*: and 1.75 million of *Everyday Cookbook*. Delia Smith's popularity is enhanced by television; the book of her Christmas series sold 300,000 copies.

6. Roland Barthes, *Mythologies*, p.11. Barthes, in his essay on food, distinguishes between people having a sense of the past rather than a past reality.

Oxo offer considerable symbolic security to those, like the Browns, who value tradition and continuity. Similarly, in referring to alcohol by its brand name, the Browns gain added value from established products that are marketed as traditional, whether they are or not. This is why they never buy a supermarket's own brand. The Joneses, in contrast, gain their added value by demonstrating the skilled selection of best-value 'plonk' which owes nothing to vintage or provenance, and thus defies time and tradition.

Much of Mrs Brown's dinners – the nibbles, starters, puddings, cheese and the alcohol – owe no place to the past but are consistent with the cuisine of the restaurants that the Browns and their friends regularly patronise. These are largely limited to steakhouse chains that change little over time and at which their dining group collectively attends to celebrate each of their birthdays. The cuisine Mrs Brown produces, and which so markedly contrasts with Mrs Jones's open, expansionary, and eclectic menus, is congruent with the range of taste evidenced at these steak houses. It gives her and her friends the template for their entertaining which, with the aid of recipes from newspapers, friends and her cookbooks, allows her to reproduce the domestic equivalents of chain restaurant catering.

Conclusions

This paper has aimed to show that for these two households, the dinner party demonstrates a range of consistent choices that makes sense of the social relationships that are important to the participants. For both the Browns and the Joneses, the dinner party involves a significant share of their resources. Explanations of motive, however, that focus on conspicuous consumption, or on the mere furtherance of good fellowship are inadequate and simplistic. For the Joneses the nature of their work makes it essential for them to move within a fluid network that is not constrained by locality or indeed by any other factors that might limit their freedom to extend and consolidate their network.
For the Browns and their friends, work serves to take the men away from the suburb and the varied nature of their employment serves to fragment them further. At the same time, however, their sharing of an equivalence of occupational status is a necessary prerequisite for mem-

bership of the dining group. It is the women, however, who form the
core of the group, which unlike the network of the Joneses, is essentially locality based and founded on the mutual support gained during
their earlier child rearing years.

For both of our households, the dinner party emerges as neither a
trivial nor a marginal event. In effectively linking the worlds of work
and leisure it offers a key indicator to demonstrate how people intri-
cately manipulate space, time, objects, resources and labour to construct their worlds and their place within them.

Bibliography

Bateman, Michael, 'Who's the Greatest Cook of All?', *Independent on Sunday*,
   3 November 1991

Barthes, Roland, *Mythologies* (Pons: Seuil, 1957).

Bourdieu, Pierre, *Distinction, A Social Critique of the Judgment of Taste* (London: Routledge & Kegan Paul, 1986), p. 79

Douglas, Mary, 'Cultural Bias', in *In the Active Voice*, (London: Routledge &
   Kegan Paul, 1982), pp. 183–254

Douglas, Mary (ed.), *Food in the Social Order: Studies of Food and Festivities in
   Three American Communities*, (New York: Russell Sage Foundation, 1984)

Douglas, Mary, and Baron Isherwood, *The World of Goods: Towards an Anthropology of Consumption*, (London: Allen Lane, 1979)

Douglas, Mary, and Michael Nicod, 'Taking the Biscuit: the Structure of British Meals', in *New Society* 30 (1974), pp. 744–7

Maslow, Abraham H., *Motivation and Personality*, (New York: Harper Row,
   1954)

Mrs Beeton's Cookery and Household Management , ed. by an anonymous team,
   (London: Ward, Lock, 1976)

Patten, Marguerite, *Perfect Cooking*, (London: Paul Hamlyn, 1972)

Petronius, Arbiter, *Collected Works, Satyricon, Tremalchio's Feast*, Loeb Classics
   (London: Heinemann, 1969), pp. 49–185

Smith, Delia, *Complete Cookery Course*, (London: BBC, 1978)

Thompson, Michael, Richard Ellis and Aaron Wildavsky, *Cultural Theory*,
   (Boulder, San Francisco and Oxford: Westview Press, 1990)

Veblen, Thorstein, *The Theory of the Leisure Class*, new edition (New York:
   Mentor Books, 1953)

Introducing children to food and table manners in Java

SRI OWEN

I

IT IS customary to think of Javanese society as highly diverse but also deeply traditional. In the cities, and even to some extent in the country-side, it may be progressive and dynamic, but the bulk of the population is conventionally regarded as conservative and reluctant to change. However, a glance at population figures will suggest that the Javanese have had to adapt to an explosion hardly less astonishing than the 1883 eruption of their small but noisy neighbour, Krakatau. Two hundred years ago, there were probably about 3 million of them. One hundred years ago, there were eight times as many. Today, there are nearly four times as many again – over 90 million, 60% of the world's fourth most populous nation, on an island slightly smaller than England.[1] Nor are they evenly distributed; the fertile areas of the north coast and the central piedmont[2] carry far more than their fair share of people and are among the most densely-occupied agricultural areas in the world.[3] And the Indonesians are becoming city dwellers, by choice or necessity; Jakarta now has about 12 million people and is expected to grow to 17 million by the year 2000; Bandung and Surabaya are expanding at a comparable rate.

1. Population figures drawn from Ricklefs, p. 116, and Lombard, III, 52; both quoting, in part, Widjojo Nitisastro, chapter 9.

2. Traditionally, the north coastal towns were outward-looking trading and fishing communities. In the interior, the rice-farming kingdoms were inward-looking, conservative and hierarchical. Lombard analyses the effect this split has had on Javanese history.

3. Clifford Geertz (1963) is the classic study of how intensive rice cultivation allowed ever-growing numbers of tiny farms and landless labourers to occupy the over-crowded island of Java. Geertz's work has inspired many challengers, however.

Yet Javanese society, subjected during two centuries to stress and a pace of change that might be expected to cripple a 'traditional' social structure, has coped and survived. How it has done this could form the subject of a long and complex investigation.[4] In this paper, all I want to do is to suggest a few ways in which attitudes to food, and in particular to the food-education of children, may have contributed to this stability and adaptability. Very little has been written on the subject; most of my comments are based on experience and observation. I had better start by saying a little about myself.

I was born in central Sumatra; my father was of a comfortably-off Minangkabau family, my mother half-Javanese and half-Sundanese. Because they were Dutch-educated and came from different islands, my parents spoke Dutch together most of the time. They were both teachers, and my father started and ran a very successful school, which was good enough for the Dutch authorities to want to incorporate it into the official education system. My parents were also passionate nationalists, however, so my father refused to give up control of his school and he and my mother did not encourage their children to speak Dutch; my sisters and I grew up speaking the 'new' national language and the local language of wherever we happened to be living. We did not stay in Sumatra very long. For a number of reasons, among them the approach of the invading Japanese armies, we went to West Java, then to Central Java. Today my married sisters are bringing up their children, some of whom are now young adults, in Jakarta, in a small town in Central Java and in the brash new-frontier atmosphere of Pontianak, on the coast of West Kalimantan. My knowledge of childhood in Indonesia is, I suppose, unavoidably middle-class, but it has spanned a good half-century of time and a wide spectrum of political and economic circumstance.

2

Despite its volcanoes – even because of them – Java has always been a fertile island, adaptable not only to wet rice farming but to the growing of a huge variety of tropical and sub-tropical fruits and vegetables. It

4. See, for example, Clifford Geertz (1960) and Hildred Geertz.

has always supported much livestock and vast numbers of poultry. Most parts of the island are within a few hours' journey of the sea, and rivers, lakes, tanks and flooded fields produce great quantities of fresh-water fish. Therefore, at least until World War II, everyone normally had enough to eat, and all except the very poorest had a fairly healthy diet. There was always the danger of a bad year, a local shortage, a drought, possibly the loss of a crop; the problems were often created or made worse by colonial policies. But, by and large, malnutrition and starvation were not widespread or chronic. Then the Japanese occupation and the struggle for independence wrecked the economy and dev-astated roads, bridges, railways and irrigation systems. Throughout the nineteen-fifties and early sixties rice had to be imported in ever-increasing quantities, so that the new Indonesia found itself ever deeper in debt. In the 23 years from the Japanese invasion to the fall of President Sukarno, malnutrition became common; at the time the ex-pression 'third world' was invented, Indonesia was indeed a Third World country.

However, its food problems are not as deep-rooted as those of, say, sub-Saharan Africa, and there has never been any doubt that it has the potential to lift itself out of them. The new order that took over in 1965 introduced policies that were at least somewhat more logical and less doctrinaire than previous ones had been, and the development of the country's industrial base and mineral resources – particularly oil – im-proved its balance of payments. Population growth has been checked, to some extent by government policy but mainly by increasing prosper-ity and urbanisation. New rice technology and the introduction of high-yield varieties has made even Java, in a good year, self-sufficient in her staple food.[5] Needless to say, the rich have benefited more from these improvements than the poor. Whether even this gradual and patchy improvement will continue is far from certain; but that is not to deny that it has taken place.

Modest prosperity, city life, television, foreign travel – and at a more fundamental level a high literacy rate and steadily-improving educa-tion, at least in primary schools – all these have made Indonesians more

5. Mears gives an exhaustive account of the early part of the rice revolution. Much has happened since his book was written, but my impression is that the situation has gone on developing along the lines he describes.

aware of what goes on in the world outside, and of the life-chances that they ought now to be expecting and demanding. Among these changing attitudes and expectations are all those that concern food: which is hardly surprising, given the importance that food has always held for them.

From what has been said, that importance will be clear; the fundamentals of Javanese life have remained pretty constant. Communal action was always desirable among irrigated-rice growers, because water has to be shared. The community might feast one week and be back at subsistence level the next. But there was plenty of variety of tastes and textures in natural ingredients, so that feasts were not just blow-outs, but gave scope to cooks to show off their skill and to eaters to develop their powers of discrimination. Much depended on the behaviour of the weather, mysterious diseases of crops and the still more alarming mysteries of the local volcano, so that a strong sense of respect developed for whatever unseen powers controlled these things. Work as one might, one must resign oneself to the final decisions that these powers made. One other point may be worth making – the Javanese, especially since they became (for the most part) Moslems, have never had anything very interesting to drink; at table, therefore, all their attention has been given to the food.

These attitudes survive in the countryside, which is typically a landscape of small villages occupying palm-shaded platforms among irrigated rice fields; the average farmer owns or rents a tiny patch of land, on average less than half a hectare, which he works with the help of his family and which is sufficient to feed the people who work it, with a small surplus of cash crops which can be sold. The pattern among the new urban white-collar and blue-collar workers is obviously quite different.[6] Although wages and salaries may still be paid partly in rice, particularly to government employees, and although many functionaries get an 'official' house and car as part of their perks, in most families husband and wife both have to have full-time jobs if they are to make

6. Generalizing about Javanese villages, towns and cities leads one towards pitfalls at every step. It is difficult to define, in western terms, what these words mean in the Javanese environment. In writing this section, I had in mind the rather special conditions of Jakarta, and much even of Jakarta is made up of village-like units which still retain links with the surrounding, but retreating, countryside.

ends meet. The children are looked after during the day by a relative or a paid help. Because the man and woman both work, they often share the housework and the cooking; although Javanese men expect their wives to look after them and fuss over them, they do not, as a rule, expect to order them around, and the position of wife and mother has always carried a great deal of respect and considerable, if limited, powers.

Finally, Indonesians have become – or perhaps always were – very conscious of what makes them healthy or is bad for them. They read and talk about calories, vitamins and nutritional values, and they worry about cholesterol – though not, as far as I can tell, about the enormous intake of sugar that most Javanese are accustomed to. Health anxiety has always made them vulnerable to potions, quack medicines, and nowadays to the dishonest marketing of commercial drugs, pills and food supplements; but, with a healthier as well as a fuller and more regular diet, the younger generation are growing up taller and heavier than their parents.

3

Traditionally, babies are breast-fed at least until they are nine months old (and this is still regarded as a fairly reliable method of birth control). Babies get a lot of attention and are carried everywhere, usually astride the mother's or elder sister's hip. European visitors routinely comment on how rarely one hears an Indonesian baby cry, or a parent shout angrily or raise a hand against a child. Standards of behaviour, however, are generally agreed on and are strictly enforced. From experience and observation, I would say that physical punishment is not as rare as foreigners may think; but a public display of anger or impatience brings terrible loss of face to a Javanese or Balinese, who has been brought up to value self-control as his or her contribution to universal order.[7] If

7. Javanese beliefs and attitudes are complex, often ambiguous. A great deal has been written about them; two illuminating contemporary studies are Lombard, op. cit., and Ward Keeler. The extent to which traditional attitudes, inculcated through upbringing, education, *wayang* performances etc etc, are being changed by the stresses of big-city life (in Jakarta) or tourism (in Bali) is a topic that needs a lot more research. An interesting text for the early days of these changes is Selosoemardjan. Note that people of other islands do not necessarily share Javanese values in full; here, as in so many aspects of life, broad statements about 'Indonesians' can be very misleading.

self-control snaps under extreme pressure, the victim may run *amok*, but as I have never known a child do this at the dinner-table I shall not pursue the subject.

Babies in Java and Sumatra never used to be given dummies, though these have become rather common in the last thirty years or so. Weaning is a fairly gradual process, and the child is spoon-fed, or more often hand-fed, until perhaps the age of five. As mother has probably gone back to work by this time, feeding will be the responsibility of an elder sister, aunt, grandmother or nanny. The whole process of teaching the child to eat is taken in a relaxed, laid-back sort of way; food is never, never forced on the child, either by threats or bribery, though hearty eating is certainly encouraged. Eating between meals is not usually thought worth commenting on, though the hopeless task of keeping children away from sweets is attempted. Its lack of success can be judged from the greatly-increased number of fillings that children now have in their teeth. This may simply reflect better dental care, but I used to astonish British dentists with my gleaming, perfect teeth until I was past the age of 50. My teeth, if not the rest of me, probably benefited from a wartime diet; for years, we had no sweets except raw sugar cane, which is less damaging than refined sugar because you have to grind the cane vigorously with your teeth to get anything from it at all. And you only want to suck sugar cane for a short time, because it gives you a furry tongue. When my friends and I nibbled, we nibbled boiled (not fried) peanuts and soybeans.

For whatever reason, Javanese children, though mischievous, are usually good-tempered and not inclined to throw food about or have tantrums. This is not to say that family life is always harmonious or free from stress – far from it. Nor are parents or carers easy-going in all other respects; until quite recently, for example, everything possible was done to force a left-handed child to use its right hand for eating as well as writing, since to use the left hand for any social purpose is regarded as the height of bad manners.

Most Indonesians, even city-dwellers, prefer to eat with their hands, although they have been quite used to spoons and forks from their earliest years. (Not so used to knives, however, because you don't need a knife to eat Javanese food; it has all been cut up beforehand.) To eat rice and meat neatly and gracefully with the fingers requires, of course, much more skill than to handle cutlery. It also makes people conscious of the texture of food before they put it in their mouths, and makes them think of food as something you get close to, instead of something vaguely dirty which you keep at arm's, or fork's, length. At a village feast – a wedding reception, say – everyone will usually sit on mats on the ground, and the food will be served on banana-leaf plates without any cutlery. At a comparable function in town, or in a well-off house-hold, people will eat standing up or perched on any available seat, still using their fingers or at most a spoon or a fork.

Not surprisingly, most Javanese have little experience of solitude and no taste for it. Around every meal-table there are usually a good many chairs. But it must be said that families do not always sit down on them at the same time. The main meal is usually lunch, and everyone should be there; but when all except the very youngest or oldest have schedules or work to do, the cooked food may be laid out on a side table quite early in the morning and may stay there until midnight, stone cold (but no one minds this in the tropics), while people help themselves when-ever convenient. To this extent, meals are casual and unsupervised. However, the norm is for everyone to sit down together, and any child who is able to sit up at table and, within reasonable limits, fend for itself is expected to do so. The nearest grown-up will help the child to the food it asks for; all the dishes are on the table together, so there is no right or wrong order of dishes or combination of them. There are no 'bogey foods' that children in Java universally dislike (though I remem-ber getting very tired of boiled yams and tapioca during the war).

The old English middle-class tradition of bringing up children in another part of the house, and of bringing them in to see their parents only to say good-night, would be unimaginable in Indonesia. I admit that as a small child I ate with the lesser members of the family in my grandmother's kitchen rather than with my father and mother in their smart dining-room; but that was only because I found the food better and the conversation easier to take part in. Even at the age of three or four, it was taken for granted that I was free to choose. Before their fifth birthdays, most children have started to eat adult food, and from five onwards they are eating chopped or crushed chilli peppers – a couple of years later they have graduated to whole chillies, and after that they will never feel that a meal is complete without them.

The atmosphere at family meals, and indeed at more formal social functions, is usually relaxed and fairly noisy. There may be a moment's silence for prayer, a brief *Bismillah* from the head of the table. The Javanese enjoy high formality – Clifford Geertz has said that in extreme circumstances a polite conversation becomes almost operatic – but 'manners' start long before one gets anywhere near a table, and the idea of 'table manners' as such scarcely exists. It is perfectly in order for anyone at the table to express uninhibited enjoyment of what they are eating; the British ideal of eating quietly, as if you were somehow ashamed of what you were doing, seems to us strange. My grand-mother told us not to drink water with the meal, because it would make the rice swell up inside us and we should feel too bloated to enjoy her excellent cooking. There is always soup on the table to wash the food down. To aid digestion, she told us to chew every mouthful 32 times – 'like the Prophet Mohammed'. My English husband was told by his grandmother to do exactly the same thing – 'like Mr Gladstone'. You are not obliged to burp or belch at the end of the meal, but no one will mind if you do.

The family is a hierarchy in which precedence goes by age, so no one is in any doubt as to where he or she fits in; males have some advantage over females, but not much. You have been brought up from birth to treat elders with respect, speak when spoken to, observe the carefully-graded subtleties of the Javanese language, and not be pushy; you take it for granted that these attitudes remain in force at table as they do in every other aspect of life. The only times I recall the 'elders first' rule being deliberately broken was when times were at their hardest in the nineteen-forties, when there was not enough food for everyone and parents filled their children's plates first before they helped themselves to whatever was left. I remember how embarrassed I felt when I first came to England and my father-in-law insisted on carving the joint and piling my plate with meat, potatoes and vegetables before he served even his own wife; this is most un-Javanese behaviour.

Small western-style dinner parties were a part of middle-class social life even thirty years ago, and are much more so today. Children – the host's and the guests' – certainly used to attend these, unless they could persuade their parents they didn't want to, or unless their good behaviour was really not to be relied on. (There is no such thing as 'a proper bed-time' in the tropics; children, like their parents, sleep when they feel sleepy or as their other commitments allow.) I would like to think that listening to grown-up conversation provided a liberal education for the child, though I doubt if this was very often the case. Nowadays, small children tend to be pushed off to watch television and teenagers find their parents' food, guests, conversation and clothes so utterly boring that they stay well away. In well-off homes, too, dinner party hosts may produce unfamiliar foods (potatoes, pasta, sausages) which the children don't like. Just the reverse happens when a child has a birthday; the party is eagerly attended by every adult friend and relative who can cadge an invitation or gatecrash, and the sticky rice cakes and jellies are devoured by everyone. Other standard dishes for birthdays are *lemper* (sticky rice cakes stuffed with spiced steamed chicken) and *pisang goreng* (fried bananas).

Clearly, from what has been said, Javanese families like to eat at home; restaurants do not have anything like the appeal they have in Europe. They are too expensive for most people, and the Indonesians are not particularly good at running them. But they do of course exist, and in Jakarta, at any rate, are becoming much better and more frequent. Most of them cater for families rather than for (say) businessmen; their menus are simple, and offer local food (or that of some other region of Indonesia that is well-known for its cooking – Padang, in Central Sumatra, for example) for conservative tastes. This pattern has changed in the past fifteen years as Kentucky Fried Chicken shops have opened all over Indonesia; if the family goes out for dinner, it is often – as in the U.S.A. – the children who decide where to go. The influence of imported TV shows guarantees peer-group prestige for those who eat Kentucky Fried rather than the local product (which is usually a great deal better). In the past, street food was much more popular than restaurant food and often better; halfway between the itinerant satay-peddler and the established eating-house was the *warung*, a semi-permanent food stall often specialising in one or two classic dishes. Street food is still big business, but standards, I fear, are declining; because street food was accessible and cheap, and most of it was healthy because it was cooked in front of you, this was one of the great joys of an Indonesian childhood and provided for many of us a wider education in food and eating than we got at home.

The notion that everyone should as a matter of course be explicitly taught to prepare and eat food is probably as strange to Java as it is to Britain. Perhaps for this reason, the last twenty years have seen a flood of cookery books published in a country where previously cookery books were unknown.[8] Jakarta has its cookery schools and its gourmet magazines just as London does. On the other hand, we have generally welcomed, or at least tolerated, small children of both sexes who want to come and help in the kitchen; indeed, the traditional Javanese kitchen, with no labour-saving devices of any kind, has often relied on child labour. Most of the basic cookery techniques and dishes that I regard as the foundation of my knowledge today I learned, almost without realizing I was learning, in the kitchens of my grandmothers and aunts and of course my mother – though in fact my father enjoyed cooking more than she did, and was better at it. I also accompanied whoever was to cook to market and learned about choosing meat and vegetables, shopping around, bargaining, and menu-planning on the basis of what produce was available.

4

If I am to draw conclusions from this rather anecdotal evidence, they must be somewhat on these lines. First, food in Java, and as far as I know in all the regions of Indonesia, is one of the most important areas of life-experience, but it has not become a specialised sub-culture as it has, for example, in France or China. There are no Indonesian foodies, except perhaps among the sophisticated bourgeois of Jakarta. There is no 'culinary tradition', there are no famous chefs and the cook is not highly regarded in the household or the restaurant, although there is a tradition of street-food cooking as something of a performing art. Guests who eat in your house show their appreciation of the food by eating a lot and going back again and again to help themselves. They take it for granted that the food is plentiful and good, and only modern city dwellers are likely to tell you about it when they say good-bye.

8. The first, and still the most comprehensive, all-Indonesian cookbook was *Mustika-rasa*, assembled by the Departemen Pertanian (Department of Agriculture) and published in Jakarta in 1967. It is still an interesting guide to regional dishes, but difficult to cook from. The best periodical devoted to food and cooking is the monthly *Selera*.

Secondly, food and table manners reflect and support social values and attitudes but are not used to teach or enforce them. From what I have heard and seen in England, it seems to me that they are so used in this country, or were. English children are sent off to wash their hands before they sit down to eat; Javanese children are brought up to wash their hands as soon as they get dirty, and I think it is fair to say that it would not occur to the average child to sit down without washing. In the same way, grown-ups are automatically careful that food is scrupulously clean, partly because they understand the risks of infection, partly because Islam insists on ritual purity, but also because they are almost obsessively clean people, even in circumstances where cleanliness is very difficult to achieve.

A rather different example comes back to me from my childhood: my father suffered from asthma, and his doctor forbade him to eat certain foods. It was therefore assumed that no one in the family would eat those foods. This was not because of any dog-in-the-manger attitude on my father's part, or any belief that what was bad for an asthmatic must be bad for everyone, but merely an extension of the principle that you do not take advantage of someone by doing in front of him something he would like to do but can't.

There is probably a third conclusion lurking in the evidence, but I do not feel confident enough to draw it dogmatically. It concerns the traditional Javanese ritual meal, the *selamatan*, or its Sumatran equivalent, the *kenduri*. These meals are given, usually to one's near neighbours, to mark or commemorate any special occasion: a certain number of days after a birth or a death; a promotion at work, success in an examination; or the beginning or completion of the building of a new house – there are all sorts of reasons for holding a *selamatan*, at which a chapter of the Koran may be read, a few speeches made, a prayer or two recited, and some quite simple food offered – often the food will not even be eaten on the spot, but the guests will take it to their own homes. At the other end of the scale, a *selamatan* may be a really big affair, a wedding or funeral that costs the family many years' savings; but these are becoming less common, as are the harvest-home celebrations that were such an unforgettable part of childhood.

Yet the basic *selamatan* still, as far as I have been able to observe from rather infrequent return visits to Java, remains a pattern of social behav-

71

iour, still governed, like so much of Asian life, by strict rules of reciprocity and obligation. This survival, and whatever changes may be taking place within it, need to be seen against the greatly-increased strictness of religious observance, not only for the Islamic majority but for everybody, in the years since 1965. The thwarting of an attempted Communist coup on 30 September in that year, and the country-wide massacres that followed, showed the easy-going nominal Moslems, Christians and others that they had better identify themselves clearly as non-atheists. Indonesian society remains, generally, as tolerant as ever; you can follow what religion you please; but you are expected to be positive about it. For Moslems (90% of the population overall, and in many areas virtually 100%), this tendency is strengthened by people's awareness of the general resurgence of Islam and a wish to identify with it. Thirty years ago, only a minority observed the fast of Ramadan with real strictness; now, almost everyone does, and the contrast in atmosphere is very striking. To the extent that fasting not only expresses but promotes and strengthens religious and social solidarity, I think it may be an exception to the rule that Indonesian foodways are not used to 'teach' anything outside or beyond themselves. The *selamatan*, however, is a much more ancient, pre-Islamic observance. I hope to find out more about its present-day character and significance on future visits to Java and Sumatra.

Bibliography

Departemen Pertanian (Department of Agriculture), *Mustikarasa* (Jakarta, Departemen Pertanian, 1967)

Geertz, Clifford, *The Religion of Java* (Glencoe, Illinois: Free Press, 1960)

– *Agricultural Involution* (Berkeley and Los Angeles: University of California Press, 1963)

Geertz, Hildred, *The Javanese Family* (Glencoe, Illinois: Free Press, 1961)

Keeler, Ward, *Javanese Shadow Plays, Javanese Selves* (Princeton University Press, 1987)

Lombard, Denys, *Le Carrefour javanais* (Paris: Ecole des Hautes Etudes en Sciences Sociales, 1990)

Mears, Leon A., *The New Rice Economy of Indonesia* (Yogyakarta: Gajah Mada University Press, 1981)

Nitisastro, Widjojo, *Population Trends in Indonesia* (Ithaca: Cornell University Press, Ithaca, 1970)

Owen, Sri, *Indonesian Food and Cookery* (London: Prospect Books, 2nd edition 1986)

– *Indonesian and Thai Cookery* (London: Piatkus Books, 1988)

– *The Cooking of Thailand, Indonesia and Malaysia* (Cambridge: Martin Books for Sainsbury's, 1991)

– *Exotic Feasts* (London: Kyle Cathie, 1991)

Ricklefs, M.C., *A History of Modern Indonesia* (London: Macmillan, 1981)

Selosoemardjan, *Social Change in Jogjakarta* (Ithaca and New York: Cornell University Press, 1962)

We Chinese eat a lot
Food as a symbol of ethnic identity in Kuala Lumpur

SORAYA TREMAYNE

How do people in 'mass' societies preserve their sense of distinction? How do they maintain their commitment to their localities, to their age, gender and religious groups, against all the homogenizing pressures of modern society? A crucial answer lies in people's resourcefulness in symbolizing their communities and groups. *Symbolizing Boundaries, Identity and Diversity in British Cultures*, edited by A.P. Cohen.

THE present paper draws upon material from a study of street-food and the hawkers selling this food, conducted in Malaysia between 1986 and 1988 for the Centre for Cross-Cultural Research on Women at Oxford. Here I propose to concentrate on certain key aspects of the study: the symbolic meaning of food and the way in which street-food stalls highlight the differences between the ethnic groups of this multi-cultural society.

The prime purpose of street-food stalls is, of course, to provide cheap, fast food. However, the food stalls in Malaysia represent much more than this: they can be viewed as the public and visible markers of ethnic boundaries and, as such, as a microcosm of each ethnic group within the context of Malaysian society as a whole.

In this paper I hope to demonstrate how food, and the eating thereof, are concrete manifestations of ethnic identity in Malaysia; and how governmental policy towards the different groups and their street-food hawkers serves to accentuate the ethnic boundaries between the two main groups, the Malays and the Chinese. Street-food, in this paper, is defined as a cooked meal sold by hawkers from mobile stalls in the street, with seating facilities.

Background

Malaysia is composed of three major ethnic groups: 56% are Malays, 34% Chinese and 8% Indians. There are several other ethnic groups, but they are not significant for the purposes of this paper.[1]

The majority of Malays still live in rural areas in spite of rapid and continuous urbanization since Independence in 1957. The Chinese are mainly town dwellers and the Malaysian Indians can be found both in towns and rural areas.

Until Malaysia gained its independence from Britain, the Chinese and Indians owned and controlled 34% of the businesses while the *bumiputras* (meaning the sons of the soil, and referring to the indigenous Moslem natives of Malaysia) had 4%. 62% of the economy was in the hands of foreign-based companies.[2] The Chinese entered the higher-paid professions; the Malays, on the other hand, wielded political power through their royal rulers – the Sultans – and dominated the rural economy as farmers and fishermen (Mahathir, p. 26). Most of the Malaysian Indians, mainly Hindu by faith, were engaged in the plantations, while the Moslem Indians were – and still are – guest-workers.

Today, roughly 60% to 70% of businesses are Chinese-owned and 25% are in the hands of *bumiputras* (see note 2).

Before Independence, Malays and Chinese had worked alongside one another despite their ethnic and religious differences. They may not have intermarried or mixed socially, but they tolerated and did business with one another. After Independence the Malays, with their well-educated political elite, continued to maintain their political dominance. The younger generation of Malays, however, realized that political power without economic strength was not effective. They argued that the rural Malays were living in ignorance and poverty, and that they should be able to participate in all the economic activities of the country and to have their fair share of the income from these (Mahathir, *The Malay Dilemma*, p. 32). The New Economic Policy (NEP) was prepared as a result of the violent intercommunal riots in May 1969 in the wake of the general elections, during which the Alli-

1. *Year Book of Statistics*, pp. 29–30.
2. S.G. Redding, *The Spirit of Chinese Capitalism*, pp. 29–30.

ance government had suffered severe reverses at the hands of predominantly non-Malay opposition parties (Enloe, *Multi-Ethnic Politics*,
1970).

The NEP aimed to eradicate poverty and redress the ethnic balance.
Effectively, the *bumiputras* believe that they should be given a 56% share
in the economic activities and more opportunity in government and
business. The pressure resulting from the measures taken to implement
the NEP caused a great deal of resentment and conflict between the
different ethnic groups, since it resulted in a complete change in the
economic structure of the country. Tension built up between the Chinese and Malays, and the cultural and religious differences which had
been dormant for decades began to surface. The Malays started to stress
their identity as a Moslem nation, and the Chinese – whose livelihood
was threatened by the NEP, and whose identity was weakened because
they were becoming second-class Malaysians – began to differentiate
themselves, in a variety of ways, from other ethnic groups. The Malays
had an advantage over the Chinese in that Islam unified them as a
coherent force, while undermining the regional and subcultural
differences that existed. The slight linguistic variations, the ethnic mix
with the Thais in the North and Indonesians in the South, and other
such differences were overlooked in favour of being considered
bumiputras. The Chinese, on the other hand, belonged to six major sub-
ethnic groups, each group with its separate dialect, professional speci-
alities and regional provenance. Many Chinese spoke only their own
dialect and could not communicate with the other sub-ethnic groups;
they had to find unifying factors in order to create a degree of solidarity
amongst themselves.

The following passage from a report, on *Corporate Strategies for Malaysia* (written by Business International Asia/Pacific Ltd. in 1981), also
highlights how, in a less intentional way than the NEP, the religion and
culture of the Malay ruling elite also serve to discriminate against the
Chinese and prevent their assimilation into Malaysian society:

Two basic features characterize the tension between the two ethnic groups: the
economic conflicts, and religious differences. Certain principles in Islam play
an important indirect role in maintaining tension between the two communities. Islam forbids intermarriage with non-Moslems, and provides not only a
body of religious and ethical beliefs but a comprehensive code for everyday life

as well. The religious factor (Moslem Malays/non-Moslem Chinese) had been a bar to intermarriage, which is the most common practice for gradually overcoming intergroup barriers. In Thailand, for example, the so-called Chinese problem is being overcome by assimilation of the Thai and Chinese ethnic groups at all levels of society since no doctrine prevents intermarriage. Malays, however, foresee no end to the unassimilable group of non-Moslems living in their midst. Islam is a democratic faith and essentially does not discriminate on the basis of race. Thus conversion would be one route to intermarriage and eventual assimilation. Here, however, two points of Islamic doctrine make it difficult for non-Moslems to convert: dietary habits (for example, the prohibition on eating pork for Moslems), and the pervasive influence of Islam on daily life. The religious factor mentioned above directly affects the way that Chinese businessmen attempt to protect themselves in situations where they cannot rely on law. A method widely used by Chinese businessman elsewhere is to marry off daughters to high-ranking officials in their adopted countries, relying on kinship to protect them and advance their interests. In Malaysia the Chinese do not have as ready access to this option. They must seek protection through legal or other channels, which has become a root cause of conflict.

There is the exceptional case of intermarriage between the Chinese and Malays, which has resulted in the emergence of a sub-ethnic group called Babas (referring to men) and Nonyas (referring to women) or The Straits Chinese (Penang, Malacca and Singapore). Babas and Nonyas are the offspring of migrant Chinese men who married the local Moslem Malay women. They became 'Malay in form, but remained Chinese in essence', as they like to describe themselves. The Chinese men, who did not become Moslem, adopted the Malay dress and language which gradually evolved into a dialect. However, even the dress which was Malay in form was made with Chinese material. Although these groups are numerically and politically insignificant as far as the economy is concerned, it is interesting to note that the principal surviving feature of Baba and Nonya culture is their cuisine, known as Nonya food/cuisine.

Indians form a distinct cultural entity, as far as their culture, religion, language and cuisine are concerned, and their influence on most aspects of Malaysian culture is visible. Representing only 8% of the total population, however, their role in the struggle for economic power – the main cause of confrontation between the Malays and the Chinese – is not a significant one. Nor do the other two groups view them with hostility or as a threat. The Indians themselves, however, view the Malays in the same way as do the Chinese, and feel that they have been pushed out of the way in favour of the Malays. Nonetheless, when they have to make a decision they usually side with the Malays, because they do not trust the Chinese and reckon that their interests are closer to those of the Malays. When appropriate I shall refer to the case of Indians to highlight inter-ethnic feelings; but the Malays and Chinese remain the focus of this paper.

Street-food as a microcosm of ethnic differences

Faced with the threat presented by the new political situation, the Chinese responded by articulating their feelings in a number of ways. Some of these expressions of feeling concerned the Chinese community, encouraging them to unite culturally; others provoked cultural confrontation with the non-Chinese, especially the Malays. The expression of this separate identity can be found in several institutions which are purely Chinese and which are practised with more force by migrant Chinese outside China than in mainland China: festivities and celebrations are examples of these. At a more visible and day-to-day level, one of the most striking examples of ethnic division between Malays, Chinese and Indians is crystallized in the city streets where food is consumed in public from stalls. In no other social institution is such a strict and visible line drawn. Each ethnic group sells its own food and operates in segregation from the others. In other public places, such as office canteens and shopping malls, there are separate areas allocated to different ethnic groups. Here the dividing line is drawn mainly between Moslem and non-Moslem food.

Cooked food bought from hawkers, who operate from push carts from a fixed location and who have seating facilities for their clients, is the most popular and widespread form of public eating in Malaysia. The selling of street-food is essentially an urban phenomenon, as in Indonesia too.[3]

Street-food vendors in developing countries are generally classified by planners and policy makers as falling into the category of the infor-

3. Sri Owen, *Indonesian Food and Cookery*, London, Prospect Books, 1986.

mal. Hawkers are generally considered as the poor, who make a meagre living by selling food in the corners of streets (see McGee and Yeung, Tinker, Smart). Although most of the hawkers in Malaysia fall into the lower-income bracket, the magnitude of the street-food operation and its culturally complex character make Malaysia an exceptional case compared to other countries. Hawking touches on so many social and political institutions that it can be seen as a microcosm of Malaysian society. A short discussion including some facts and figures will indicate the extent of the hawkers' operation in general and the position of each ethnic group in particular.

Scale of hawking

The city of Kuala Lumpur is the main location for this study. I also made a survey of food stalls in Penang, Kota Baru, Kota Kina-Balu and Kuching to provide a comparison.

Kuala Lumpur, at the time of the study, had a population of 1.2 million inhabitants according to the official figures, with a majority of 65% Chinese. Before urbanization brought waves of newcomers (mainly Malays from rural areas), the Chinese formed around 85% of the population of Kuala Lumpur. At that time the great majority of stalls were run by the Chinese. With the arrival of large numbers of migrants and the change in the ethnic composition of the city, the number of food stalls has increased dramatically to cater for the need of the newcomers. The following figures are taken from the 1980 census and the Hawkers' Management Department of the City Hall of Kuala Lumpur. They will give an idea of the changes which stem from growing urbanization and the effect of the NEP.

The official number of licensed food hawkers is 25,000, although the associations of hawkers and some of the officials of the City Hall, reluctantly and off the record, admit that there are at least three times as many hawkers who operate without a licence. If we multiply 75,000 by three – the number of people required to run a cooked-food stall – we are faced with 200,000 people directly involved in selling street-food. This is approximately 20% of the total population of Kuala Lumpur. In addition, thousands of businesses are indirectly dependent on the street-food business: food markets, ice delivery, fuel delivery (most hawkers use gas, kerosene and charcoal at the same time for different purposes). With the closure of some of the central markets, the increasing number of middle-men involved in delivering meat and vegetables and other services involves an additional large number of people.

Another set of statistics which helps confirm the above comes from the Department of Transport and the Police. These claim that two million meals per day are served in public places in Kuala Lumpur. Without doubt, at least three-quarters of these are provided by street-food sellers.

The rate of increase in the number of food stalls is also remarkable. The Hawkers' Department of the City Hall receives between 100 and 150 application forms per week for new licences. Usually one-third of the applicants receive a licence. According to official figures, the total number of hawkers (food and non-food) increased from 8,300 in 1972 to 15,000 in 1979 and to 36,000 in 1986.[4]

Finally, the most relevant set of figures in this study is the change in the ethnic proportions of licensed hawkers. In 1975 there were 8,300 Chinese hawkers, 1,200 Malays and 811 Indians. In 1988, the number of Malay hawkers had gone up by seven times to 8,500. The number of Chinese and Indians had nearly doubled to 16,500 for the Chinese and 1,500 for the Indians. The Social and Economic Research Unit's (SERU) study of hawkers states: 'New entrants into hawking are mainly *bumiputras* as indicated by the large percentage (69%) of them in the age groups under 40 years. This implies that *bumiputras* are venturing into the business sector, though into the more traditional and small scale ones such as the hawking of food'.

Although the figures do not specify the percentage increase of the Chinese and Malay population for the years given, it is clear that the increase in the number of Malay stalls is out of proportion compared to the total increase in the Malay population, and to the increase in the population of other ethnic groups. One might also guess that the number of Chinese hawkers who operate without a licence is much higher than admitted, or guessed at, and does not figure anywhere.

4. The figures and statistics are not always consistent and do not always add up. They are meant to give a general idea of the changes.

Stalls and their customers

One of the most remarkable features of the streets of Kuala Lumpur is that they give the impression that everybody is eating all the time. The constant flow of customers, combined with the noise and steam and smell of cooking at the stalls, creates a lively and colourful atmosphere. The customers come from all walks of life. Wealth and social class are not divisive factors. The most obvious divisive element is religion rather than ethnicity. Islamic eating practices and food taboos forbid Moslems from eating certain food such as pork, or food prepared in a 'non-Islamic' way. One can therefore see Moslem Indians eating at Malay stalls and vice versa. In finer analysis, one observes that ethnic differences between Malays and Chinese deter the few Moslem Chinese, who are rarely seen at Moslem food stalls.

The stalls are spread out throughout the city. In some areas such as China Town they are exclusively Chinese, in others such as Kampong Baru they are Malay, and in the central and business areas of town there is a mixture of all three groups. In this case they stand in rows alongside one other, but do not mix.

The majority of the customers of stalls (between 60 and 70%) are regulars. This applies to all ethnic groups. Going to stalls serves more than one purpose. Stalls, especially those operating outside the business areas, serve as a community centre for their customers, where they can meet friends, business contacts, future spouses and newcomers from rural areas. Politicians also use the stalls as a forum for their activities (this is practised in a more explicit way by Malay politicians). Buying and selling drugs and prostitution are two other invisible activities harboured by the stalls. Receiving and exchanging news is crucial for people in the informal economy, who need to form or modify their strategies (often short-term) accordingly. They do not always trust the official news and often follow rumour which is not necessarily baseless. The stalls' role as a place for the spread of information is very important. A BBC report during the Tiananmen Square unrest in China suggested that the fastest means of communication with the rural areas was via the stalls.

Stalls' customers come from a variety of backgrounds and use the stalls for differing purposes. Stalls operating in the daytime mainly attract employees ranging from office workers to construction workers, and passers-by. Night stalls, which cater for night-workers and people without cooking facilities, serve a more leisurely customer-type: family and young people's outings, couples wishing to remain anonymous, and even lonely old people. Malay and Indian stalls, which sometimes have a video and entertain their customers with films on boxing and wrestling, have a high number of old women as their regular customers.

Food as a reference to ethnic identity

Talking about food, and the eating thereof, is often used to convey a sense of superiority and as a distinctive cultural statement by all the ethnic groups studied, but is most noticeable among the Chinese. Talking about food and eating is a preoccupation with the Chinese, who are interested in food in its wider context and implications (creating the right balance between 'heating' and 'cooling' food, medicinal effect of ingredients etc.). When the Chinese insist that 'We Chinese eat a lot', they are demonstrating their love and appreciation for food and refering to the richness and variety of Chinese cuisine. Several people told me that the reason for this 'obsession' with food is that for people in China in the old days there was no other way of spending their money; they therefore spent it on food. The reality does not accord with this statement, since the majority of migrants were people pushed out a few generations ago by the scarcity of food and the hardship of life in China. Furthermore, examination of the diet of many Chinese workers from lower-income groups reveals that the average person does not 'eat a lot'; most Chinese have two meals per day accompanied by some snacking. Eating a bowl of noodles when meeting a business contact, or drinking tea when selling insurance or other services at a stall, is done to create a bond rather than to satisfy the appetite.

At a symbolic level, food is used by the Chinese as a reference point to reinforce cultural identity: 'We Chinese' and 'eating a lot' refer to a dream and a myth, conveying a sense of belonging to China, of security provided by the abundance of food, and a message of success.

In the following passage, Redding stresses the importance of ethnic solidarity among the overseas Chinese, and the significance of their success in relationship to this ethnicity.[5] He points out 'the slowness of the assimilation of the overseas Chinese into the host cultures of Malaysia, Indonesia and the Philippines' and explains that:

Accounts of retention of ethnic separateness are common, and this feature would appear to have a long-standing and consistent history. Although it inevitably results from many forces, there are three principal causes which come to mind as determinants: firstly, the Chinese are resented for their success and band together defensively; secondly, they perceive that Chinese culture is superior to its alternatives; thirdly, it may simply be more humanly comfortable, at a very basic level, to associate with one's own kind.

Redding elaborates on the outstanding success of the migrant Chinese in ASEAN countries and the pride they take in this success and argues that:

They would not be Chinese if they did not, at the same time, understand with full sensitivity, the effect of their success on people in the host culture, and the kind of resentment which might ensue. In consequence a wary and defensive insistence on the maintenance of their own group solidarity is entirely predictable.

A logical extension of such success is to point to the source as Chinese civilization itself. If seen retrospectively, and the traditionalist perspective tends to ensure this, and if seen romantically (not difficult at a long remove from the events), then Chinese civilization has massive authority based on its achievements. It is not surprisingly still a guiding beacon, and in consequence a shared focus, universally understood and strongly cohesive in its workings.

Indians often draw attention to their food, which is popular with both Malays and Chinese, by saying that most of the Malaysian cuisine is based on the Indian.

Malays use the reference to food not to establish their ethnic identity (they do not see any threat to their identity), but to convey their sense of unity as a Moslem nation. The most frequent context of symbolic reference to food is in distinguishing themselves as Moslems who abhor the pork-eating habits of the Chinese. I have even heard some Malays say that the Chinese have a 'cold body' because they eat pork. The sense of modesty imposed by Islam prevents the Malays from making public their likes and dislikes to the same extent as do the

5. Redding, p. 58.

Chinese. Malays on the whole do not introduce the topic of food unless prompted, and even then they do not make a public issue of it.

All customers of stalls, regardless of their ethnic origins, prefer the informality and 'relaxed' atmosphere of the stalls to restaurants. They also think that stall food is cheaper and tastier, and is served fast. For the Chinese the additional attraction of stall food is the proof of its freshness, since the food is cooked in front of the customer, whereas some Indian and Malay food such as curries are cooked beforehand and reheated.

An interesting point is that both Malays and Chinese, at an individual level, are prepared to go to one another's houses and be entertained in their restaurants, but they will almost never go to each other's stalls whether accompanied by the host or not. They do not wish to be seen by their own group to eat publicly at the 'others' food stalls – or risk being given the cold shoulder by the 'others'. Crossing the ethnic boundaries in such a public way, especially if unaccompanied by one of the members of the host group, is considered an intrusion. Food when consumed publicly is used as a marker of cultural identity, whereas when consumed privately it sheds its symbolic significance.

Attitudes towards one another's food

The Chinese and Malay attitudes towards each other's food differ greatly and are not reciprocal. The views that are expressed in the form of anecdotes or beliefs clearly reflect underlying cultural and political differences and feelings. While Malays avoid Chinese food (except *halal* food) and articulate their views about the Chinese eating habits in strong terms, the Chinese do not express any 'formalized' or 'derogatory' opinions about Malay food. They may occasionally send indirect messages, using food as indirect means to refer to Malays themselves. In saying: 'but there are no Malay food stalls, Malays do not have stalls, only the Chinese have stalls', and other such denials, they are in fact expressing their opinion on the Malays and their ability to run businesses. One can detect a certain sense of patronage on the part of the Chinese. They remain to be convinced of the competence of Malays as efficient businessmen. At the same time, the Chinese are – on the whole – adventurous, like to try new food, and will eat Malay food happily.

Hawkers and the organization of food stalls among different groups

Supporting and controlling organizations

Hawking is a relatively insecure profession, because it depends on many – potentially changeable – factors, including changes in population movements, town planning and government policies. Smart's study of hawkers in Hong Kong confirms this finding.[6] Hawkers, therefore, have to employ certain strategies to help secure their work and its continuity, and to allow them to survive. Being a hawker in Kuala Lumpur entails more than simply buying a pushcart and setting it up in a corner. In the process of establishing themselves in business (and afterwards), hawkers normally find themselves involved with several formal and informal institutions, some of which are supposed to support them and some to control them. Once more the structure of the stalls and the type of institutions associated reflect ethnic differences and the position of each ethnic group in society. An analysis of the way the food hawkers organize themselves clearly reveals how, at grass-roots level, the ethnic differences prevent any kind of occupational unity from developing among Malaysians.

Formal organization: the authorities

The attitude of the Malaysian authority towards hawkers is, on the whole, a positive one, compared to many other developing countries. They realize that the service provided by the hawkers is essential, and one that no other institution can replace. But they also reckon that the scale of hawking, and the problems created by such large numbers of people involved, have to be taken seriously. One of the most important duties of the Department for the Management of Hawkers is to ensure that every hawker has a licence and is healthy and fit to handle food. The Department issues new licences and renews old ones. Licensing is one of the areas in which the NEP has apparently, been implemented successfully, in that proportionally more licences are granted to Malay applicants than to the Chinese. I have already discussed the scale of hawking and the change in its ethnic composition. In practice, those

6. J. Smart, *The Political Economy of Street Hawkers in Hong Kong*, p. 134.

Chinese hawkers who already have a licence try to renew it, but many do not apply for a licence to set up new stalls, or continue their operation without one. They assume, rightly or wrongly, that they will not be granted a licence because they are Chinese. This group usually operates outside the central and business areas of the city and remains within its own community (either the area where they live, or where the community is purely Chinese). In some cases bribery is practised to appease the enforcement officers.

Malay hawkers either apply for a licence and, in majority of cases, receive one; or do not apply and, when approached by enforcement officers, rely on their ethnic identity and sense of brotherhood, using negotiating and delaying tactics. If they have an influential friend, they may even threaten the enforcement officers.

In the case of Indian hawkers, most of the foodstalls are run by Moslem Indians, many of whom are guest-workers. Usually an older man, possibly a second-generation guest-worker, marries a Malay woman and obtains a licence in her name. He then brings his 'brothers' from his home town in India as helpers. Some of the Indian stalls I have studied employ up to seven workers who all share a very large bed in a small room and otherwise spend their life in the street, mainly at the stall. The Hindus and Buddhist Indians resident in Malaysia often run drink stalls.

Semi-official organisations

A second type of organization is the 'mediating' institution, such as the hawker associations or member of parliament, whose main role is to facilitate the relationship between hawkers and the authorities. The associations help their members to obtain licences and loans, and form pressure groups to protect their interests. In Malaysia, hawkers do not form a single united association. Associations are based on the ethnic origins of the hawkers rather than their profession. Malays and Chinese have their separate associations, and Indians receive their support from the Indian Chamber of Commerce. If they are Moslem Indians, they are allowed to join the Malay associations.

Malay associations of hawkers have a large number of members. Malays favour collective working. The concepts of co-operation and mutual help (*Gotong Royong*), and consensus (*Muafakat*) are prescribed values in Malay culture, and form the pillars of traditional decision-making among the Malays. Malay hawkers are also encouraged by the help given by their associations in obtaining interest-free loans from MARA (Majlis Amanah Rakyat), the People's Trust Council, which is funded by the Government with the aim of accelerating *bumiputra* economic development.

The Chinese are traditionally more individualistic than the Malays, and do not trust any person or organization outside their immediate family circle.[7] Many of them however join their associations against a 'rainy day'. The Chinese do not have access to interest-free loans, but neither do they resort to bank loans. Their usual route for borrowing is from informal sources such as moneylenders and relatives.[8]

Members of parliament, as another 'mediating' element, have more sporadic contact with hawkers. Hawkers form a considerable number and force as constituents in every area of the city. But it is mainly at the time of elections and other political events, when the politicians need the support of their constituents, that they communicate with them. There are, however, some politicians, especially Chinese ones, who have made a name and reputation for themselves by keeping the hawkers constantly on their agenda and fighting for their rights. This applies especially to issues relating to resettlement of hawkers from crowded areas to the outskirts of the city, or to purpose-built shopping malls and covered markets.

Informal organizations

There are a number of informal, and sometimes illegal, groups heavily involved in either protecting or controlling the hawking business. These have their roots in different socio-economic institutions which vary among different ethnic groups. The most relevant are moneylenders, debt-collectors and protection groups.

Moneylenders

Almost every first-time hawker needs to borrow money to set up stall. The main expense, especially for those operating in the central areas of

7. For a better understanding of the Chinese individuality see Redding, p. 58.
8. *A Socio-Economic Study of Hawkers*, Annex 1.

the city, is the 'tea money' they have to pay to take over a site. 'Tea money' is the cash paid to the outgoing hawker by the newcomer, and the sum involved varies greatly depending on the profitability of the site. In some cases it can amount to as much as £12,000. This transaction is illegal; the officials 'do not want to know about it' and refer to it as 'hanky panky money'. Depositing tea money creates a complex bond between the newcomer and the resident hawkers, and goes beyond a purely financial agreement. I would like to emphasize that tea money is not a mere depositing of money, but also a guarantee on the part of the newcomer that he will conform to the rules of hawking, because if he does not he will be forced out by others who, if necessary, will call in the protection groups to get rid of him. Recovering one's tea money in such a case is not easy, and it may be lost altogether. Tea money thus becomes the proof of the credibility of the newcomer, who shows that he either has sufficient funds to invest, or can borrow and repay his debts. Some of the Chinese cases I studied borrowed money even if they did not need to, just to establish a reputation as good borrowers. The depositing of tea money is practised among all three ethnic groups but more often among the Chinese and Indians than the Malays who, as discussed, have access to government loans. The most usual means of borrowing money is from the moneylenders.

Debt-collectors

Moneylenders, in turn, have to make sure that they get their money back. To this end, they call on debt-collectors to collect debts. This latter group is generally referred to as gangsters. In the majority of cases in fact, it consists of young men wishing to set up their own businesses, who have to give their services free to the established and powerful underground institutions running the gangster and protection groups before they are allowed to start their own business. Although all three ethnic groups have their debt-collectors and gangsters, this means is used on a larger scale and in a more obvious way by the Chinese.

Protection groups

Protection groups are a permanent part of the of the people, especially those in lower-income groups, in the informal sector of the economy in Kuala Lumpur. Protection is a very widespread practice, and is used to extract money not only from people who run businesses, but from a cross-section of society including new migrants living in lodging houses without any connections. Hawkers are no exception. Whether a hawker needs protection or not, he will have to pay a regular sum to a protection group to protect himself from raids by other groups. Details of the way the protection groups operate are not relevant to this paper. The important point is that raids, kidnapping, or any other form of violence or conflict, remain strictly within ethnic boundaries and do not cross into the other groups. Despite the underlying tension between the ethnic groups, confrontation is avoided at all costs.

Conclusion

In this paper I have attempted to show how we can gain an insight and understanding of ethnic differences and feelings which exist between the Malays, the Chinese and to a lesser extent the Indians, in Malaysia by examining the social and cultural aspects of street-food, the organization of foodstalls, and the driving forces, values and motivations of people involved in selling street-food.

Analysis of the formal and informal means that people use to set up their businesses and sustain them demonstrates the level of interaction between these groups and the way each group receives, interprets and reacts to the political and economic measures introduced by authorities. To this end I have used street-food as a significant example, and a complex one which involves several formal and informal official and underground components. Food has been considered here as a symbol of ethnicity rather than in its more concrete and economic context.

The political changes which took place in Malaysia after Independence, and the intercommunal conflicts, led to hostile feelings between the Malays and the Chinese. The cultural and ethnic differences became publicly apparent when the Chinese realized that the new economic policy would limit their participation in the economy, and threaten their livelihood.

The Malaysian Chinese are second- or third-generation migrants from China. Like all migrants who have been uprooted and thrown into a new environment, they needed to strengthen their sense of identity and to preserve China as their cultural reference point. The fact that they could not intermarry with the Malays prevented them from becoming more integrated into a 'Malaysian' society, and from being assimilated to their host country. The Chinese therefore created cultural boundaries around themselves to protect this identity. These boundaries, which began as demarcation lines, gradually turned into fortresses. After the introduction of the NEP the Chinese resorted to a number of means to protect their economic interest and preserve their position in society. Being essentially urban dwellers relying on networks and contacts, they developed exceptional skills in creating a balance in their relationship with the formal institutions and authorities on the one hand, and the informal and often underground organizations on the other. Every Chinese hawker I have met has friends among the CID and the underground world, and plays these forces against each other.

For Malays, who consider themselves to be natives of Malaysia (as opposed to migrants), the trauma of being uprooted by being thrown into an urban situation is of a different nature. In the case of the rural to urban migrants, the problems are not those of food shortages, insecurity or homelessness, but those of confusion: the drastic change in circumstance of leaving the peaceful and secure village and community (*kampong*) and wandering into the city. A young person who comes from a paternalistic culture, where total protection and support is provided by the community for its members, and problems are solved in council form and by consensus, suddenly finds himself or herself faced with loneliness and no support from kin. Instead he or she is offered help from the government, and encouraged to defend his or her political and economic 'rights' as a Malay and a Moslem.

The tension of *bumiputras* versus migrants, and Moslems versus non-Moslems causes deep friction between the two groups. Although leaders from both ethnic groups are trying to modify the differences and find ways of reconciling them, at grass-roots level the feeling of hostility is still strong within both groups. 'We Chinese' as opposed to 'We Malaysians', is frequently the opening sentence for most conversations. The recent policy of the Malaysian Government allowing the Chinese to visit China (something they were not previously permitted to do) is having an impact on the Malaysian Chinese. Those who have returned from a visit to their homeland in China feel that 'it is better to be a Chinese in Malaysia than a Chinese in China'. This feeling is not yet widespread, however, and will take time to filter through to other Chinese in Malaysia.

As we have seen in the case of hawkers, the Chinese have adopted a 'paranoid' view of the policies devised by the authorities, and have tried to circumvent them. They try to strengthen their bastion of Chineseness by recreating a miniature China and remain as a group apart, using direct and indirect messages to convey this. To this end, food-stalls become one of the most effective signals. They represent a cultural unity acting as a haven, with well-defined boundaries within which each ethnic group can withdraw, and from which symbolically they can challenge the 'others'. The public can observe them segregating themselves in the street, and eating their own food which is special to them and exclusive of other groups. In addition, each ethnic group conducts many of its social and business activities from the stall in a very discreet way. When the Chinese refer to 'eating a lot' they are referring to a cultural ideal, symbolized in food.

Bibliography

Published Sources
Cynthia H. Enloe, *Multi-Ethnic Politics: The Case of Malaysia,* Research Monograph Series, University of California, Berkeley: Center for South and Southeast Asian Studies, 1970.
Mahathir Bin Mohamad, *The Malay Dilemma*, Kuala Lumpur, 1970.
T. G. McGee & Y. M. Yeung, *Hawkers in South East Asian Cities, Planning for the Bazaar Economy*, Ottawa, 1977.
T. McGee, *Hawkers in Selected Asian Cities, a Preliminary Investigation*, Hong Kong, 1970.
Sri Owen, *Indonesian Food and Cookery*, London, Prospect Books, 1986.
S. G. Redding, *The Spirit of Chinese Capitalism*, Berlin nd New York, 1990.
Josephine Smart, *The Political Economy of Street Hawkers in Hong Kong,* Hong Kong, 1989.
Symbolising Boundaries, Identity and Diversity in British Cultures, edited by A. P. Cohen, Manchester, 1986.
Irene Tinker, 'Street Food: Testing Assumptions about Informal Sector Activ-

ity, by Women and Men', *Current Sociology*, vol 35, no 3, Sage Publication, 1987.
Year Book of Statistics, Department of Statistics, Malaysia, 1987.

Unpublished Sources
A Socio-Economic Study of Hawkers in Kuala Lumpur, Socio-Economic Research Unit (SERU), (unpublished, Kuala Lumpur, 1987).
Corporate Strategies for Malaysia, an In-depth Guide for Responding to the NEP (unpublished, Kuala Lumpur, 1981).
Deraf Lapuran, Penjaja Dan Penjajaan Di Bandaraya Kuala Lumpur: Kedaan Semasa, Masalah Dan Cadagan, by Dr Rokiah Talib & Dr Mohd Fawzi Haji Yacoob (unpublished, Kuala Lumpur, 1987).

2

Food in cultures from the Renaissance
to the nineteenth century

The Intensification of Italy
Food, wine and the foreign in seventeenth-century travel writing

CHLOE CHARD

In the many commentaries on Italy written by French and English travellers during the eighteenth century, descriptions of food and wine are relatively rare: far less attention is accorded to the gastronomic aspects of Italy than to objects of commentary such as landscape, architecture and antiquities, painting and sculpture, and manners and social customs. Where eighteenth-century travel books do in fact mention Italian food and wine, they are often violently condemnatory. Lady Miller's *Letters from Italy* (1776) provides the following account of an evening 'at a village called Maschieri':

... in the dirtiest of all possible inns, and the most miserable bed, 'we courted sleep in vain,' after having supped upon, what think you? a pork soup with the *bouilliée* in it, namely a hog's head, with the eye-lashes, eyes, and nose on; the very food the wretched animal had last eat of before he made his *exit* remained sticking about the teeth; we wanted neither 'nose of Turk, nor Tartar's lip,' and had there been a tiger's chawdron for the ingredients of our cauldron for sow, (at least hog's blood was not wanting) 'to make the gruel thick and slab,' we should have been able to have raised ghosts from the charmed pot. This soup was removed by a dish of broiled housesparrows. Need I say we went to bed supperless.[1]

Seventeenth-century travel writings, on the other hand, not only include an abundance of descriptions of food and wine, but also assume

1. Miller, II, 89–90. For similar expressions of horror and disgust, see, for example, II, 186–7 and Samuel Sharp, *Letters from Italy*, 45–6.

The author would like to thank Tim Knox, Helen Langdon, Todd Longstaffe-Gowan and Vincent Woropay for reading and commenting on earlier drafts of this paper; she is also very grateful to Gillian Riley, for drawing her attention to Giacomo Castelvetro's *Brieve racconto di tutte le radici di tutte l'erbe di tutti i frutti che crudi o cotti in Italia si mangiano*, and generously supplying her with a copy of the treatise.

that Italian wines and foodstuffs deserve quite as much attention as Italian art and architecture – an assumption that is obliquely voiced through seventeenth-century travellers' selections of features to be noted: Jean Huguetan's *Voyage d'Italie* (1681) includes, for example, the following brief assessment of Vicenza: 'Les Palais y sont beaux; le vin y est excellent, et la campagne tres fertile.'[2]

The status of wine as a worthy object of commentary is sometimes affirmed directly – though always with a self-protective gesture of irony. John Raymond's *Itinerary Contayning a Voyage Made through Italy* (1648) describes Albano as a town that 'deserves seeing, if not for the Antiquity, yet for the good Wine; one of the best sorts in *Italy*'. The same travel book comments on the villa of Caprarola: 'In the Garden the Cataracts of water, are very admirable; But that for which this place is most spoken of, is the Sellar.'[3] In Richard Lassels's *Voyage of Italy* (1670), the traveller also pauses to consider the two rival attractions of Caprarola, and concludes by making a similar choice: 'Having walked this garden about, youl deserve after so much water, a little wine, which will not be wanting to you from the rare *cellar* lyeing under the great *Terrasse* before the house: and perchance youl think the *wineworks* here as fine as the *waterworks*.'[4]

Among the many commentaries on food and wine that seventeenth-century travel writings include, moreover, expressions of pleasure and approbation predominate overwhelmingly over complaints and criticisms. Even the most unenethusiastic accounts of Italy written during this period usually exempt Italian gastronomy from their condemnation: Richard Fleckno's morose description of Rome in his *Relation of Ten Years Travells in Europe, Asia, Affrique, and America* (1654?) concedes that 'good meat there is, delicious wine, and excellent fruit', before hastily explaining away these merits with the observation: 'but that is the Climats vertue, and none of theirs'.[5]

Opposition and Intensification

Rather than viewing the disparity between the comments of seventeenth-century travellers and those of travellers from the succeeding

2. 245–6.   3. p.267, p.65.   4. I, 249.   5. p.34.

century as the product of some vast diminution in the quality of Italian food itself, it is possible to see this disparity as the product of a series of changes in the rules governing what can be said and written about Italy, and about southern Europe in general – changes that take place between about 1680 and 1730.[6]

In both seventeenth-century and eighteenth-century travel writings, the subject who utters the commentary imposes on the foreign a demand that it should proclaim its otherness as forcefully as possible, by exhibiting an unmistakeable difference from the familiar. In writings of both periods, too, one of the principal ways in which this difference is expected to manifest itself is through a display of drama more extreme than that found in the traveller's own country.

The most common strategy by which difference is affirmed in eighteenth-century travel writing is direct opposition: proclaiming a power of comparison derived from the experience of travel, the subject who utters the commentary scrutinizes the topography of foreignness for objects that provide as precise a contrast as possible to elements within his or her own native region.[7] This rhetorical device is exemplified by a passage in Hester Piozzi's *Observations and Reflections Made in the Course of a Journey through France, Italy, and Germany* (1789):

God has kindly given to Italians a bright sky, a penetrating intellect, a genius for the polite and liberal arts, and a soil which produces literally, as well as figuratively, almost spontaneous fruits. He has bestowed on Englishmen a mild and wholesome climate, a spirit of application and improvement, a judicious manner of thinking to increase, and commerce to procure, those few comforts their own island fails to produce.[8]

6. The aim of the analysis that follows is not to seek any kind of ultimate explanation for these transformations, but, rather, to locate the forms of language used to describe Italian food and wine in the seventeenth century within the wider context of an ordering of knowledge, concerned with a particular region of the foreign, which assigns to gastronomic commentary a specific set of rhetorical functions – and which, when its main themes and strategies begin to change, confers a quite different role on descriptions of wines and foodstuffs.

7. In eighteenth-century travel literature, the speaking subject can be positioned as either a male or a female traveller. Both male and female pronouns and possessive adjectives are therefore employed here when referring to writings of this period. In references to seventeenth-century travel writing, however, only male pronouns and adjectives are used, since the subject of commentary in these earlier writings is almost invariably specified as male.

8. II, 140.

Within the commentary of opposition, any expression of pleasure in the foreign raises the possibility that the traveller voicing delight is at the same time rejecting the familiar. In affirming that Italy is supplying the quality of drama which the traveller expects and demands of it, eighteenth-century travel writings regularly define Italian drama by setting it in contrast to some corresponding quality – such as tameness, insipidity, or mediocrity – that is presented as characteristic of the traveller's own country, and is invested with an inferior degree of fascination and excitement. Henry Swinburne's *Travels in the Two Sicilies* (1783–5) notes, at Taranto, 'a tameness in the prospect not unlike the insipidity of the artificial lakes and elegant swells in our fashionable gardens in England, totally different from the bold beauties of Italian landscape'.[9] Any generalized and unequivocal preference for the foreign over the familiar is, however, carefully avoided in writings on Italy during this period. A commentary on Venice in Piozzi's *Observations and Reflections*, for example, begins by noting the 'striking' quality both of that city and of Italy as a whole, but then, assuming that the delights of the traveller's own country are called into question by this expression of pleasure in the foreign, hastily reaffirms these delights:

I do believe that Venice, like other Italian beauties, will be observed to possess features so striking, so prominent, and so discriminated, that her portrait, like theirs, will not be found difficult to take, nor the impression she has once made easy to erase. British charms captivate less powerfully, less certainly, less suddenly: but being of a softer sort, increase upon acquaintance; and after the connexion has continued for some years, will be relinquished with pain, perhaps even in exchange for warmer colouring and stronger expression.[10]

A more covert method of denying any preference for the foreign is to ensure that expressions of pleasure are always counterbalanced by expressions of censure; in eighteenth-century travel literature, praise and delight constantly alternate with criticism and condemnation. Among these expressions of censure are complaints about food and wine.

Such complaints are particularly useful in challenging the ability of one particular domain of objects – those objects that form part of the terrain – to supply the traveller with pleasure and benefit. Eighteenth-century travel writings are full of accounts of the superior drama of the

9. II, 46.   10. I, 150–1.

Italian countryside – a drama derived from the aesthetic qualities of wild, mountainous scenery (the qualities that Swinburne describes as disappointingly absent from Taranto). Praise of wild sublimity, however, is easily combined with a form of censure: the suggestion that human mismanagement of the terrain threatens to deprive it of the pleasures of natural fertility.[11] By employing food and wine as metonyms for the terrain from which they are produced, criticism of Italian gastronomic standards strongly reinforces such a suggestion: the natural plenty of Italy cannot be so very impressive, it is implied, if all that is set before the traveller is the sort of meal described by Lady Miller.

In seventeenth-century commentary, on the other hand, the foreign is presented not through the strategy of opposition but, rather, through that of intensification: the traveller identifies Italy as different from northern Europe by claiming that, while it incorporates many features that are also found in England or France, it displays these features in an intensified form. As in eighteenth-century travel writing, the subject of commentary registers a strong desire to discover a dramatic difference from the familiar within the topography of the foreign: this difference, however, is implicitly designated as a difference of degree rather than of kind.

The element of drama, therefore, is never, in this earlier form of commentary, placed in direct opposition to any contrasting quality within the familiar; instead, it is greeted as an effect produced by an unusual intensity, concentration, or extremity within objects and attributes that are in themselves perfectly familiar – such as the 'huge Citrons' observed by John Evelyn in Genoa in 1644, which strain credulity not because of their exoticism but simply because of their size: they are described as fruits 'that one would have believed incredible should have been supported by so weake branches'.[12] The drama that the foreign supplies is very precisely identified with intensification rather than with unfamiliarity, or with any contrast to the familiar, in the description of the Campania Felix in Fynes Moryson's *Itinerary* (1611): 'Here the beautie of all the World is gathered as it were into a bundle.'[13]

---

11. See, for example, Sharp, 49–50.   12. *Diary*, p.99; diary entry for 17 October 1744.
13. III, 106.

The absence of any structure of opposition, in seventeenth-century travel writing, allows the subject of commentary to express delight in the foreign without at the same time implying any denigration of the familiar. Expressions of pleasure, therefore, require no disavowal, of the kind constantly voiced in eighteenth-century travel writing through expressions of censure, but are allowed to proliferate without qualification or restraint. Censure is not entirely excluded from commentary on the foreign, but occupies a minor role, as a subsidiary strategy of intensification; such censure, moreover, is often amused and indulgent rather than vehemently condemnatory.[14] The lack of any sense that the delight and approbation aroused by the foreign require some counterbalance is clearly demonstrated by comparing Piozzi's commentary on Venice with a passage from Moryson's *Itinerary*:

Italy worthily called the Queene of Nations, can never be sufficiently praised, being most happy in the sweete Ayre, the most fruitfull and pleasant fields, warme sunny hils, hurtlesse thickets shadowing groves, Havens of the Sea, watering brookes, baths, wine, and oyle for delight, and most safe forts or defences as well of the Sea as of the Alpes. Neither is any part of Europe more inhabited, more adorned with Cities and Castles, or to be compared thereunto for tillage and husbandry.[15]

In seventeenth-century literature of the Grand Tour, then, there is no particular need for the traveller to criticize Italian food and wine. On the contrary, the rhetoric of intensification imposes a strong demand for affirmations of gastronomic excellence. The instance of superior intensity that seventeenth-century accounts of Italian travel place at the centre of their imaginative topography of the Grand Tour is the overwhelming fertility of the terrain – the very form of pleasure, in fact, that eighteenth-century travel writing seeks to subtract from this topography. As in this later form of commentary, food and wine serve as metonyms for the land from which they are produced. Praise of food and wine, therefore, provides confirmation of the dramatic fruitfulness of the Italian countryside.

14. For an example of light-hearted censure, see the account of the people of Genoa ('ils n'ont pas la reputation d'être plus Saints que les autres ') in Jacob Spon, *Voyage d'Italie, de Dalmatie, de Grèce, et du Levant*, I, 34.

15. III, 105.

Incomparability and profusion

In affirming the superior intensity of the foreign, both in accounts of food and wine and in descriptions of other domains of objects, travel writings make constant use of the theme of incomparability.[16] This theme, of course, entirely precludes the strategy of symmetrical opposition: the object of commentary is cited as one that destabilizes any such attempt at balanced assessment. While a declaration of incomparability presupposes an initial attempt at comparison, there is no need at all for the objects of comparison to be taken from the traveller's own country: on the contrary, a stronger affirmation of intensity is produced by designating as the area of scrutiny either Italy itself – the land within which rival points of incomparability may be expected – or some conspicuously vast sweep of terrain, such as Europe, the whole world, or the whole range of geographical locations within the traveller's experience or imagination. (The last of these categories is often indicated obliquely, through a generalized designation of a particular feature as incomparable.) The description of Padua in Edmund Warcupp's *Italy, in its Original Glory, Ruine and Revival* (1660), for example, asserts that 'the bread they make here is the whitest of *Italy*; And the wine is by *Plinie* accounted amongst the most noble and excellent.'[17] Jean Gailhard's *Present State of the Princes and Republicks of Italy* (1650) observes that, in Italy, 'the Palate is satisfied with the best fruits, and other delicacies, and the rarest wines in *Europe*'.[18] In Jean-Jacques Bouchard's journal of 1632, the traveller's account of the gastronomic pleasures of Sorrento includes the observation: 'Il se prend

16. Like the themes of profusion and excess, and many other characteristic features of the rhetoric of intensification – the allegory of Paradise, for example – this theme of incomparability is not limited to writings on Italy and southern Europe, but is employed in descriptions of a wide range of different regions, both during the seventeenth century and for some centuries before it. Mary B. Campbell, in *The Witness and the Other World: Exotic European Travel Writing, 400–1600*, identifies in Columbus's journals, and in other Renaissance writings concerned with the New World, a number of the same effects of language that appear in seventeenth-century writings on Italy (see 165–209). Reasons of space, within the present study, preclude any attempt to chart the precise continuities and discontinuities that are established between literature of the Grand Tour and forms of travel writing concerned with more exotic locations.

17. p.19.   18. 1–2.

aussi en cette coste un poisson qui est le plus delicat de tous ceus que jamais j'aye mangé.'[19]

The second theme that serves to establish the superior intensity of the foreign is that of profusion – as deployed in Moryson's description of Capua as 'a place abounding with all dainties', or his observations of the Duchy of Spoleto: 'the soile of this Dukedome is most fruitfull, of corne, wine, almond, and olive trees, and of most sweet fruits'.[20]

It is possible for the traveller to vaunt the pleasures of gastronomic incomparability and profusion in a particularly hyperbolic manner, moreover, because fruits, wines, and the plants that produce them are, in seventeenth-century travel writing, invested with an ability to gratify not only the sense of taste but various of the other senses as well – usually, the senses of sight and smell. John Clenche's *Tour in France and Italy* (1676) supports the description of Italy as 'most of it fertile, beyond expression', by a declaration that 'its Wines are incomparable, and of infinite variety and delicacy, pleasing at once both scent and tast'.[21] George Sandys's account of Posilippo, in his *Relation of a Journey* (1615), elaborates the theme of profusion through a multiplication of sensory pleasures, in noting 'those orchards both great and many, replenished with all sorts of almost to be named fruite trees: especially with oranges and lymons, which at once do delight three senses.'[22]

In descriptions of food and wine, as in other areas of commentary, accounts of incomparability and profusion are supported by a series of highly intensificatory rhetorical tropes. One of the tropes most commonly employed is a hyperbole of enumeration, in which the traveller testifies to Italian abundance by uttering an extensive list of natural products, natural or artificial 'wonders', works of art, or other noteworthy objects – not necessarily all from a single category. Sandys provides a hyperbolically enumerative survey of Sicily: 'Vines, sugar-canes, hony, saffron, and fruites of all kindes it produceth: mulberry trees to nourish their silke-wormes, whereof they make a great income: quar-

19. II, 428; the commentary identifies the fish by informing the reader that 'il s'appelle *lecciuola*, c'est le *glaneus* des anciens, en Provence ils l'appellent *biche* ou *cabrolle*.'

20. I, 108, 101. 21. p.122.

22. p.262. See also, for example, Evelyn, p.96 (16 October 1644), Raymond, unpaginated introduction (describing the 'most ravishing beauty' of the orange tree), Gailhard, 1–2, and Fleckno, p.22.

ries of porphyre, and serpentine. Hot bathes, rivers, and lakes replenished with fish...'[23] Evelyn comments on the countryside between Capua and Naples: 'Here likewise growes Rice, canes for Suggar, Olives, Pomegranads, Mulberrys, Cittrons, Oranges, Figgs and infinite sorts of rare fruits.'[24]

A second form of hyperbole regularly adopted in seventeenth-century travel writings is a hyperbole of accumulation. Gilbert Burnet's *Some Letters. Containing an Account of what Seemed Most Remarkable in Switzerland, Italy, &c* (1686) progresses through several examples of mere gastronomic excellence, at Chavennes, in northern Italy, before introducing a climactic instance of incomparability: 'Both here and in the Grisons the meat is very juicy, the Fowl is excellent, their Roots and Herbs very tastful, but the Fish of their Lakes is beyond any thing I ever saw.'[25] The same trope is employed to describe one of the delicacies of Pesaro, in François Misson's *Nouveau Voyage d'Italie* (1691): 'Les Olives en sont admirables, mais les figues surpassent tous les autres fruits, en bonté et en réputation.'[26]

Another of the tropes employed as a strategy of intensification is a hyperbole of substitution: a relatively modest object within the foreign is said to resemble some more intensified object within the familiar. The source of intensity, within this substitution, is often size. Burnet's commentary on Chavennes includes the observation: 'I never saw bigger Grapes then grow there, there is one sort bigger then the biggest Damascene Plums that we have in England.'[27] Moryson's *Itinerary* remarks on Italy in general: 'All the fields are full of fig trees, not small as with us, but as big in the body as some Appel-trees, and they have broad leaves.'[28] William Bromley's *Remarks in the Grande Tour of France and Italy* (1692) notes, in Naples, that 'whereas I rarely saw in the Pope's Dominions Orange-Trees, unless in Pots, and preserved with Care and Art; here they appeared as Apple-Trees in our *English* Orchards, so frequent and so large.'[29]

23. p.235.   24. p.169 (29–31 January 1645).   25. p.94.

26. I, 216. See also, for example, Warcupp, p.4, describing the cherries of Marostica, and Huguetan, 164–5, describing two different sorts of mustard.

27. p.93.   28. III, 110.

29. 282–3. See also Bouchard, II, 427–8, for a variation on the substitution of large for small, in which figs and grapes resemble pears and plums not in size itself but in firmness.

A very common hyperbole of substitution is the observation that winter in the South resembles the more intensified season of summer, as it is experienced in northern Europe. At Fondi, Moryson declares: 'The Orange trees at one time have ripe and greene fruites and buds, and are greene in winter, giving at that dead time a pleasant remembrance of Summer.'[30] Evelyn comments on Naples: 'The very winter here is a summer ever fruitefull, & continualy pregnant, so as in midst of February we had Melons, Cheries, Abricots and many other sorts of fruite.'[31]

The rhetoric of self-conscious extravagance

So far, in all the seventeenth-century commentaries cited, the subject uttering the account of the foreign has claimed to be observing the objects of commentary, or has, at least, in references to tasting and smelling, established a claim to some kind of first-hand empirical engagement with the topography. The claim to speak with the authority of the eye-witness is one that occupies a crucial role in travel writing of the succeeding century: it is essential that the traveller should leave the reader in no doubt that he or she has actually observed the objects of commentary in person, on the spot. This claim is maintained, to a great degree, through the dominant role assigned to visual observation among the strategies by which the topography is translated into discourse: the commentary is structured as a series of observations, to which responses and reflections are appended, as reactions provoked by the visual spectacle that the traveller confronts. Information about the objects described is, therefore, usually presented within the framework of accounts of the experience of viewing these objects: in Piozzi's *Observations and Reflections*, for example, a historical narrative is encapsulated in a declaration of eye-witness acquaintance with a particular spot: '*I have examined* the place where Sylla massacred 8000 fellow-citizens at once'.[32]

In the seventeenth century, however, the speaking subject regularly adopts various positions that differ sharply from that of eye-witness observation, or from any on-the-spot empirical engagement with the objects of commentary. One such position is that of a writer, self-

30. I, 105.   31. 182–3 (8 February 1645).   32. I, 381 (italics added).

consciously deploying particular forms of language, which in no way claim to be unmediated transcriptions of the experience of viewing the terrain, but which, on the contrary, are presented, more or less overtly, as displays of rhetorical artifice and ingenuity.

When occupying this position, then, the subject recognizes his task as one of constructing a rhetoric of hyperbole, which will affirm as strongly as possible the intensity and drama of Italy; such a recognition, by precluding the detachment available to the traveller as observer, actually places him in complicity with Italian intensity and drama. A passage from *Coryats Crudities* (1611), by Thomas Coryate, for example, incorporates a hyperbole of substitution in which all pretence at direct observation of the topography is abandoned, and the traveller, instead, openly treats the natural world as a store of signs, to be selected and combined at his own whim; the dominance of literary contrivance over eye-witness experience is emphasized especially strongly by the declaration that the hyperbole employed is in fact borrowed from a friend: 'To conclude this introduction to Lombardy, it is so fertile a territory, that (as my learned and eloquent friend *M. Richard Martin* of the middle Temple once wrote to me in a most elegant letter) the butter thereof is oyle, the dew hony, and the milke nectar.'[33]

In another hyperbole of substitution, the disregard of any need for a show of eye-witness observation is all the clearer for the confidence with which the traveller, in seeking out the intensificatory term of the substitution, ventures, quite unambiguously, beyond the domain of empirical investigation: Raymond describes Frascati as 'a place of such ravishing delights, as fitter's for the Gods to inhabit then men', and Coryate employs the same substitutive formulation to affirm the incomparability of Lombardy: 'For it is the fairest plaine that ever I saw, or ever shall if I should travell over the whole habitable world: insomuch that I said to my selfe that this country was fitter to be an habitation for the immortall Gods then for mortall men.'[34]

Rhetorical ingenuity and self-conscious artifice are proclaimed especially ostentatiously through the use of allegory – a figure in which reference to a world outside language assumes only a secondary place, half-obscured by reference to the origin and structure of the allegory

33. p.93.   34. p.117; p.99.

itself.[35] In all the three main allegories employed within seventeenth-century accounts of the Italian terrain, the origin that supplies this primary point of reference is located within literary and mythological tradition: these three recurrent tropes are the allegory of Italy as Paradise, the allegory of a benevolent Mother Nature exerting herself on Italy's behalf, and the allegory of Bacchus and Ceres fighting over which of them can confer the greatest benefits on Italy. (The first of these, while unmistakably invoking Christian and classical mythology, does in fact incorporate within its etymology a precise empirical observation: that Italian fruitfulness is manifested much more strongly in the growing of plants – as in a 'paradise', or garden – than in the raising of animals.[36])

Many commentaries introduce the allegory of Paradise as the climax of a description, consolidating the observations of profusion and incomparability that precede it. Moryson's description of the gardens of Naples deploys it as the culmination of a hyperbolic expression of pleasure, which progresses through a declaration of incomparability and an enumerative account of abundance:

> On all sides the eye is as it were bewitched with the sight of delicate gardens, as well within the City, as neere the same. The gardens without the wals are so rarely delightfull, as I should thinke the Hesperides were not to be compared with them; and they are adorned with statuæs, laberinthes, fountaines, vines, myrtle, palme, cetron, lemon, orange, and cedar trees, with lawrels, mulberies, roses, rosemary, and all kinds of fruits and flowers, so as they seeme an earthly Paradice.[37]

A passage from *Coryats Crudities*, describing the view from the tower of Milan Cathedral, employs the allegory in the same culminatory and consolidatory role:

> The territory of Lombardy, which I contemplated round about from this Tower, was so pleasant an object to mine eyes, being replenished with such unspeakable variety of all things, both for profite and pleasure, that it seemeth

35. For accounts of allegory that emphasize its preoccupation with its own origin and structure, see, for example, Paul de Man, 'The Rhetoric of Temporality' and Joel Fineman, 'The Structure of Allegorical Desire'.

36. Moryson, III, 108, describes Italy as 'being like a most pleasant Garden, and having few Pastures'.

37. I, 112.

to me to be the very Elysian fieldes, so much decantated and celebrated by the verses of Poets, or the Tempe or Paradise of the world.[38]

The use of allegory in passages such as these, however, is relatively restrained in comparison to the extended elaboration of the second main allegory – that of a benevolent Mother Nature – within the general survey at the beginning of Lassels's *Voyage of Italy*; self-consciously figurative language is here allowed to proliferate to a point where it entirely engulfs the description of incomparability and profusion, incorporating within its various twists and turns the allegory of Bacchus and Ceres. No observation is left unallegorized: even hyperbolic enumeration, a trope within which eye-witness experience usually predominates over literary ingenuity, is here assimilated into a subsidiary allegory of Italy as a body, 'sweating out' its abundance of natural products:

> For the Country it self, it seemed to me to be *Natures Darling*, and the *Eldest Sister* of all other countryes; carrying away from them, all the greatest blessings and favours; and receiving such gracious lookes from the *Sun* and *Heaven*, that if there be any fault in *Italy*, it is that Mother *Nature* hath cockered her too much, even to make her become Wanton. Witnesse luxuriant *Lombardy*, and *Campania* antonomastically *Fœlix*, which *Florus*, *Trogus* and *Livy* think to be the best parts of the world, where *Ceres* and *Bacchus* are at a perpetual strife, whether of them shall court man the most, she by filling his barnes with corne; he by making his cellars swimme with wine: Whiles the other parts of *Italy* are sweating out whole *Forests* of *Olive-trees*, whole woods of *Lemmons*, and *Oranges*, whole fields of *Rice*, *Turky wheat*, and *Muskmillons*, and where those Bare Hills, which seem to be shaven by the Sun and cursed by Nature for their barrennes, are oftentimes great with child of pretious *Marbles*, the ornaments of Churches and Palaces, and the Revenews of *Princes*: witnesse the *Prince* of *Massa*: whose best Revenues are his Marble Quarries: *Nature* here thinking it a farre more noble thing to feed Princes, Then to feed sheep.[39]

The display of ingenuity becomes so ebullient, by the end of this passage, that it verges on irony: the 'Bare Hills' are initially specified as unpromising material for assimilation within the allegory, but are then triumphantly made to bear witness to the benevolence of Nature. Such a display emphasizes the movement of the allegory beyond the conventional and inherited origins that it invokes, and firmly establishes the

---

38. p.99; see also 92–3 and p.120, for other allegories of Paradise.   39. I, 1–2.

position of the subject as a writer, adjusting literary tradition to the demands of a specific text and context. At the same time, however, the subject is also positioned as a scholarly compiler, overtly mapping out the origins of the allegory of Bacchus and Ceres by reference to specific texts (the works of *'Florus, Trogus* and *Livy'*). In Ellis Veryard's *Account of Divers Choice Remarks, as well Geographical as Historical, Political, Mathematical, Physical and Moral, taken in a Journey through the Low-Countries, France, Italy, and Part of Spain* (1701), this position is again adopted; classical texts are again cited, more vaguely, in introducing the same allegory, and the strategy of citation is extended to the allegory of Nature:

The temperateness of the Air, and great abundance of all things necessary for the preservation of Life, made *Pliny* imagin Nature to have been in a merry Mood when she made it, and induc'd the Poets to feign Bacchus and Ceres at variance, and emulously contending which shall most contribute to the delight and benefit of the Inhabitants.[40]

In both these two allegorical passages, the position of scholar converges almost seamlessly with that of writer: the emphasis on the activity of literary composition is increased yet further by the invocation of precursors in hyperbolic language, while the structure of allegory, with its reference back to origins, not only proclaims literary artifice but also readily accommodates a scholarly naming of sources. This position is not limited to the context of self-consciously literary passages, but assumes a much more pervasive role in determining the forms of language through which knowledge of the foreign is ordered in the seventeenth century. It is assumed, during this period, that the objects of commentary are determined to a large degree by their 'fame' – that is, by the reputation and accretion of mythical, historical and anecdotal narrative that they have acquired. As a result, the work of consulting, summarizing, and quoting any secondary sources that may offer information about that fame – in particular, classical textual sources – is defined as a major part of the task of topographical description. The assessment of 'fame' or 'esteem', through direct or indirect reference to such sources, may largely or entirely displace first-hand observation: accounts of particular places regularly proceed by listing the events and

40. p.262. See also Warcupp, 255–6.

attributes for which these places are famous, without pausing to describe what they look like.[41]

Accounts of food and wine, too, frequently adopt this same strategy of scholarly compilation, and note the 'fame' conferred on particular wines and foodstuffs by classical texts or proverbs, or established by common 'esteem', or simply by the judgement of others who have tasted them. As in the allegories quoted above, citation of such sources is often employed to authenticate hyperbolic expressions of pleasure. Moryson's account of vinous incomparability in Spoleto consists simply of a quotation from Martial (translated as 'If with *Spoleto* bottels once you meet, | Say that *Falerno must* is not so sweet.')[42] *Coryats Crudities* supplements the subject of commentary's own view that the wines to be found in Venice are 'singular good' by the story of another traveller, who, tasting the 'toothsome and delectable' wine of '*Lagryme di Christo*' in that city, 'uttered this speech out of a passionate humour: *O Domine Domine, cur non lachrymasti in regionibus nostris?* that is, O Lord, O Lord, why hast thou not distilled these kinde of teares into our countries?'[43]

Excess

The two allegories of Nature and of Bacchus and Ceres can both readily be made to produce a particularly strong effect of intensification by locating within the topography of the Grand Tour not simply profusion but excess. Lassels's survey of Italy begins by describing Nature's immoderate favouritism, and emphasizes the unrestraint induced in the country itself by such extreme indulgence ('if there be any fault in *Italy*, it is that Mother *Nature* hath cockered her too much, even to make her become Wanton'). Lombardy is described not merely as abundant but as positively luxuriant, and Bacchus and Ceres, in their 'perpetual strife' – itself immoderate – produce corn and wine at a rate that clearly exceeds the rate of consumption. The foodstuffs named in the hyperbole of

41. See, for example, Evelyn's description of Montefiascone (p.115; 4 November 1644).

42. I, 101; the lines translated are given as '*De Spoletanis quæ sunt curiosa lagenis | Malveris, quam si musta Falerna hibas*'.

43. 287–8.

enumeration are classified as products of excess, rather than of mere profusion, by the metaphor of 'sweating out' – with its reference both to an uncontrollable physical exudation and to the extremity of heat that induces sweat. Nature's decision to feed Princes rather than sheep represents a movement beyond the limitations of mundane essentials, towards more ambitious and self-aggrandizing aims.

In Veryard's survey of Italy, too, Nature is bent on indulging her own caprice rather than following the dictates of sober responsibility, while Bacchus and Ceres are presented as ebulliently unrestrained in their behaviour, and their unrestraint produces a corresponding excess of wine and food – sufficient to exceed the satisfaction of need, and contribute to positive 'delight'.

Seventeenth-century travel writings regularly transmute the theme of profusion into that of excess. Bouchard's description of Fondi mentions a natural fruitfulness that goes beyond expected boundaries, and produces a dramatic excess of supply over demand: 'il y a aussi quantité de beaus jardins tous plantez d'orangers et citroniers qui rompent, tant ils sont chargez de fruit, qui se perd à faute de gens qui le recueillent.'[44]

Other travel writings affirm that Italian profusion far exceeds demand by observing that in Italy it is possible to obtain food and wine without paying for it. Evelyn notes: 'At Fundi... we had Oranges & Citrons for nothing, the trees growing in every corner infinitely charged with fruite, in all the poore people's Orchyards.'[45] Coryate relates that on the road between Brescia and Bergamo, 'I did oftentimes borrow a point of the law in going into their vineyardes without leave, to refresh my selfe with some of their grapes. Which the Italians like very good fellowes did winke at, shewing themselves more kind unto me then the Germans did afterward in Germany'.[46] The ease with which both food and wine are obtained for nothing is emphasized particularly strongly, as a feature of his native country affectionately remembered by an Italian in exile, in Giacomo Castelvetro's *Brieve racconto di tutte le radici di tutte l'erbe di tutti i frutti che crudi o cotti in Italia si mangiano* (1614).[47]

In seeking out points of the greatest possible intensity, the subject of commentary, in seventeenth-century travel writing, not only scruti-

44. II, 171.   45. p.168.   46. p.341.   47. p.39, p.48.

nizes the topography of the Grand Tour for instances of immoderate profusion of the kind just cited, but also registers a strong impulse to extend the scope assigned to the theme of excess, by moving from profusion and unrestraint in natural productiveness to unrestraint in consumption of the fruits of that productiveness. Such a move would seem an easy rhetorical manoeuvre to accomplish, since the social behaviour of the Italians is constantly classified as excessive in other ways. (Often, such excess is presented as mirroring or echoing the extravagant abundance of natural fertility in Italy, as in Misson's description of Naples as 'un Paradis habité par des diables', and in Raymond's comment on the large number of courtesans in that city: 'as the gardens are fild with Oranges, so the houses want not for Lemmon.'[48]) Travel writings regularly comment on the opportunities for excessive consumption that Italy offers. Bouchard's journal states that 'les Capuans sont encore aujourdhui fort delicieus en toutes choses, et surtout en manger', and notes that the traveller himself, in Capua, was treated 'fort friamment et splendidement, avec quantité de pasticeries, confitures et pastes, et autres galanteries de sucre'.[49] Evelyn's diary describes the traveller arriving, in Naples, 'at the 3 Kings, a Place of treatement of excesse, as we found by our very plentifull fare all the tyme we were in Naples, where provisions are miraculously cheape, & we seldome sat downe to fewer than 18 or 20 dishes of the most exquisite meate & fruites'.[50]

Opportunities for excess are sometimes elaborated yet more hyperbolically: Sandys's account of Posillipo begins by asserting that 'the name doth signifie a releaser from cares; for that the wine (wherewith this mountaine is richly furnished) is an approved remedy for those consuming infirmities'; the commentary then goes on to quote a number of classical texts that vaunt the pleasures and advantages of unrestrained indulgence in wine, and emphasize that 'the mind is now and then a litle to be cherished, and set free from an over-sad sobrietie'.[51] In Warcupp's description of the countryside around Gaeta, 'whose hills are plentifully fraught with good wines', the allegory of 'an important combate between the Father *Liberio* the Finder of wine, and *Ceres* the Goddesse' is preceded by the suggestion that these wines possess a

48. I, 292; 141–2.   49. II, 449.   50. 169–70 (31 January 1645).   51. p.216.

particular ability to satisfy the 'gusto' of those 'who delight to drink well and to be intoxicated'.[52]

Accounts of excess in consumption of food and wine, however, seldom attribute extreme bibulousness or *gourmandise* to the Italians themselves; where they do so, such unrestraint is always limited to the inhabitants of a particular area, as in Bouchard's commentary on Capua, quoted above, or to the period of carnival, described by Moryson as one of 'unspeakable luxury in meate, wantonnesse, and all pleasures'.[53] In attempting to maintain and extend the theme of excess, seventeenth-century travel writings energetically wrestle with the problem that the Italians are very firmly classified as 'sparing' in eating and drinking. Castelvetro, in a paragraph of his treatise entitled 'perché gl'Italiani mangino più erbaggi e frutti che carne', begins by presenting the consumption of vegetables as a reaction to a failure in natural profusion – a relative scarcity of meat – but then argues that vegetables are in fact eaten out of preference, as a response to extremes of heat.[54] Moryson, noting a similar moderation in the consumption of meat by the Italians, attempts not only to restore the theme of profusion but also to insist that the traveller has observed positive gluttony: 'howsoever they are not so great flesh-eaters as the Northerne men, yet if the bread bee weighed, which one of them eates at a meale, with a great Charger full of hearbes, and a little oyle mixed therein, beleeve mee they have no cause to accuse Northerne men for great eaters.'[55]

The strategy most commonly employed to ensure that Italy is invested with a high degree of intensificatory excessiveness in eating and drinking is that of simply transferring attention from the behaviour of the Italians themselves to the conduct of travellers in Italy. When elaborating the theme of excess in relation to social behaviour in general, seventeenth-century travel writing regularly maps out the topography of the Grand Tour as one of danger and temptation for the foreigner.[56]

52. 255–6.   53. III, 50.   54. p.37.   55. III, 113.

56. This emphasis on danger almost completely disappears in the eighteenth century, when travel is defined an as activity that entails a much greater degree of detachment – the detachment of the spectator confronting a distanced visual spectacle. The debauches of young travellers, in eighteenth-century travel writings, are usually accorded little attention; where they are in fact mentioned, they are often blamed on the folly of the travellers themselves, rather than on the temptations of Italy.

A letter addressing a traveller in James Howell's *Epistolæ Ho-Elianæ*, for example, constructs an allegory of Nature that unfolds in such a way as to locate within Nature's favouritism a danger of corruption not only for the Italians but also for the Englishman in Italy:

You are now under the chiefest clime of wisdom, fair *Italy*, the darling of Nature, the Nurse of Policy, the Theater of Vertue; But though *Italy* give milk to *Vertue* with one dug, she often suffers *Vice* to suck at the other, therefore you must take heed you mistake not the dug; for there is an ill favord saying, that *Inglese Italionato, è Diavolo incarnato*; An *Englishman Italianat*, is a Devill incarnat.[57]

Moryson's description of 'the most fertile Plaine of *Capua*' links generalized temptation to profusion and excess of fruitfulness through the proleptic figure of Hannibal, prefaced to the two hyperbolic allegories of Paradise and of Bacchus and Ceres; the narrative of the collapse of Hannibal's military campaign against the Romans, in the face of Capuan luxury and debauchery, provides an anticipatory frisson of danger, in suggesting the allurements encountered by the contemporary traveller, which further intensifies the vision of natural extravagance: 'The Capuan delights, corrupting the Army of *Hanniball*, are knowne to all the World. This Province is an earthly Paradise, where *Bacchus* and *Ceres* strive for principalitie.'[58]

Another narrative of temptation to excess, anticipating future departures from moderation, focuses on a traveller who, unlike Hannibal, limits his unrestraint to the field of drinking. Descriptions of Montefiascone, on the main route between Florence and Rome, emphasize the dangerous pleasures of the local wine by recounting the story of the German or Dutch bishop who died after drinking too much of it, and was buried in the local church of S. Flaviano. (It is from this story, travel writings maintain, that the wine acquired its name, *Est Est Est*: the bishop sent his servant on ahead to write *Est* on the doors of inns supplying good wines – or, according to another version, on vessels containing these wines – and on reaching one particular inn, or bottle, the servant was so enraptured that he repeated this affirmation two or three times.)[59]

57. III, 51.   58. III, 106.   59. See, for example, Evelyn, p.115 (4 November 1644), Huguetan, p.45, and Bromley, p.320.

With reference to a further proleptic figure, 'the Emperour *Fredericke* the Third', *Coryats Crudities* emphasizes the gastronomic incomparability and profusion of Venice by noting an instance of temptation to excess in eating. Having described, at some length, 'the marveilous affluence and exuberancy of all things tending to the sustentation of mans life' in that city, Coryate focuses, in particular, on a 'speciall commodity..., which is one of the most delectable dishes of a Sommer fruite of all Christendome, namely muske Melons'. A hyperbolic account of the abundance of these melons is followed by a direct warning about the dangers posed by their excellence:

> But I advise thee (gentle Reader) if thou meanest to see Venice, and shalt happen to be there in the sommer time when they are ripe, to abstaine from the immoderate eating of them. For the sweetnesse of them is such as hath allured many men to eat so immoderately of them, that they have therewith hastened their untimely death: the fruite being indeed γλυκύ πικρον, that is, sweete-soure. Sweete in the palate, but sowre in the stomacke, if it be not soberly eaten. For it doth often breede the *Dysenteria*, that is, the bloudy fluxe: of which disease the Emperour *Fredericke* the Third died by the intemperate eating of them...[60]

Eating, drinking, appropriation

At the same time as they hyperbolically transmute profusion into excess, these accounts of the dangers of immoderate eating and drinking also put forward the consumption of food and drink as a model-metaphor for the appropriation of the foreign. Throughout the period of the Grand Tour, the subject uttering a commentary on the foreign is required to display an ability to appropriate the topography that he or she encounters – in other words, to demonstrate that he or she is able to utilize it for his or her own purposes, by extracting pleasure and benefit from it. In eighteenth-century travel writing, the central model-metaphor for this task of appropriation is the viewing of works of art: the subject of commentary confronts the foreign as a distanced pictorial spectacle, and enjoys and criticizes it from a position of detachment, in

60. 257–8.

the manner in which he or she might enjoy and criticize a painting.[61] In seventeenth-century commentary, on the other hand, the subject's powers of appropriation are affirmed through the presentation of the topography as one that actually offers itself up to him for consumption – for a mode of enjoyment analogous to the enjoyment of food and drink.

The accounts of temptation to excess just cited might all seem more concerned with the loss of control than with a positive ability to appropriate. In each case, however, the traveller who is placed in the position of vulnerability is not the traveller uttering the commentary, but a traveller whose adequacy to his task is in some way in doubt; the speaking subject indicates through his recognition of the dangers that he himself is better able to deal with them, and can even derive authority from his status as the object of seductive blandishments on the part of the foreign. In the allegorical account of Italy as 'the darling of Nature' in Howell's *Epistolæ Ho-Elianæ*, quoted above, the young traveller to whom the letter is addressed is designated as one in danger of succumbing to temptation, but the subject who delivers the warning speaks from the privileged, authoritative position of one who, it is implied, has survived such temptation, and has at the same time enjoyed the opportunities for both baneful and beneficial consumption of Italian pleasures that have been offered to him.

The possibility of positively devouring foreign delights is, in this passage, described metaphorically: the allegory refers to the various undefined pleasures that Italy offers, both virtuous and vicious, as the milk of a mother who is herself a favourite child. Such metaphors of food and drink are quite often employed in seventeenth-century writings, reinforcing the definition of the foreign as an object of active consumption rather than mere passive spectatordom: the reference to ingestion within the title of Thomas Coryate's travel book is emphasized particularly strongly when this title is announced in full: *Coryats*

61. For an example of the way in which the viewing of works of art operates as a model-metaphor for the appropriation of other objects, see Laurence Sterne's *Sentimental Journey through France and Italy*, p.84: describing his own primary purpose as that of observing women, in order 'to spy the *nakedness* of their hearts', the traveller-narrator declares: 'I conceive every fair being as a temple, and would rather enter in, and see the original drawings and loose sketches hung up in it, than the transfiguration of Raphael itself.'

Crudities. Hastily gobled up in five Moneths travells in France, Savoy, Italy, Rhetia commonly called the Grisons country, Helvetia alias Switzerland, some parts of high Germany, and the Netherlands; newly digested in the hungry aire of ODCOMBE in the county of Somerset, and now dispersed to the nourishment of the travelling members of this kingdome.[62]

In commentaries that describe the foods and wines of Italy directly, rather than introducing the topic of gastronomy metaphorically, these foods and wines nonetheless acquire a metaphorical function: in addition to operating as metonyms for the terrain of overwhelming fruitfulness from which they are produced, they also serve as metaphors for Italy in general, in its role as a topography of intensified pleasure, to be assimilated through an act of appropriation that will cause the traveller little difficulty, since it is no more daunting than the activities of eating and drinking.

Since allusions to food and wine so strongly affirm the traveller's powers of appropriation, it is hardly surprising that they recur so often in seventeenth-century travel writing, nor that accounts of temptation to excess – whether presented directly or proleptically – are deployed to suggest a topography that energetically entices the traveller into consuming it.

Bibliography

Bouchard, Jean-Jacques, *Journal*, edited by Emanuele Kanceff, 2 vols, continuous pagination (Turin: G. Giappichelli, 1976; the journal is concerned with the years 1630 to 1632)

Bromley, William, *Remarks in the Grande Tour of France and Italy. Lately Performed by a Person of Quality* (London, 1692)

Burnet, Gilbert, *Some Letters. Containing an Account of what Seemed most Remarkable in Switzerland, Italy, &c.* (Amsterdam, 1686 [1687]; first published in Rotterdam, 1686)

Castelvetro, Giacomo, *Brieve racconto di tutte le radici di tutte l'erbe di tutti i frutti che crudi o cotti in Italia si mangiano*, edited by Emilio Faccioli (Mantua: Gianluigi Arcari, 1988)

62. See also, for example, the use of a gastronomic metaphor to describe the Italian character ('... *Of the best wines you make the tartest vinegar*') in James Howell's *Instructions and Directions for Forren Travell*, p.55.

[Clenche, John,] *A Tour in France and Italy, Made by an English Gentleman, 1675* (London, 1676)

Coryate, Thomas, *Coryats Crudities. Hastily gobled up in five moneths travells in France, Savoy, Italy, Rhetia comonly called the Grisons Country, Helvetia alias Switzerland, some parts of High Germany, and the Netherlands. Newly digested in the hungry aire of ODCOMBE in the County of Somerset, and now dispersed to the norishment of the travelling members of this kingdome* (London, 1611)

Evelyn, John, *Diary*, edited by E.S. de Beer, (London: Oxford University Press, 1959)

Fleckno, Richard, *A Relation of Ten Years Travells in Europe, Asia, Affrique, and America* (London, [1654?])

Gailhard, Jean, *Present State of the Princes and Republicks of Italy* (London, 1668; first published in 1650)

Howell, James, *Instructions and Directions for Forren Travell. Shewing by what Cours, and in what Compas of Time, one may Take an Exact Survey of the Kingdomes, and States of Christendome, and Arrive to the Practicall Knowledg of the Languages, to Good Purpose* (London, 1650; first published in 1642)

H[owell], J[ames], *Epistolæ Ho-Elianæ. Familiar Letters Domestic and Forren; Divided into Six Sections, Partly Historicall, Politicall, Philosophicall, upon Emergent Occasions*, 6 parts (London, 1645)

[Huguetan, Jean,] *Voyage d'Italie Curieux et Nouveau* (Lyon, 1681)

Lassels, Richard, *The Voyage of Italy*, 2 parts (Paris, 1670)

Miller, Anne, Lady, *Letters from Italy, Describing the Manners, Customs, Antiquities, Paintings, &c of that Country, in the Years 1780 and 1781, to a Friend Residing in France, by an English Woman*, 2 vols (London, 1776)

Misson, François Maximilien, *Nouveau voyage d'Italie, fait en l'année 1688. Avec un mémoire contenant des avis utiles à ceux qui voudront faire le même voyage*, 2 parts (The Hague, 1691)

Moryson, Fynes, *An Itinerary, Containing his Ten Yeeres Travell through the Twelve Dominions of Germany, Bohmerland, Sweitzerland, Netherland, Denmarke, Poland, Italy, Turky, France, England, Scotland, and Ireland*, 3 parts (London, 1617)

Piozzi, Hester Lynch, *Observations and Reflections Made in the Course of a Journey through France, Italy, and Germany*, 2 vols (London, 1789)

Raymond, Jo[hn], *An Itinerary Contayning a Voyage Made through Italy, in the Yeare 1646, and 1647* (London, 1648)

Sandys, George, *A Relation of a Journey begun An: Dom: 1610. Foure bookes containing a description of the Turkish Empire, of Ægypt, of the Holy Land, of the remote parts of Italy, and Ilands adjoyning* (London, 1615)

Sharp, Samuel, *Letters from Italy, Describing the Customs of Manners of that*

Country, in the Years 1765, and 1766, second edition (London, 1767; first published in 1766)

Spon, Jacob, *Voyage d'Italie, de Dalmatie, et de Grèce, et du Levant fait aux années 1675 et 1676*, 4 vols (Lyon, 1678)

Sterne, Laurence, *A Sentimental Journey through France and Italy by Mr. Yorick, with The Journal to Eliza and A Political Romance*, edited by Ian Jack (Oxford: Oxford University Press, 1984)

Swinburne, Henry, *Travels in the Two Sicilies in the Years 1777, 1778, 1779, and 1780*, second edition, 2 vols (London, 1790; first published 1783–5)

Veryard, E[llis], *An Account of Divers Choice Remarks, as well Geographical as Historical, Political, Mathematical, Physical and Moral; Taken in a Journey through the Low-Countries, France, Italy, and Part of Spain; with the Isles of Sicily and Malta. As also a Voyage to the Levant* (London, 1701)

Warcupp, Edmund, *Italy, in its Original Glory, Ruine and Revival, Being an Exact Survey of the whole Geography and History of that Famous Country* (London, 1660). Translated from Itinerario, overo nova descrittione de' viaggi principali d'Italia, an Italian version of Franciscus Schottus, *Itinerarii Italiae rerumque Romanarum libri tres*)

Secondary works

Campbell, Mary B., *The Witness and the Other World: Exotic European Travel Writing, 400–1600* (Ithaca and London: Cornell University Press, 1988)

de Man, Paul, 'The Rhetoric of Temporality', in *Blindness and Insight: Essays in the Rhetoric of Contemporary Criticism*, second edition (London: Methuen, 1986)

Fineman, Joel, 'The Structure of Allegorical Desire', in Stephen Greenblatt, *Allegory and Representation* (Baltimore and London: Johns Hopkins U.P., 1981)

The gastronomic Michelangelo

GILLIAN RILEY

WHAT we know about Michelangelo's lifestyle is what his biographers Condivi and Vasari told us in his lifetime, with the tacit approval of their subject. Later historians have perpetuated this myth of the rugged genius, with a mind on higher things than the gross pleasures of the table or the niceties of clean linen, in whom the agonies and ecstasies of the creative struggle engendered the miseries of self-neglect and the deprivations of a puritanical austerity. Vasari's very unappealing story of the leather knee-boots seems to bear this out: Michelangelo wore them for so long that when he removed them the skin of his legs is alleged to have peeled off as well. In a detail from Raphael's *School of Athens*, 1510–12, we have a portrait of a tousle-headed, pensive young sculptor in a workman's smock and soft leather boots, sitting on his own, disdaining the *bella figura* of his fellow artists posing alongside Plato, Aristotle and Pythagoras. Our Michelangelo crouches over a block of stone, scowling at a letter from home. About this time his valetudinarian old father was constantly writing from Florence that most irritating of all parental exhortations to 'wrap up well dear, eat properly and be sure to keep your head covered in cold weather.' None of which Michelangelo did, and fell ill as a result. But these letters tell us little about Michelangelo's actual way of life. Perhaps others might shed more light.

Five volumes of letters exist, a detailed record of the artist's professional life from which his biographers have reconstructed a tangled web of confused briefings, impossible dead-lines, conflicting loyalties, treacheries, exhortations, accusations, exonerations, triumphs and reconciliations of that most tempestuous of sixteenth-century artists. Michelangelo hoarded all his papers and correspondence, accounts, records of transactions and rough drafts of his own replies. Perhaps somewhere embedded in all this could be found some information about his eating habits.[1]

1. P. Barocchi and R. Ristori, *Il Carteggio di Michelangelo*, Florence 1965–83.

On the back of one of these letters Michelangelo drew us the most helpful clue of all – a set of illustrated menus.[2] The letter was sent on 18 March 1518 while Michelangelo was at Pietrasanta, arranging for the purchase and transport of marble for work on the church of San Lorenzo in Florence and the gigantic funeral monument for the late Pope Julius II. Michelangelo, with typical perversity, had been reluctant to follow his clients' instructions to buy marble from Pietrasanta, in Florentine territory and hence cheaper than the quarries of Carrara, but eventually capitulated, after years of squabbling and recrimination. There were compensations, however, in the *douceur de vivre* of life in his new surroundings, the woods, meadows, vines and chestnut groves of this pleasant, fertile plain, in a dip in the mountains. There is no way of knowing when or why he wrote out these lists of simple Lenten fare on the back of it. Thumbnail sketches illustrate each item, the pictures getting more and more out of synch with the text, which must have been written down first. Unlikely to have been done as a shopping list for a servant, when this could have been explained perfectly well verbally, it is probably a way of illustrating, in a relaxed and lighthearted way, for some friend or drinking companion, how well it is possible to eat during Lent.

Commentators always use this as an illustration of Michelangelo's austere tastes, but in fact a more detailed perusal shows that even at this early stage in his career he had an appreciation of the pleasures of good food: simple ingredients, carefully prepared and elegantly presented.

Here is the list:

pani dua	two bread rolls
un bochal di vino	a jug of wine
una aringa	a herring
tortegli	tortelli
una insalata	a salad
quatro pani	four rolls
un bochal di tondo	a jug of full-bodied wine
un quartuccio di bruscho	a quarter of dry wine
un piattello di spinaci	a dish of spinach
quatro alice	four anchovies
tortelli	tortelli

2. Letter from Bernardo Niccolini, 18 March 1518, Archivio Buonarroti, Biblioteca Laurenziana, Florence, (X.f.578, verso).

sei pani	six rolls
dua minestre di finochio	two bowls of fennel
una aringa	a herring
un bochal di tondo	a jug of full-bodied wine

These elegant little meals are a long way from the comparatively rustic fare of Annibale Carracci's *Mangiafagioli*, in which a coarse-mannered but not base character devours with enthusiasm but no nicety, a dish of black-eyed beans, clutching his bread in a none too clean fist.[3]

Each dish on the sketched menu is presented in an appropriately shaped pot: the salad in a wide, shallow dish with a neat tiny plinth, the spinach piled in a smaller bowl, the four anchovies draped elegantly over the curved mouldings of their basin, the stewed fennel in round, rimmed bowls; only the herring swims in mid-air while the tantalisingly mysterious *tortelli* have no container to convey some sense of scale to their writhing *contraposto*.

Recipe books of the period[4] show just how well it was possible to eat during Lent or on lean days, when the Church forbade the consumption of meat and meat-derived products.(Sometimes milk, cheese and butter were excluded, sometimes not. By the mid sixteenth century the papal kitchens were reluctant to do without dairy products.)

The herring would have been salted, then common fare throughout Europe. Michelangelo might have eaten it, after soaking to remove excess salt, dressed with olive oil, chopped herbs and onions with a squeeze of lemon or some vinegar or verjuice.

If the menus were drawn soon after receipt of the letter in May, the salad could have been a *mischianza*, identical to the mixture of herbs and salad plants so lovingly described by Giacomo Castelvetro a century later,[5] and loving recreated today by the Lancellotti family in Modena,[6] decorated with blue borage flowers and dressed with fruity Tuscan olive oil, possibly from the Buonarroti's own estates.

The little bread rolls were made from fine white flour, a luxury which

3. Annibale Carracci (1560–1609) *The Bean eater*, Rome, Galleria Colonna.

4. See Bibliography.

5. Giacomo Castelvetro, *The Fruit, Herbs & Vegetables of Italy*, translated and edited by Gillian Riley, London, Viking, 1989.

6. Da Lancellotti Ristorante, Via G. Matteotti 20, angolo via Grandi 120, 41019 Soliera, (MO).

can be seen, on the tables of the well-to-do, in banquet scenes and still lives of the period.

The *piattello* might have contained any of the glorious spinach recipes of Renaissance cuisine: at its simplest, freshly picked spinach leaves cooked gently in their own juices and eaten tepid with a dressing of virgin olive oil and salt; or the leaves, once cooked, turned in hot butter or oil with garlic, anchovies and raisins and served with a dusting of sugar and cinnamon; or alternatively tossed in butter and mixed with grated Parmesan cheese and ricotta, and bound with eggs and breadcrumbs to make a more substantial dish. This last mixture could also have been the filling for the *tortelli*.

The *minestra*, a dish somewhere between the consistency of a stew and a soup, might have been coarsely chopped fennel simmered slowly in its own juices, or a little vegetable stock or almond milk and olive oil, thickened with breadcrumbs and ground almonds, and seasoned with salt and pepper.

Anchovies would make the perfect foil to this delicate dish. From the drawing they appear to have been taken from their barrel, washed of the salt in which they had been preserved, soaked perhaps in milk to remove more salt, dressed with oil and herbs and draped over the generously moulded rim of their bowl.

The *tortelli* are more of a problem – the nomenclature of pasta is confusing enough in present-day Italy, where different things are made in different ways and called by different names in every region, sometimes every town. The history of pasta is a real can of worms. Early cookery texts name and describe some interesting ways of making and serving pasta with familiar names but somewhat strange ingredients: a sweetened short pastry is wrapped round a mixture of cheese, herbs and dried fruits and simmered in stock or fried and called *ravvioli*. A dough of flour, breadcrumbs, eggs, sugar and spices is made into little dumplings, shaped and patterned on the curve of a small cheese or nutmeg grater, and cooked in broth or almond milk and served with a seasoning of sugar and cinnamon, and called *maccheroni*. Michelangelo's drawing is not a great help here. The first image might indicate the torsion involved in shaping *tortellini*, twisting the filling in its diagonally folded, tiny squares of pasta, round the index finger of the left hand to make shapes 'like so many little bonnets, *annolini* we sometimes call them' as Scappi wrote in 1570.[7] But the lower sketch shows somewhat ambiguous objects, amorphous lumps, more round than twisted, which could be filled shapes of pasta dough, or little pasties or turnovers, or the doughnut-like *ravioli*, also known as *maccaroni*, in the sixteenth century, or the *tortelli* or *tortelloni*, as they are called in Parma or Modena today. If Michelangelo the perfectionist craftsman had spent as many hours toiling away at the kitchen tables of Pietrasanta as he had on the harsh rock-face of the Carrara quarries he would have been better equipped to draw his *tortelli* from life, and drawn them better – *La man che ubedisce al intelletto*...

The jugs of wine, *tondo* and *brusco*, would have been the local vintages, full-bodied and dry, of the region. They were very good. Pope Paul III praised them years later, on one of his journeys.

Back in Rome, Michelangelo could have enjoyed wine from the Roman vineyards, the best were around Porta San Pancrazio, and outside the Porta Sant' Agnese and on the estates of nobles and cardinals within the walls. These produced a purer wine than much of the local plonk, which was often 'improved' with cinnamon, cloves and that old favourite, elderflowers. Or he could have enjoyed some of the special wines kept carefully in his own cellars.

Cheese, butter and eggs do not feature on the menus, for Michelangelo was a stricter observer of Lent than his friends and clients in the Papal court. But fine cheese, as we shall see, was something he cared about. Towards the end of his life he thanked his nephew, Lionardo for a consignment of red and white chickpeas, beans and peas, saying how he was glad to have them in time for Lent, since his poor health made it difficult for him to be as strict as he would have wished.

These elegant little Lenten meals are not *cucina povera*. Michelangelo was proposing modest, but sophisticated, menus, to be enjoyed at leisure rather than scoffed between bouts of creative fervour. He always believed, and certainly wanted to give the impression, that he struggled single-handed, without support or sympathy, with the herculean tasks imposed on him by intractable patrons and malign providence. Although recent research on the ceiling of the Sistine Chapel reveals the work of various hands, Michelangelo always insisted that he finished his masterpiece single-handed. These menus imply the existence of a

7. Bartolomeo Scappi, *Opera*..., 1570, reprinted Bologna 1981.

skilled back-up support team in the kitchen as well as the studio. He must have been living in Pietrasanta, as in Rome, in the comfortable style to which his upwardly mobile, if not noble, family aspired, rather than grappling alone on the bare rock face with the obdurate and stubborn forces of nature. Untrustworthy and incompetent his workmen in the quarries may have been, but the little sketches of food imply the existence of considerable domestic skills at home.

Michelangelo eventually moved back to Rome, after enduring four harrowing years caught up in the disaster of the failed Florentine Republic, the siege of Florence and the consequent devastation of his property and land in the surrounding countryside. Documemnts survive from 1530,[8] during the period after the upheavals, when Michelangelo was supplying wheat, millet and barley to his tenant farmers to replant their ruined fields. He was buying these from Giovanbattista Figiovanni, a business associate in Florence, at the high prices on the fluctuating grain market.

Despite the devastation caused by the Sack of Rome in 1527, Michelangelo was glad to return to his comfortable house near the *Macel de' Corvi*, (destroyed only recently to make way for the massively ugly monument to Vittorio Emmanuele); leaving the narrow, confined streets of the bustling commercial city of Florence for the dream-like *rus in urbe* of Renaissance Rome, with its gardens and orchards and vineyards among the ruins of classical palaces and temples, its picturesque mediaeval towers and tenements, its elegant modern palaces, and the ring of pilgrim churches and the basilica of St Peter's, focal point of the faith which was the mainspring of his existence.

Although Michelangelo had a deep attachment to his native city, and throughout his life invested in property and land in and around Florence, Rome was where his heart was. The affection and support of patrons and friends like Vittoria Colonna and his close friendship with Tommaso de' Cavalieri were a welcome antidote to the tiresome behaviour of his father and brothers, who appear to have been both grasping and incompetent.

Working on commissions in Florence in 1533, Michelangelo missed the calm and comforts of his Roman home, with its airy loggia, terrace

8. William Wallace, 'An unpublished Michelangelo document', *The Burlington Magazine*, vol 129, March 1987.

and gardens. His friend Bartolommeo Angelini wrote reassuring letters: 'Your house is watched over all the time. I go there often during the day – the hens and their master the cock are flourishing and the cats miss you dreadfully, though not enough to put them off their food...'

In another letter Bartolommeo tells how he sold off all the inferior wine, and will buy in some of better quality for when Michelangelo returns. In July 'the heat is intense, but we survive and the figs are doing well.' In August 'the house and garden and animals are well, but we all miss you. The muscat grapes are ripening and Tommaso will have his share if they survive the magpies'. A fortnight later they are still not quite ripe but the figs in the courtyard are doing fine, the little animals are all well and there has been a bit of rain so the garden has had a drop to drink. Michelangelo's replies do not survive, but the kind, soothing letters continue through the summer. By early October the peaches and pomegranates are ripe, a basketful goes to 'Messer Tomao' and one to a friend's little boy. 'They have been really beautiful this year.'

As well as letters the friends exchanged sonnets, Bartolommeo said his own was 'a sonnet only in name, alas, more of a *pesce pastinacha.*'. (Boiled parsnips dipped in flour and fried in oil were a cheap substitute for fish, so a fish got up like a parsnip would have been a somewhat strange confection). In another letter he claimed to be more adept at frying sausages than writing verse.

Later in life Michelangelo found countless excuses not to return to Florence, even at the insistence of the powerful Medicis. His father and brothers were dead, all his friends were in Rome and there was so much work in hand there, (finishing off St Peter's). His nephew Lionardo, now a grown man with a young family of his own, was in the impossible situation of being treated as a delinquent small boy, and at the same time being expected to administer the family estates in Florence with a competence that was forever being undermined by his irascible uncle. Biographers have been hard on Lionardo, he is portrayed as a cringing toady, sucking up to his rich uncle, or as a cold, cynical opportunist, unfeeling and unresponsive, late for the deathbed and grasping over the legacy. An impossible situation for a worthy, ordinary young man overwhelmed by the burden of his responsabilities – sole heir to a towering genius and fanatical book-keeper, the greatest artist of his age and the most exacting landlord. He did his best. He tried hard. But he could not win.

He endured the saga of the shirts. 'Lionardo', raged his uncle in 1540, 'you astonish me, a peasant would be ashamed to wear them, such coarse, rough stuff! I did not ask for them! I do not need them! When I do I'll send you the money to buy some.' Thirteen years later the hapless Lionardo got it right: 'Lionardo, the shirts have just arrived, all eight of them; they are really beautiful, the cloth is especially fine... thank Cassandra (Lionardo's wife) for me and let me know if there is anything she would like me to send her from Rome.'

Presents from Florence kept arriving. They shed some light on Michelangelo's tastes. Every year in June or July a consignment of Trebbiano would arrive. Fragrant, straw-coloured, refreshing and much prized throughout Italy, this Tuscan wine was served at Papal banquets and was always a prestigious gift, a status symbol in the hierarchy of offerings and sweeteners. '4 July 1556, Lionardo, I have been too busy to write and thank you for the Trebbiano. It arrived, thirty-six *fiaschi*, and is the best you ever sent me. But I am sorry you went to such expense, particularly since I have so few friends left to share it with.'

Trebbiano wine was appreciated by the master of the cellars of Pope Paul III Farnese, Sante Lancerio, who accompanied his master on journeys in Italy and abroad during the years of his pontificate, 1534–49. A manuscript in the Biblioteca Ariostea in Ferrara contains his account of the wines sampled during the Pope's journey across Italy to set up the Truce of Nice in 1538.[9]

According to Lancerio *Montefiascone* was no good, in spite of its reputation, *Montepulciano*, very good. In Pietrasanta and Massa di Carrara the Cibo family entertained His Holiness with a selection of their excellent wines, perhaps the same as the jug wine on Michelangelo's menus. In Nice the people are no good and the wine even less good. Then back home via La Spezia where both red and white wines are excellent... so much so that half the party, sleeping off the effects in the olive groves, got left behind when the Pope's retinue departed by sea, and had to make the next stage of the journey overland on foot, further than most of them had ever walked in their lives, remarked Lancerio unfeelingly.

9. *I vini d'Italia, giudicati da Papa Paulo III Farnese e dal suo Bottigliere Sante Lancerio,* Tallone Editore, 1981.

The manuscript also contains an account of the wines in Pope Paul's cellars in Rome, dedicated in 1559 to Cardinal Guido Ascanio Sforza:

Trebbiano wines are sent to Rome from the Florentine states of Valdarno di Sopra and many other places, but the best are those of San Giovanni and Figghine. Most of it comes in flasks packed in carts, or in special box containers. Trebbiano is a delicate wine, not appropriate to every kind of food, for it is very light and subtle. To enjoy it at its best the colour should not be too dark, but golden, with not too sharp an aroma and a rounded taste, neither sweet nor acid, with a hint of quince. His Holiness enjoyed it greatly when of this quality, but not to drink with everything. Messer Bindo Altoviti used to have good Trebbiano wines sent to him in Rome and presented them to the Pope who drank them in the autumn, between the new and the old vintages.

Michelangelo also gave flasks of Trebbiano to his friends. The same year that Lancerio was writing in praise of Trebbiano the unfortunate Lionardo got an incandescent letter from his uncle: 'Lionardo, I received the Trebbiano, not without rage and shame, for I made a present of some without tasting it, assuming it to be good, to my enormous discredit. However good it might have been, you should not have sent it, this is the wrong time anyway.'

A week later he was still fulminating: 'Lionardo, I wrote to you about the receipt of the Trebbiano and how without tasting it first I gave several flasks away, assuming them to be as good as the ones you usually send, which caused me rage and shame. They may have left you in good condition but the carrier could have got up to some mischief on the journey. Anyway do not send me anything more unless I ask you, because everything upsets me...'

Michelangelo was now in his seventies and in poor health, as he had explained in a letter the previous year: 'As to how I am, I am not well, with all the afflictions of old age – the stone, so that I can't urinate, and pains in the side and back so that I often cannot manage the stairs on my own; and I get so irritable which makes everything worse.'

But the presents kept on coming. The annual gift of cheeses would arrive during the New Year; on 7 January 1559 he wrote to thank Lionardo for the 'fifteen *marzolini* and fourteen pounds of sausages, I am very glad of them, particularly the *marzolini*, because there is a shortage of such things.'

Marzolini were a speciality of Florence. They were hard cheeses, lightly salted and matured for about a year, and much esteemed as a luxury, something it was good to give as presents and be seen to have on one's table. A helpful description of them is to be found in Pantaleone da Confienza's *Summa lacticiniorum*, published in Turin in 1477:

Marzolino cheese is commonly called Florentine cheese because it is made in Florentine territory, in Tuscany and Romagna. They are round, fairly big cheeses, about a good *braccio* wide and a span, or six cubits deep. They are very clean and brilliant, and when mature a lemony wax colour. They are made for the most part with sheeps' milk, though some add some cows' milk as well. They are fairly compact in consistency and consequently without holes. They have a good flavour when hardened with time and last well, depending on their size. I think this is partly due to good handling and also the dry fodder of the animals. The method of keeping them is not negligible either. They are esteemed cheeses and exported all over – I have even eaten them in France. They make desirable presents.[10]

Platina, Bartolomeo Sacchi, had published a few years earlier his manual on health and good living, *De honesta voluptate et valetudine*. Descriptions of ingredients, their properties and how to cook them, include a few paragraphs on cheese:

Two cheeses at present vie for supremacy – the *marzolino*, as the Tuscans call it, made in Tuscany in March, and the *parmigiano* of the cisalpine regions, which is also called *maggengo* after the month of March.[11]

While Michelangelo was partaking of simple but exquisite little meals with a few choice friends, his patron, Paul III might have been sitting down to the elegant but far from frugal banquets prepared by his friend, Cardinal Campeggi's cook, Bartolomeo Scappi, later to become *cuoco segreto* to Pius V. In his *Opera*, published in Venice in 1570, Scappi gives a comprehensive repertoire of recipes and kitchen precepts, which includes a very long section of banquet menus. These make exhausting reading, even though we know that the guests selected what they fancied from the dazzling array of dishes, rather than consuming the lot. Among the cheeses of quality in these menus are *marzolino* and *parmigiano*. The *marzolini* were specified as being 1½ or 2 lbs in weight, somewhat smaller than one might imagine from Pantaleone's

10. Pantaleone da Confienza, *Trattato dei Latticini*, a cura di Emilio Facioli, Milan 1990.
11. Bartolomeo Platina, *Il Piacere Onesto e la Buona Salute*, edited by Emilio Faccioli, Turin, Einaudi, 1895. p.50.

description, nearly a century ago, served cut in half on a dish from which diners would presumably cut off the portions they wanted.

Michelangelo himself may well have been a guest at some of these banquets. He was on friendly terms with his patron, Pope Paul III, who in 1535 commissioned him to paint the Last Judgement on the altar wall of the Sistine Chapel. The contract also makes Michelangelo a formal member of the papal household, with emoluments and dining rights.[12] A later contract, in 1549, giving Michelangelo complete control over the rebuilding of St Peter's, calls him 'our beloved son, Michelangelo Buonarroti, a member of our household and our regular dining companion...'[13]

As a regular dining companion of the Pope Michelangelo would have eaten at what was probably the most luxurious table in Europe. He may have enjoyed many of the dishes described in Scappi's book, not all of them as rich and complicated as the pies and exquisitely spiced sauces of the ceremonial dinners. A mixed green salad in early March, a tart of spinach, green herbs and cheese from Scappi's native Bologna, a dish of crisp raw fennel with the desert wines at the end of the meal, are all reminiscent of the list jotted down so many years ago.

More luxurious presents – hams and fresh local cheese from Casteldurante, arrived during the 1550s from Cornelia Colonelli Brunelli, the widow of his friend and assistant, Francesco Amatori, known as Urbino. The death of Urbino in 1556 was a tragedy for Michelangelo who had come to depend on the younger man, who had worked for him for twenty five years as housekeeper, works overseer, studio manager, confidante and companion. 'I made him rich, he was to support and cherish me in my old age', wrote Michelangelo bleakly. Instead he found himself responsible for Urbino's young wife and two small children, administering their inheritance and dealing – with almost saintly patience – with the attempts of her litigious and grasping family to get their hands on the money, prudently stashed away in a bank in Rome. Cornelia wrote him long, gushing letters, affectionate, egregious, naïve, demanding, prudently backed up with well-timed gifts of local *prosciutto*, cheeses, and sausages: 'Friday 1 January, 1557, ... Since today is

12. Linda Murray, *Michelangelo, his Life, Work, and Times*, London, Thames & Hudson, 1984. p.158.

13. Murray, p.203.

New Year's Day, when it is our custom to greet our masters, I am sending your honour a little present of *guaimo* cheese, eight pounds in weight...' And in April 1558, 'I am sending you two hams and two pairs of *guaime*, which we would like you to enjoy for our sakes.'

Unwell and overwhelmed with commissions, Michelangelo still found time to return the kindnesses; in January the following year Cornelia writes from Casteldurante: *'Magnifico e come padre amantissimo*, I received your letter together with some bitter oranges and lemons, for which I thank you as much as I know how.'

Cornelia and Lionardo continued to send little luxuries to Michelangelo, even when he claimed to be too old to enjoy them. Neither were exactly disinterested. Both were astute enough to calculate what was most likely to appeal to their exacting benefactor. Their presents are therefore a fairly accurate indication of his gastronomic tastes.

A series of accounts from his apothecaries also throws light on Michelangelo's tastes. These list mainly medicaments, and are a helpful source of information about his health and that of his household. But embedded in the lists of ointments, syrups, cordials, suppositories and purges we find slabs of marzipan, boxes of *cotognata* (quince paste), sweet fruit jellies, melon seeds, honey, cinnamon, a sugar loaf, currants, almonds, spices and a restaurative dish of chicken and spices for Urbino on his sick-bed.

In conclusion it seems possible that a fresh look at the available information could enlarge our understanding of Michelangelo's character, and show him to be not a closet foodie but a voluptuary in the best sense of the word. His portraits, too, show a face with laughter lines beneath the beetling brows, a kindly smile lurking round the austere mouth. The young painter who embellished the ceiling of the Sistine Chapel with areas of gorgeous, shimmering colour, radiant draperies, tender scenes of domestic life, and sensitive portraits of women and children as well as God in all his *terribilità*, became the towering genius who still needed news of his cats and chickens, found time to exchange humorous sonnets with his caretaker, and took pleasure in giving and receiving little presents of special cheeses and wines. We can be sure that love of food alone would not have made him the dining companion of Popes and cardinals, but an ungracious rejection of the pleasures of fine living would certainly have been an obstacle. It is unlikely that his conversations with the virtuous and intelligent Vittoria Colonna, poet and widow of the Marchese of Pescara and his close friend since 1537, would have assumed our own self-consciously pompous 'foodie' high seriousness but it is possible that the intense spirituality of their relationship was softened by the amenities of Roman life, with conversations on the vine-shaded veranda in a lambent evening light, sipping golden Trebbiano and picking at the vermilion globules of pomegranate seeds, watching Cornelia's babies playing with the kittens on the terrace below, with cows grazing among the ruins of the Forum in the distance.

It seems that for too long Michelangelo's character might have been diminished by the conventional approach of historians, begun in his lifetime by Vasari and Condivi, who present him as an austere kill-joy with a high-minded detachment from earthly pleasures. This investigation of his appreciation of the fine simplicities of Italian gastronomy will, I hope, go some way towards redressing the balance.

Bibliography

P.Barocchi and R.Ristori, *Il carteggio di Michelangelo*, Florence, 1965–83.

Pantaleone da Confienza, *Trattato dei Latticini*, edited by Emilio Faccioli, Milan, 1990.

Emilio Faccioli, *L'arte della cucina in Italia*, Turin, Einaudi, 1992

Sante Lancerio, *I vini d'Italia, giudicati da Papa Paulo III e dal suo bottigliere Sante Lancerio*, Alpignano, Tallone Editore, 1981.

Linda Murray, *Michelangelo, his life, work and times*, London, Thames and Hudson, 1984.

Cristoforo Messisbugo, *Libro nuovo*, 1557, reprinted Bologna, Arnaldo Forni, 1980

Bartolomeo Platina, *Il piacere onesto e la buona salute*, edited by Emilio Faccioli, Turin, Einaudi, 1985.

Gillian Riley, *Renaissance Recipes*, San Francisco, Pomegranate Artbooks, 1993

'Superior Vegetables'
Greens and roots in London
1660–1750

MALCOLM THICK

Introduction

The extent of vegetable consumption by the well-off in London in the century following the Restoration has not been fully explored. Commercial vegetable growing was rapidly expanding around the capital in the late seventeenth and early eighteenth centuries. This paper will examine the complexities of consumption and taste for vegetables at this time, and consider how producers responded to new types of demand. The focus is on middle-class and upper-class Londoners because it was they who were most caught up in what has been called the 'Consumer Revolution' of the eighteenth century. This phenomenon marked a transformation in the attitude of people towards the acquisition of goods and services: 'More men and women then ever before in human history enjoyed the experience of acquiring material possessions'. Consumption was stimulated by fashion, a desire for novelty in everything, food, and more particularly, vegetables, included.[1]

I

In this period, reliable contemporary statistics of domestic consumption are few and are, at best, informed guesses. Two statistical pioneers, Gregory King in the 1690s and Jacob Vanderlindt in the 1730s, include

1. N.McKendrick, J.Brewer, J.H.Plumb, *The Birth of a Consumer Society*, p.1. This work provides a wealth of evidence and analysis of consumption in the eighteenth century.The author is aware that Carol Shammas (see bibliography) has recently challenged the intensity of the upturn in consumer spending in the eighteenth century. She does, however, detect a trend towards the consumption of more ephemeral and fashionable goods at this time.

some data on fruit and vegetable consumption in their works and, helped by Peter Earle's interpretation of these early statistics in his book on middle-class Londoners, I have investigated the money spent on vegetables by the well-off in the capital.[2]

Vanderlindt estimated that food and drink cost a seven-member 'family in the middling station of life' £76 16s. per annum in 1734, 33% of total expenditure. Gregory King divided his consumption estimates into many income bands and his per capita figures for middle-class food consumption in 1695 range from £5 to £20 per annum, say £35 to £140 for seven-member households. King costed fruit and vegetable consumption on a national per capita basis at 4s.4d. per annum in 1695, 5.75% of his estimated total per capita food bill. Applying this percentage to the total food bills for the middle classes outlined above, we arrive at annual expenditure on fruit and vegetables of £4 7s. for Vanderlindt's household and between £1 19s.6d. and £7 18s.1d. for King's households.[3]

These figures, modest but significant elements in household expenditure, sit oddly with a statement by Richard Bradley in 1726 that 'It is not very rare to see Bills from Fruiterers and Herb-shops, of one Winter's standing, to amount to Sixty, Eighty, an Hundred, and sometimes an Hundred and Fifty Pounds, where the Families are large'. Bradley, author of works on botany, agriculture, gardening and cookery, Professor of Botany at Cambridge, and one intimately acquainted with both commercial gardening around London and the marketing of vegetables in the capital, is an author whose opinions should not be dismissed lightly.[4]

It may be possible to reconcile Bradley's figures with those of the statisticians. Bradley includes upper-class as well as middle-class households in his statement; presumably the ostentatious consumption of the very rich might account for his highest estimates. Households of the aristocracy were large: Gregory King thought 'Temporal Lords' headed 40 member households, whilst knights had families of 13. Such households spent large sums. King estimated that England's leading

2. Peter Earle, *The Making of the English Middle Class*, pp.269–281.   3. Earle, p.271.

4. Richard Bradley, *A General Treatise of Husbandry and Gardening*, p.150; Richard Bradley, *Country Housewife and Lady's Director*, Introduction by Caroline Davidson, pp.10–31.

families each laid out £2,400 per annum, a total which might include significant purchases of fruit and vegetables. Bradley was writing of London, surrounded by the biggest concentration of market gardening, where the largest part of a rich household's consumption of vegetables would be purchased, rather than home-grown. He included fruit in his figures. Imported fruit was expensive, as were exotics like grapes and pineapples produced in England in greenhouses; these would inflate the bills. But the most significant reason why Bradley may have been right was the willingness of the well-off in the early eighteenth century to consume vegetables which were expensive to produce and commanded high prices at market.[5]

II

Detailed comments on food are not plentiful in diaries or literature of this period and such as there are tend to mention the main, meat ingredient of a meal, not vegetables on the side. Some of the best evidence comes from foreign visitors. The oft-quoted passage in the memoirs of Henri Misson, dating from the 1690s, bears repeating :

Generally speaking, the English Tables are not delicately serv'd. There are some Noblemen that have both French and English Cooks, and these eat much after the French manner; but among the middling Sort of People they have ten or twelve Sorts of common Meats, which infallibly take their Turns at their Tables, and two Dishes are their Dinners: a Pudding, for instance, and a Piece of Roast Beef; another time they will have a piece of Boil'd Beef, and then they salt it some days before hand, and besiege it with five or six Heaps of Cabbage, Carrots, Turnips, or some other Herbs or Roots, well pepper'd and salted, and swimming in Butter: A Leg of roast or boil'd Mutton, dish'd up with the same dainties, Fowls, Pigs, Ox Tripes, and Tongues, Rabbits, Pigeons, all well moistened with Butter, without larding: two of these Dishes, always serv'd up one after the other, make the usual Dinner of a Substantial Gentleman, or wealthy Citizen.[6]

Pehr Kalm, a Swede visiting London in 1748, also ate dinners whose main ingredient was butcher's meat; he noted, however, that 'they take

5. Gregory King, *Natural and political conclusions upon the state and condition of England*, edited by G.Chalmers, pp.48–9,67.

6. Earle, pp.276–7; *Englishmen at rest and play*, edited by R. Lennard, pp.233–4.

turnips, potatoes, carrots, &c from the dish, and lay them in abundance on their plates'. Kalm also mentions other vegetables commonly eaten; lettuce, salad sprouts, cabbage, spinach, turnips, and green peas.[7]

These are observations of the ordinary, day-to-day meals of middle-class Londoners; Misson also commented on the French cooks employed by the nobility. French influences were not new; in the first decade of the seventeenth century Sir Thomas Overbury characterised a 'French cook in England' as one who produced salads, vegetables, mushrooms, and sauces in abundance but little meat and small portions. He fed not 'the Belly, but the palate...He dares not for his life come among the butchers, for sure they would quarter and bake him after the English fashion, he's such an enemy to beef and mutton'. Despite such criticism, a French cook was a mark of status; Pepys recorded in 1660 how Lord Mountague, finding his fortune much improved, 'did talk very high how he would have a French Cook and a Master of his Horse'.[8]

Many fought a rearguard action against French cookery into the eighteenth century. Richard Steele lamented the demise of roast beef and plain cooking in 1710 and a poet satirically regarded French cuisine as so essential that the lack of it at Public Schools and Universities interrupted the 'Progress in Learning'. But by 1750 the ubiquity of ragouts, omelettes, fricassees, and other made dishes in cookery books indicates that French cooking had made a marked impression in the kitchens of the better-off in England, despite the continuation throughout the period of a tradition of more robust and rural recipes in middle- and even upper-class cooking, which tempered the influence of French cuisine on all but a small circle of the the richest London households. Hannah Glasse expressed the ambiguous attitude to French cookery at the time when she condemned 'the blind Folly of this Age, that they would rather be impos'd on by a French Booby, than give Encouragement to a good English cook', but nevertheless gave English cooks many French-influenced recipes to try. French cuisine, with its imaginative use of vegetables and smaller emphasis on meat, must have

7. Pehr Kalm, *Kalm's Account of his Visit to England on his Way to America in 1748*, edited by J.Lucas, pp.7,14.

8. H.Morley, *Character Writings of the Seventeenth Century*, pp.84–5; Samuel Pepys, *Everbody's Pepys*, edited by O.F.Morshead, p.55.

contributed something to the increased demand in London for garden produce, especially high quality crops which were expensive to culti-vate.[9]

The increasing taste for gardens, a trend clearly discernible after the Restoration in much of society, fostered more interest in vegetables and fruit amongst the middle and upper classes. In the 1660s John Worlidge, a reliable observer, found 'scarce a cottage in most of the southern parts of England, but hath its proportionate garden, so great a delight do most men take in it', and John Aubrey thought that 'in the time of Charles II gardening was much improved and become common'. The Earls of Bedford, who hired an experienced gardener to improve their kitchen gardens at Woburn after 1671, represented a general trend amongst the nobility. Writers justified producing ever more books on gardening for the gentry by pointing to its expansion – John Laurence wrote in 1717 of 'Gardening being of late Years become the general Delight and Entertainment of the Nobility and Gentry, as well as the Clergy of this Nation'. Two years later, George London and Henry Wise thought another book necessary because 'Of late years ... Garden-ing and Planting have been in so great Esteem'. An early historian of horticulture looked back in 1829 on gradual improvements in gardening in the seventeenth century which 'burst forth in splendour in the 18th Century'. Recent research has confirmed that there was a steady, if small, annual expenditure on gardens by the middle classes at this time.[10]

The gardens of the gentry were not all for ostentatious display; most included a kitchen garden where fresh vegetables and wall fruit were grown. Stephen Switzer, an early eighteenth-century seedsman and nursery gardener, observed: 'whoever has a good Cook, or reads the Books which are published in that Art, will soon find... how much... Plants that grow in a Garden contribute to the making a good Dinner;

9. A.Wilbraham & J.C.Drummond, *The Englishman's Food*, p.214; *The art of cookery in imitation of Horace's Art of Poetry*, pp.3–4; Hannah Glasse, *The Art of Cookery Made Easy*, Preface; E.Smith, *The Complete Housewife*, Preface; Stephen Mennell, *All Manners of Food*, pp.83,88–9,125–7.

10. John Worlidge, *Systema Horti-Culturae*, p.175; G.Scott-Thomson, *Life in a Noble Household*, pp.150; Miles Hadfield, *A History of British Gardening*, p.127; John Lawrence, *The Clergy-Mans Recreation*, Preface; George London & Henry Wise, *The Complete Gard'ner*, p.i; George W.Johnson, *A History of English Gardening*, p.147; Lorna Weatherill, *Consumer Behaviour & Material Culture,1660–1760*, p.103.

how much, if moderately us'd, to Life and Pleasure itself.' Many of the gentry migrated to London for the social 'Season' in the winter months and, although some produce was no doubt sent from gardens at home, most of their accustomed vegetables were bought from market gardeners (note that Bradley, quoted above, refers to bills for 'one *Winter's* standing'). This demand stimulated high-quality production.[11]

III

Part of the motivating force pushing vegetable consumption forward was the publishing trade; in books and periodicals, people of some wealth read what they should be wearing, sitting on, hanging on the wall, planting in the garden, and, from the pages of more and more books on cookery and household management, what they should eat and how it must be prepared and presented. From an examination of seventeen of the more than one hundred published cookery books of the late seventeenth and early eighteenth centuries, some conclusions have been drawn on the consumption and taste for vegetables in the middle and upper classes.[12]

Cookery books are an indirect indication of diet, the authors' choice of recipes not necessarily being what readers in fact ate. Book purchasers, however, would not buy what they did not intend to use. The books were aimed at a narrow section of society, the middle and upper classes, but were often, within those bands, passing on the tastes of those at the top of the scale to those slightly below. Thus Lamb's *Royal Cookery* outlined the dining habits of the Royal Household and leading aristocracy to an upper-middle-class readership, whilst Hannah Glasse's clear and logical text was for the lower-middle-classes, as was Sarah Harrison's *Housekeeper's Pocket Book*, which contained fashionable dishes whose ingredients 'might be purchased at a moderate Expence'.[13]

The books have some limitations for the historian of vegetables. Many advise how to choose meat and fish at markets; no author comments on vegetables. More seriously, many cookery books mention

11. Stephen Switzer, *Country Gentleman's Companion*, pp.v–vi.

12. Virginia Maclean, *A short-title catalogue of household and cookery books, 1701–1800*.

13. Lamb; Glasse; Harrison, p.iv.

vegetables rarely, particularly those little-influenced by French cooking. In others, however, they are found in some variety. Maybe the basic English way of cooking and presenting vegetables was so simple and straightforward as to merit no mention in all but the most methodical texts. Where general directions are given they are very simple.[14]

The *Compleat Housewife* (1753) offers the following advice on how 'To dress Greens, Roots, etc.':

When you have nicely picked and washed your greens, lay them in a cullender to drain, for if any cold water hang on to them they will be tough; then boil them alone in a copper sauce-pan, with a large quantity of water, for if any meat be boiled with them it will discolour them. Be sure not to put them in till the water boils.

Individual directions are then given for preparing ten vegetables; for French beans the advice is:

Take your beans, string them, cut them into two, and then a-cross, or else into four, and then a-cross, put them into water with some salt; set your sauce-pan full of water over the fire, cover them close, and when it boils put in your beans, with a little salt. They will be soon done, which you may know by their being tender; then take them up before they lose their fine green, and having put them in a plate, send them to table with butter in a cup.[15]

Detailed instructions on making salads are rarely found in the cookery books, but commercial gardeners were producing lettuces, cucumbers, cress, celery, radishes, chervil, and other fleshy herbs, in abundance, and Stephen Switzer in 1727 wrote, 'It would be endless for me to enumerate the improvements that have been made in lettuce, and all the salletings'. John Evelyn's *Acetaria* of 1699 stands out as the only work to concentrate on salad-making. Was Evelyn so comprehensive (and long-winded) on the subject that no-one wished to add to his work? Or were salads, like boiled vegetables, considered too obvious an item of food to spend time on? In *Adam's Luxury and Eve's Cookery* (1744), a book devoted solely to the growing and cooking of vegetables, 'To dress a Salled' takes up under half a page at the very end of a chapter entitled 'Receipts which could not come under any of the foregoing Heads'.[16]

14. Glasse, pp.15–18; Smith, pp.14–16.   15. Smith, pp.14–16.

16. Stephen Switzer, *Practical Kitchen Gardener*, p.vii; *Adam's Luxury and Eve's Cookery*, p.187.

If not plain boiled and buttered, many vegetables were subjected to only slightly more elaborate treatment before serving. Artichokes, asparagus, cauliflowers, endive, and mushrooms were all to be served with cream, gravy, or a white sauce. Some recipes elevate the vegetable dish to the status of a 'made dish'. 'Farced Cucumbers', a 1744 recipe, involved stuffing the hollowed-out cucumbers with a mixture of cooked vegetables, egg yolks, and bacon; tying them up; stewing; flouring, and finally frying them before sending the dish to the table with a sauce of claret, lemon peel, butter, and allspice. Cabbages and lettuces were also 'farced'. Book after book gives recipes for vegetable ragouts and fricasees. These were served as side-dishes or with meat in either of the two courses commonly eaten. Hannah Glasse has many vegetable recipes in a section headed 'a Number of pretty little Dishes, fit for a supper or Side-dish, and little Corner-dishes for a great Table'. The arrangement of many small dishes of vegetables on larger plates set amongst meat dishes in some of Patrick Lamb's table settings of 1705 show clearly what Hannah Glasse meant.[17]

Vegetables were added to meat dishes and pies; some, such as artichoke bottoms, asparagus, and cauliflower, being frequently used. Mushrooms were also often put in for flavouring. Some combinations of vegetables and meat, for example, chicken and asparagus, cucumber sauce with lamb, tongue and cauliflowers, were obvious favourites.[18] Vegetables enhanced and garnished meat dishes: Patrick Lamb wrote of lettuce ragout, 'We serve these Lettuces under a Leg of Mutton, or with Partridges, Chickens, Pullets, Ducks a la Braise, &c, in the same manner as we do other Ragoos of Legumes'. Boiled and hashed mutton was, in 1701, to be served on sippits with 'Artichokes and colliflowers about the Mutton'. Cauliflowers, perhaps because of the pleasing appearance of the white florets, were a frequent garnish; thus the monthly bill of fare in the 'Family Magazine' of 1743 lists Cauliflower with Neats Tongue, Boiled or Fried Udder, Venison, Mutton, Beef, Calves Head, Ham and Chickens and Roast Sirloin. Conversely, one meat dish might be accompanied by a variety of ragout according to taste and season. Patrick Lamb suggested Duck with a ragout of green

---

17. *Adam's Luxury and Eve's Cookery*, p.133; Glasse, p.111; Lamb.
18. E.Smith, pp.66–7; Lamb, p.46; *Family magazine*, pp.20–26.

peas, artichokes and asparagus tops, celery, cardoons, chicory or cucumber.[19]

Some widely available vegetables were scarcely mentioned in cookery books of the period. Many included few or no references to roots (carrots, turnips, parsnips, and beets).[20] Books where roots were included were written for the lower middle classes or country people. *Adam's Luxury and Eve's Cookery* (1744), with many recipes for roots, advertised its contents as 'a great Variety of cheap, healthful, and palatable Dishes...Designed for the Use of all who would live Cheap, ... particularly for Farmers and Tradesmen in the Country', Sarah Harrison's book provided a bill of fare full of root dishes for 'the frugal Mistress of a family' with ingredients which 'might be purchased at a moderate expense'. Roots were the cheap food of the London poor and so were shunned by many who could afford better. A rare mention of them in the distinctly aristocratic *Royal Cookery* of Patrick Lamb is apologetic; 'Beets, Are a Sort of Root, that for being common ought not to be despised'.[21]

Roots, along with cabbages and dried beans, had been inferior food in London for some time. John Parkinson wrote in 1629 that although Turnips are 'often seene as a dish at good mens tables', 'the greater quantitie of them are spent at poore mens feasts'. A miserly gentleman in a comedy of 1632 was despised for feeding his family on roots and livers. Roots, cabbages and beans came to London markets by the cartload in enormous quantities after the Civil War; at between 2d. and 6d. a cartload, the toll from turnip carts at Leadenhall Market alone was £260 in 1696. By the middle of the eighteenth century roots were still a staple of the poor. In 1760 Philip Miller, the distinguished gardener, thought that carrots 'provide great comfort to the poor'. The lowly status of the root was reinforced by its increasing use as animal fodder; turnips were, by the middle of the eighteenth century, as likely to be eaten by cattle and sheep as people.[22]

19. Lamb, p.117; *Complete caterer*, pp.77–9; *Family Magazine*, pp.20–6.

20. Salmon; Lamb; Bailey; *The Pastry Cooks Vade Mecum*; *The Complete Cook and A Queens Delight*; *Complete caterer*.

21. *Adam's Luxury and Eve's Cookery*, title p.; Harrison, p.iv; Glasse, Preface; Lamb, p.26.

22. John Parkinson, *Paradisi in sole*, p.509; J.Massinger, *The City madam*, Act I Scene i; P.V.McGrath, 'The Marketing of Food,Fodder, and Livestock in the London Area

Despite their inferior status, roots were eaten in some quantity by the middle classes (as Misson and Kalm recorded). But they were not the vegetables favoured by those who could afford better, and they were definitely not fashionable. What vegetables were most prized? Those which occur frequently in the cookery books examined are: artichokes, asparagus, cauliflowers, cucumbers, French and kidney beans, green peas, lettuce, mushrooms, and spinach, with broccoli also gaining in popularity later in the period. These may be considered the favoured, 'superior' vegetables of polite London society, and the recipes in which they were included may explain their appeal.

Some vegetables – asparagus, artichokes, and lettuces in particular – had been firm favourites for a long time. Throughout the seventeenth century they occur in cookery books and other literary sources. Ben Jonson mentions widespread eating of artichokes and lettuce in 1616. Both a fictional prostitute in the 1630s and Samuel Pepys in the 1660s enjoyed asparagus. Maybe such vegetables were liked simply because their texture and taste found widespread satisfaction; in eighteenth-century terms, they were 'delicate'. (This widely used epithet also however, connoted superiority and gentility). These, and most of the other superior vegetables, could be served in many ways or had particular virtues which were widely exploited in cooking. Asparagus was boiled and buttered, covered in various sauces as a side-dish, extensively used to flavour stews, used as a pie ingredient and as a garnish for chicken and other dishes. Lettuce was the basis of many salads and was a frequent ingredient in cooked dishes. Cauliflower was a favourite garnish. Mushrooms flavoured and coloured ingredients and were a mainstay of French cookery; the Muse in the poem *The Art of Cookery* was instructed to sing of 'the man that did to Paris go, That he might taste their Soups, and Mushrooms know.'[23]

in the Seventeenth Century', pp.195–6; H. Le Rougetel, *The Chelsea Gardener*, p.137; Malcolm Thick, 'Market Gardening in England and Wales' in *The Agrarian History of England and Wales*, Vol V.ii, edited by Joan Thirsk, p.532.

23. Ben Jonson, *Epigrammes*, 33, 'On the famous voyage'; John Murrell, *Two Books of Cookerie and Carving*; *The Complete Cook and A Queens Delight*; *The Court and Kitchen of Elizabeth, commonly called Joan Cromwell*; Massinger, Act III Sc i; Charles Cooper, The English Table in History and Literature, p.65; *The Art of Cookery, In Imitation of Horace's Art of Poetry*, p.79; *The Diary of Samuel Pepys*, edited by Henry B. Wheatley, 1946, vol vi, p.263.

Broccoli, increasing in favour in the early eighteenth century, was relatively new to England, although mentioned as a delicate vegetable by Evelyn in 1699. The seed was imported from Italy. Bradley wrote in 1723: ''tis a plant which has been cultivated privately in some few Gardens in England, for about three years', but commercial production had not begun. He planned to produced a pamphlet on its culture. Another writer, Stephen Switzer, gave pride of place to it in a small work on new vegetables in 1728. Broccoli is a good example of the eighteenth-century quest for novelty which led both to the introduction of new vegetables to tempt the rich and to the development of new varieties of established crops.

Some new varieties had little to commend them but novelty; Bradley complained: 'We have great varieties of Lettuce, many of which have been more esteem'd for their Rarity then for their Goodness.' Evelyn, in 1699, could remember when melons were rarely cultivated and 'an ordinary melon would have been sold for five or six shillings'; in 1744, however, it was suggested: 'To enumerate all the different Sorts of This Fruit, would be not only endless, but impossible, there being annually new Sorts brought from abroad, a great many of which proved good for little'.[24]

A final characteristic of superior vegetables is that they were, for much or all of the year, more expensive than roots. Richard Bradley's market reports bear this out and it is seen clearly in J.C.Loudon's survey of Covent Garden prices in 1822, which reveals that although the price of roots such as carrots varied little over the year, rising only with the new crop, some other vegetables were unobtainable for parts of the year and, at other times, commanded a high price. This premium was occasioned by the desire of the rich for vegetables when they were scarce, a distinctly modern-sounding fashion which was nonetheless well known over a century before Loudon's statistics.[25]

24. John Evelyn, *Acetaria*, pp.16,38; Bradley, *A General Treatise of Husbandry and Gardening*, p.43; Bradley, *New Improvements of Planting and Gardening*, p.164; Stephen Switzer, *A Compendious method for raising Italian broccoli; Adam's Luxury & Eve's Cookery*, p.48.

25. J.C.Loudon, *Encyclopaedia of Gardening*, p.1062. Loudon's statistics are ouside our period but, although the population of London was then much larger and some tastes had changed, the basic conditions of supply and demand remained much the same as in the early eighteenth century. Bradley, *A General Treatise of Husbandry and Gardening*, pp.41–4,108.

In 1684 demand for out-of-season vegetables attracted moral censure: 'And verily the vanity of some deserves our wonder, who are of that Heliogabalian Stomach, to which nothing doth relish which is not dear ... onely loving Pease, when they are scarce to be had'. Evelyn was contemptuous of forced 'Early Asparagus ... so impatiently longed after', and Steele, in the Tatler, in 1710 summed up the dictates of fashion by observing: 'They are to eat every Thing before it comes in Season, and to leave it off as soon as it is good to be eaten'. Such scorn is indicative of the wide demand for out-of-season vegetables. In 1719 Richard Bradley could say: 'the Pride of the Gardeners about London chiefly consists in the production of Melons and Cucumbers at times either before or after the natural Season'.[26]

Explaining his publication of the fancy prices charged for unseasonable vegetables, Bradley wrote, 'I choose to mention the Prices of these Curiosities, that we may the better judge of their Scarcity, and compare them with Fruits of the same kind another Season.' In May 1723 he observed: 'Forward Pease were sold this Month for Half a Guinea per Pottle-basket' (equivalent to seven guineas a half-sieve, compared with 6d. for the same measure in July 1822). Loudon's price survey shows a steep decline in the price of peas in a few weeks as the main crop suceeds those first harvested, and the pea suffers a similar annual drop in culinary status, sold in quarts to the rich in May or June, and shovelled off the tail of carts to poor customers in high summer. In June 1723 Bradley reports: ' About the Middle of the Month, most of the Crops of Pease and Beans about London were ripe, and came daily in such Quantities to the Markets, that their Price was reduced to about one shilling per Bushel. In May also the rich could buy 'Collyflowers, of the right sort...for 5s. each'. He also reported that 'Kidney-Beans raised in Hot-Beds were about 3s. or 4s. per Hundred' (in March, raised in the same manner, they had been 2s. 6d. *a dozen*) and 'Mushrooms were bought for eight and ten Shillings a Basket, in St. James's Market' in March 1723.[27]

26. *The Compleat Tradesman*, p.17; Evelyn, pp.134–5; *Tatler*, March 21st,1710; Bradley, *New Improvements of Planting and Gardening*, p.116.

27. Bradley, *A General Treatise of Husbandry and Gardening*, pp.41–43, 108, 148; Loudon, p.1062; 'Peas Sold from a Cart', Wash drawing by Robert Dighton, c.1786, Museum of London.

IV

The gardeners who supplied the markets with out-of-season vegetables relied heavily on glass lights and bell-glasses to protect the crop from the elements and artificial undersoil heating in the form of 'hot-beds', rotting dung covered with soil. This technology, used on asparagus 'brings great Profit to the Gardeners near London'. Kidney beans were raised on hot-beds to sell in January, and 'Mushrooms are cultivated in Beds of Dung, so as to have them when there is none to be gathered in the Fields...as they do about Paris'. In 1744 'some People are at a great Expence to produce Pease in April or sooner, by sowing of the dwarf Pease in September and October, and transplanting them into frames'.[28]

Cucumbers, asparagus, and cauliflowers were raised in large quantities by this method, the object being to lengthen the time they were in season, and so supply the markets for much of the year. The cauliflower was a particular success, in 1744 'This excellent plant is cultivated in our Kitchen-Gardens with so much Skill, as to have them for the use of the Kitchen above half the Year'. In 1773 it was claimed that, 'Of all crops raised by kitchen-gardeners, none yield so much profit as those of colly-flowers raised under glasses; indeed, the large expenses attending them require some extraordinary profit'.[29]

Stephen Switzer, a knowledgeable London gardener, seedsman, and author, summarized the progress made in artificially lengthening growing seasons in the first quarter of the eighteenth century – progress largely achieved by commercial gardeners:

Who then, till within these few years, could have imagin'd that the cucumber, which seldom was seen heretofore (even since my remembrance, who have not been above twenty five years a practitioner in Gardening) Till the middle, or perhaps the latter end of May, seldom the beginning, that are now produced in and about London, and several places in the country, in the beginning of March; and the industrious among the Gardeners are still striving to outvie one

28. Bradley, *New Improvements of Planting and Gardening*, pp.138, 159; Bradley, *General Treatise of Husbandry and Gardening*, pp.41–3; *Adam's Luxury & Eve's Cookery*, pp.57,64.

29. *Adam's Luxury & Eve's Cookery*, pp.57,64; Richard Weston, *Tracts on Agriculture and Gardening*, p.54.

another, and will in all probability produce them in February, or sooner, and that as good or better than they have in any of the succeeding months, when they have less time to tend them.

And as the fruits that grow in the kitchen garden are so much more accelerated now than they were heretofore, so are the legumes and herbacious rooted plants, the collyflower in particular, that never shew'd its beautiful head above three of four months in the year, appears now above six or seven furnishing the tables of the curious all that while with its wholesome nourishment; and by good management mocks the severity of our unsteady climate.

The phaseolus, or kidney bean, that used not (but was thought too tender) to be sown till the beginning or middle of April, is now, by the means of frames and glasses, and that with little trouble, sown in January and February; and the fruit (if it may be so called) which used to be fit to gather heretofore not till the middle of June, is now fit for the table by the beginning of April; and which is more, by the great skill and improvement of our industrious Gardiners it continues a constant and most useful dish for every week in the year between that and the beginning of October.

Even peas and beans, that were heretofore the produce but of two or three months, furnish the table with an agreeable dish for seven or eight; viz. from April to almost Christmas; so expert are our Gardiners now in the retardation of the produce of the Garden, as well as in the bringing of it in early.[30]

All around London some market gardeners were producing fashionable vegetables for genteel tables while others were growing bulky roots for general consumption. Some areas were renowned for particular vegetables; on the Surrey bank of the Thames, for instance, Barnes and Mortlake had a reputation for asparagus, and huge quantities of cucumbers were grown under glass in the outskirts of Southwark. Individual growers defied Nature to bring vegetables to maturity out of season. Mr Jewell of the Neat Houses experimented with a variety of early crops, and Bradley named others who did the same in 1719–1720: Jewers of Battersea who raised early melons, and Gilman and Brown of Brentford who both produced out-of-season cucumbers for sale.[31]

The Neat House gardens at Westminster were regarded at the time as the best gardens for high quality vegetables. They occupied a fan-

30. Switzer, *The Practical Kitchen Gardener*, p.vii.

31. Maisie Brown, *The Market Gardens of Barnes and Mortlake*, pp.13–14; Surrey RO, Quarter Sessions, 6/12/Midsummer 1750, /62 to /105; Bradley, *General Treatise of Husbandry and Gardening*, pp. 42,109,165.

shaped area of land in the south-west corner of Westminster, beyond Tothill Fields in a bend of the Thames. The London topographer John Strype described them in 1720:

A parcel of houses most seated on the banks of the River Thames and inhabited by gardeners, of which it is of note for the supplying of London and Westminster Markets in Asparagus, Artichokes, Cauliflowers, Muskmelons and the like useful things, by which reason of their keeping the ground so rich by dunging it (and through the nearness of London they have the soil cheap) to make their crops very forward to their great profit, in coming to such good markets.[32]

A year later Bradley, who knew some of the gardeners there and was a regular visitor, wrote that the gardens 'abound in Salads, early Cucumbers, Colliflowers, Melons, Winter Asparagus, and almost every Herb fitting the Table; and I think there is no where so good a School for a Kitchen Gardener as this Place'. Regarded as the most technically-advanced vegetable gardens in the country, the nobility sent apprentices from their own gardens to the Neat Houses to learn the skills needed to produce good crops.[33]

The pre-eminence of the Neat Houses at this time cannot be explained purely by the favourable soils, irrigation channels, easy access to market via the Thames, and long-established gardening families with a considerable body of expertise and experience, important as these factors undoubtedly were. The added element in their success was the apparent ability of the Neat House gardeners to read the market for good quality and out-of-season vegetables, to supply what was required, and, as important, to put forward new products to tempt the customer. Thus, when white cabbage was more prized than green, they copied some provincial private gardeners who folded the leaves of 'Coleworts or strong Cabbage Plants' and tied them together, 'by which Means, in a Fortnight's Time, the inner Parts will become white, and eat as well as any Cabbage'. By 1721 'most of the gardeners about the Neat Houses are fallen into that Method, and have reap'd good Sums of Money from it'. Early crops from the Neat Houses beat all others to

32. John Strype, *A Survey of the Cities of London and Westminster*, Book Vi, p78. I will publish a full account of the history of market gardening at the Neat Houses in due course.

33. Bradley, *Philosophical Account of the Works of Nature*, 1721, p.184.

market: Mr Jewell, in May 1723, sent cauliflowers 'of the fine sort to market first, about the 14th'. This same man, to stimulate demand with something new, 'was the first Gardener in England that raised the young Sallad Herbs for the Winter Markets, and Kidney-Beans in Hot-beds'.[34]

The Neat House gardeners were a close-knit community. The gardens were packed together in a small area and the need to co-operate over access to land and maintenance of watercourses and pathways fostered a community spirit. Son followed father in the business and offspring were apprenticed to fellow gardeners. Such a situation engendered commercial co-operation: healthy three or four year old asparagus roots, 'of which the gardiners and neat-house men about London have always great store' were best for forcing on hot-beds, and these 'they sell to one another, when any one of their fraternity wants them, for about four or five shillings per pole'. No doubt they swapped intelligence of market conditions and new techniques of production as well.[35]

The Neat House gardeners were in regular contact with well-off Londoners who made up their main market because the gardens had, from the 1630s, been a place of resort. Some gardeners ran public houses, and others opened their gardens in the summer as places to sit and drink. Samuel Pepys went there on several occasions, to drink and enjoy the company in the evening and, one Sunday afternoon, he called by boat with his wife and bought a melon. The ease of access to the gardens may help to explain why such horticultural writers as Bradley and Switzer frequently visited them. The gardeners themselves were tradesmen of some standing who lived in comfortable houses and would have mixed socially with some of their middle-class customers.[36]

---

34. Bradley, *General Treatise of Husbandry and Gardening*, pp.108,157; Switzer, *Practical Kitchen Gardener*, p.ii.

35. Westminster City Archives, F4538; 1049/12/114; Switzer, *Practical Kitchen Gardener*, p.177. Leases and rates assessments show gardens remaining in the family from generation to generation.

36. Greater London Records Office, AM/PI (1) 1684/26; 1687/13; Westminster City Archives, 1049/3/5/68; W.Roberts, 'The London Neat House Gardens', *Journal of the Royal Horticultural Society*, 1941, p.12; *The Diary of Samuel Pepys*, edited by Henry B.Wheatley, 1946, vol. v, p.365, vii,p.51, viii, p.30.

Conclusion

Social interaction was important, therefore, both in attuning gardeners to the market and as a determinant of the taste for vegetables amongst middle-class and upper-class Londoners. This taste was influenced in particular by the spread of interest in gardening and intrusion of French cuisine into English kitchens. Both these fashions travelled down the social scale. Innovation in garden design took its lead from the monarch and leading nobility, and the tables of these members of society influenced the meals of the middle classes. But it has also been demonstrated that a more subtle influence on eating habits in London came from below, as suppliers of vegetables produced new varieties to tempt the palate or produced familiar vegetables in unfamiliar seasons.[37]

London was at the centre of the the desire for novelty and change. Each winter the leading gentry went to the capital for the Season, a round of social gatherings where changes in fashion spread very quickly. London also contained many middle-class households who stayed all year, merchants, tradespeople, and the professional classes. As well as copying the fashions of their social superiors, they formed their own circles of fashion and social emulation. Most of this latter group had no gardens and bought all their vegetables in the markets.[38]

Bernard Mandeville, summing up the influence of fashion on the rich in 1717, included both gardens and food in a list of desirable goods:

The worldly minded, voluptuous and ambitious Man, notwithstanding he is void of Merit, covets Precedence every where, and desires to be dignify'd above his Betters: He aims at spacious palaces and delicious Gardens...His Table he desires may be served with many Courses, and each of them contain a choice variety of Dainties not easily purchas'd, and ample evidences of elaborate and judicious Cookery.[39]

37. Miles Hadfield, *A History of British Gardening*, pp.151–178.
38. McKendrick, Brewer, & Plumb, pp.9–99.
39. Bernard Mandeville, *The Fable of the Bees*, 1714, edited by Phillip Harth, pp.170–1.

Bibliography

Manuscript sources
Surrey Records Office,Quarter Sessions, 6/12/Midsummer 1750, /62 to /105.
Museum of London, 'Peas Sold from a Cart', Wash drawing by Robert Dighton, c.1786.
Westminster City Archives, F4538; 1049/12/114; 1049/3/5/68.
Greater London Records Office, AM/PI (1), 1684/26; 1687/13;

Unpublished thesis
P.V.McGrath, 'The Marketing of Food, Fodder, and Livestock in the London Area in the Seventeenth Century', Unpublished London University M.A. thesis, 1948.

Secondary works
Anon.
– *Adam's Luxury and Eve's Cookery* (London, 1744)
– *The art of cookery in imitation of Horace's Art of Poetry* (London, 1708)
– *A collection of above three hundred recipes* (London, 1728)
– *The Compleat Tradesman* (London, 1684)
– *Complete Caterer* (London, 1701
– *The Complete Cook and A Queens Delight* (London, 1671)
– *The Court and Kitchen of Elizabeth, commonly called Joan Cromwell* (London, 1664)
– *The family magazine,in two parts* (London, 1743)
– *The Pastry Cooks Vade Mecum* (London, 1705)
– *Tatler* (London, 21st March,1710)
– *The English and French Cook* (London, 1674)
Bailey, Nathaniel, *Dictionarium Domesticum* (London, 1736)
Bradley, Richard, *Country Housewife and Lady's Director* (London, 1732)
– *Country Housewife and Lady's Director*, Introduction by Caroline Davidson (London, 1980)
– *A General Treatise of Husbandry and Gardening* (London, 1726)
– *New Improvements of Planting and Gardening* (London, 1719)
– *Philosophical Account of the Works of Nature* (London, 1721)
Brown, Maisie, *The Market Gardens of Barnes and Mortlake* (London, 1985)
Cooper, Charles, *The English Table in History and Literature* (London, 1929)
Earle, Peter, *The Making of the English Middle Class* (London, 1989)

Evelyn, John, *Acetaria* (London, 1699)

Glasse, Hannah, *The Art of Cookery Made Easy* (London, 1751)

Hadfield, Miles, *A History of British Gardening* (London, 1985)

Harrison, Sarah, *The House-keeper's Pocket Book* (London, 1743)

Johnson, George W., *A History of English Gardening* (London, 1829)

Jonson, Ben, 'On the famous voyage', *Epigrammes*,133 (London, 1616)

Kalm, Pehr, *Kalm's Account of his Visit to England on his Way to America in 1748*, ed. by J.Lucas (London, 1892)

Kidder, E., *Receipts of Pastry & Cookery* (London, no date,c.1720)

King, Gregory, *Natural and political conclusions upon the state and condition of England*, ed. by G, Chalmers (London, 1810)

Lamb, Patrick, *Royal Cookery* (London, 1710)

Lawrence, John, *The Clergy-Mans Recreation* (London, 1717)

Lennard, R., ed., *Englishmen at rest and play* (London, 1931)

London, George, & Henry Wise, *The Complete Gard'ner* (London, 1719)

Loudon, J.C., *Encyclopaedia of gardening* (London, 1824)

McKendrick, N., J.Brewer, J.H.Plumb, *The Birth of a Consumer Society* (London, 1983)

Maclean, Virginia, *A short-title catalogue of household and cookery books*, 1701–1800 (London, 1981)

Mandeville, Bernard, *The Fable of the Bees*, 1714, ed. by Phillip Harth (London, 1970)

Massinger, J., *The City madam* (London, 1632)

Mennell, Stephen, *All Manners of Food* (Oxford, 1987)

Morley, H., *Character Writings of the Seventeenth Century* (London, 1891)

Murrell, John, *Two Books of Cookerie and Carving* (London, 1638)

Nott, John, *The cook & confectioners dictionary* (London, 1724)

Parkinson, John, *Paradisi in sole* (London, 1629)

Pepys, Samuel, *Everbody's Pepys*, edited by O.F.Morshead, (London, 1955).

– *The Diary of Samuel Pepys*, ed. Henry B. Wheatley, (London, 1946)

Roberts, W.,'The London Neat House Gardens', *Journal of the Royal Horticultural Society* (London, 1941)

Le Rougetel, H., *The Chelsea Gardener* (London, 1990)

Salmon, William, *The Family-Dictionary* (London, 1705)

Scott-Thomson, G., *Life in a Noble Household* (London, 1937)

Shammas, Carol, *The Pre-Industrial Consumer in England* (Oxford, 1990)

Smith, E., *The Compleat Housewife* (London, 1753)

Strype, John, *A Survey of the Cities of London and Westminster* (London, 1720)

Switzer, Stephen, *A Compendious method for raising Italian broccoli* (London, 1728)

– *Country Gentleman's Companion* (London, 1732)
– *Practical Kitchen Gardener* (London, 1727)
Thick, Malcolm, 'Market Gardening in England and Wales' in *The Agrarian History of England and Wales*, Vol V.ii, ed. by Joan Thirsk (Cambridge, 1985)
Weatherill, Lorna, *Consumer Behaviour & Material Culture, 1660–1760* (London, 1988)
Weston, Richard, *Tracts on Agriculture and Gardening* (London, 1773)
Wilbraham, A., & J.C.Drummond, *The Englishman's Food* (London, 1957)
Worlidge, John, *Systema Horti-Culturae* (London, 1675)

Parsimony amid Plenty
views from Victorian didactic works on food for nursery children

VALERIE MARS

THIS paper examines changing fashions in eating, as depicted in a sample of representative Victorian child-care manuals and household books, directed at the children of parents with incomes sufficient to keep a nurse and a nursery.[1] These changes were linked to changes in the view of man's relationship to nature. In the eighteenth century nature equated with purity, and culture was seen as essentially corrupting. The more elaborate, luxurious and 'less natural' the food, the more it was seen as corrupting and unsuitable for children. As the nineteenth century progressed, this view shifted, with nature increasingly seen as subject to man's control and subjugation. Children's food similarly became the vehicle in its turn for their control and subjugation. The account that follows will consider directions suggested by a sequence of didactic sources, examining these sources for their social rather than their dietetic implications.

Ideas of suitable food for the Victorian nursery were epitomised in the ideas of Dr William Cadogan, who wrote an influential essay on the nursing and management of children, which he sent to the governors of Thomas Coram's Foundling Hospital in 1747. Although the Hospital's main purpose was to rescue and rear foundlings, this charitable foundation also pioneered new attitudes to child-care and it used Dr Cadogan's essay to promote this aim. They published it, a year later, in 1748. This is what Cadogan wrote about children's food:

There are many faults in the quality of their food: it is not simple enough, their papps, panados, gruels are generally enriched with sugar, spice and sometimes

1. I am indebted to Mary Douglas for devising Cultural Theory, the theoretical underpinning on which this paper is based.

a drop of wine; neither of which they ought ever to taste. Our bodies never want them; they are what luxury only has introduced to the destruction of the wealth of mankind. It is not enough that their food be simple, it should be also light. Several people I find are mistaken in their notions of what is light; and fancy most kinds of pastry, pudding, and custards &c. are light, that is light of digestion.[2]

This concept of luxury, of a man-made artificiality associated with mischief, was opposed to ideas of nature associated with virtue. The equation between culture and mischief was made explicit in John Armstrong's book *The Young Woman's Guide to Virtue, Economy and Happiness* (1825). Armstrong approvingly quotes Jean-Jacques Rousseau (1712–28): 'Everything is perfect as it comes out of the hands of God; but everything degenerates in the hands of man.'[3]

The *Young Woman's Guide* also admiringly quotes Dr Cadogan, and a follower of his, Dr Buchan, whose own book on child-rearing incorporated Cadogan's essay. Armstrong offers instructions that are consistent with their views:

In feeding children be sure not to cram them with unnatural mixtures [and as the child grows,] the bill of fare may be gradually enlarged, provided always that it consists of an innocent variety . . . You must be careful to feed your charge at stated and regular periods; perhaps three times a day is sufficient.[4]

Emphasis was on natural foods to be taken within a structure, but the exact details of the programme remained unspecified.

The theme of the child as conforming to a natural ideal continued with Mrs Pullan who, following the educational ideas of F. Froebel (1782–1852),[5] wrote a booklet (published in 1856) about his educational toys.[6] Though ideas of the natural continued in their original form, not everyone's ideas changed with the new fashion. Froebel used natural examples. Toys were to be used in a *kindergarten* and Mrs Pullan, using a horticultural metaphor to describe the eucational process, pursues it throughout an entire paragraph: the wild rose is first transplanted to the garden and then cultivated into a damask rose. She continues: 'the

2. p. 3.   3. p. 85.   4. p. 89.

5. Froebel advocated the kindergarten as the setting for educating the child through play.

6. Froebel had died three years before his works were translated into English, which makes his ideas contemporary with the time when the 'natural' was the accepted view.

rose [however] cannot be made to produce plums'[7] – that is, children cannot be trained against their nature. Her views on food are similarly consistent with those of Cadogan when she says: 'The food of young children can never be too simple.' Sudden changes were to be avoided, though occasional treats were allowed.

The new didactic mode took the same dietary directions and gave them new justifications, which bear the imprint of the authoritarian attitudes usually associated with Victorian childrearing. Dr Pye Henry Chavasse was the most noteworthy and long-published of these authoritarians; his book of questions and answers went through fourteen editions, from 1839 to 1885. It was directed at mothers of every station. Overt mention of 'station' was not made in earlier books – the readership could be taken as implicit. Books such as his, produced for an ever widening audience, included an increasing number of didactic works in which professional or upper class authors instructed those of lower social status, or simply the uninformed. In *Advice to Mothers on the Management of Their Offspring*, he discusses how children should be 'managed', and calls them not 'children' but 'offspring' – a term which negates any sense of individual personality.

Cassells Domestic Dictionary, 1877/9, under the heading 'Children, rearing and food of', begins: 'We know that food does for the body what fuel does for the steam engine';[8] just as the observance of mechanistic and hierarchic routines was required in order to keep the wheels of industry running, so the same principles were now brought to bear on the care of children. Roses and plums are superseded by engines.[9] The individualistic roses and plums however, were to receive some drastic pruning.

In the new class society, in which hierarchy and classification were at the core of social organisation, the different emphasis on new ways of working and domestic organisation was to produce an authoritarian rhetoric in attitudes to child-rearing. Indeed, the tone of Pye Henry Chavasse's answers appears to owe more to a vengeful deity than to the

7. p. 2.   8. p. 286.   9. Mrs Fry used engines as a paradigm for the body as early as 1828. But in keeping with the earlier mode, nature has the ascendancy over mechanics: 'The human frame is a machine, complex in its formation; and the operations of nature on it, as it reflects its mechanical laws, are often rendered dark and obscure by the mists of ignorance and prejudice.' (p. 326).

gentle authority of a Dr Cadogan. To the question, 'Have you any objection to pork for a change?', Dr Chavasse insists: 'I have the greatest objection to it. It is a rich, gross, and therefore unwholesome food for the delicate stomachs of children.'[10] When asked about sweets and cakes, Chavasse reaches an apoplectic climax: 'I consider them so much slow poison. Such things cloy and weaken the stomach and thereby take away the appetite and thus debilitate the frame. If the child is never allowed to eat such things, he will consider dry bread a luxury.'[11]

Forbidding sweets and cakes was a constant theme of the more authoritarian bias in later literature; the need to exclude such indulgencies served as a constant metaphor for control over personal choice. Why were they held in such opprobrium? Eating, for the middle-class and upper-class Victorian child, took place only in the nursery, and only at prescribed times. The food of such a child was eaten within the constraining structure of an ordered meal, at the table; promiscuous eating, in the rare instances where it was allowed, gave the child some autonomy, and emphasised his individuality – all the more so since sweets were often bought with his or her personal pocket money. Casual snacking, on the other hand, was associated with children who spent time on the streets, where they could buy food from the many stalls and walking vendors. The denial of this latter form of autonomy to nursery children effectively emphasised their class exclusivity.

Henry Mayhew, in *London Labour and the London Poor*, writes:

Men and women, and most especially boys, purchase their meals day after day in the streets. The coffee-stall supplies a warm breakfast; shell fish of many kinds tempt to a luncheon; hot-eels or pea soup, flanked by a potato 'all hot', serve for a dinner; and cakes and tarts, or nuts or oranges, with many varieties of pastry, confectionery, and fruit, woo to indulgence in a dessert; while for supper there is a sandwich, a meat pudding, or a 'trotter'.[12]

This rather arch setting out of street food, selected as a gentleman selects dinner from a caterer, was the work of a journalist writing for middle-class readers. Further on, where he lists the more substantial items sold, he says more realistically that it is from these that the 'street poor find a mid-day or midnight meal.'[13] In a long list of street food and drink, over fifty items are named; among them many sorts of sweets,

10. p. 76.   11. p. 80.   12. p. 116.   13. p. 117

cakes and pastries, all of which were forbidden to nursery children. Social division was thereby reinforced through the enforcement of structured eating habits: nursery children had to be separated from promiscuous outdoor eaters.

All of Dr Chavasse's answers are in the same tone of unflagging command, which were perfectly consistent with a view of earthly hierarchical authority. These naturally reflected the values of a perceived heavenly authority, also constructed on the same principle. Durkheim has argued that temporal morality is reinforced by religious belief. Chevasse's tone was consistent with the current religious revival, the growing numbers of non-conformists and the movement to counter apostasy, the beginning of which was marked by John Keble's Oxford sermon of 1833.

The revival of Protestantism and the growth of non-conformism gave a new emphasis to original sin. Children, who were seen as naturally full of original sin, could not now be nurtured like growing plants, but had to be disciplined until they were purged of sin: changed from the natural state and rendered fit for incorporation into man-made culture. Only as a result of this process were they able to leave the nursery and later, at the appropriate age, to progress to the schoolroom. Finally, on reaching maturity, they were qualified to join adults in the dining room where they often continued to eat a plain, but less proscribed, diet, with elaborate dishes reserved for dinner parties. A formal dinner party was, then, the most inaccessible meal of all to nursery children. Dr Chavasse's comment about children finding dry bread a luxury can now be seen in its proper context. The belief that children's original sin must be expunged meant that any tendency to untamed behaviour had to be eradicated before children could be allowed to eat with adults in the dining room.

Children had nursemaids well before the nineteenth century, but the new household management advocated such strongly hierarchic dining practices that it effectively removed children from an interactive family life. To maintain this newly required separating hierarchy, however, required a household with the resources to support a cook, housemaids and a nurse. Mrs Beeton writes of nurseries where 'the mother is too much occupied to do more than pay a daily visit'.[14] Her distant

14. p. 1014.

relationship to child-rearing parallels her similar distance from food preparation. Both involve minimum contact – daily visits to the nursery equating with daily interaction with the cook. Both food, in its uncooked state, and children are closer to nature than was consistent with the ideal of Victorian feminine gentility. In distancing herself from lower status tasks, the lady of the house was operating on the same principles as the factory manager. Division of labour was the principle on which both roles were predicated: the mistress managed the house; the master, the factory or office.

A book which was unusual, in this context, was Mrs Warren's *How I Managed My Children from Infancy to Marriage* (1865), based on personal experience of her own child-rearing. She gave her children the same dishes that she had had as a child, but made sure that hey were 'properly cooked', unlike the food she was given when young.[15] Mrs Warren is unique in referring to her own childhood; none of the other authors of such works ever alluded to their own pasts. Their silence is consistent with a view of childhood as a stage of untamed immaturity best forgotten; children, they assume, should not be valued for their individual thoughts and opinions. It is also consistent, in a time of dynamic change, with the tedecy to view the past as irrelevant to concerns of the present.

By the end of the century, Ward and Lock's *Home Book: a Domestic Encyclopaedia* (1880) included an extensive section on 'Children and What to do With Them', with a complete chapter on children's diet. The sequence of sub-headings is: 'Errors in Diet'; 'Stimulating Food'; 'Cooking for Children'; 'Eating Between Meals'; 'Punctual Meals'; 'Waste Not'; 'Meat for Children'; 'Proper Vegetables'; 'Efficacy of Salt'; 'Suppers'; 'Dessert'.[16] Such detailed coverage of every aspect of childhood feeding illustrates the lengths to which social control through eating could be exercised. The logical extension of this control was the use of purgatives, which also feature in many of the books on child-care. (Victorian choices of purgative methods are, however, outside the bounds of this paper.)

As might be surmised, there was a reaction against such a high degree of control. The Arts and Crafts movement represented an analagous

15. p. 34.　　16. p. 438–441.

reaction against the controls of industry, embodying as it did a return to natural forms and individual craftsmanship. In keeping with its contents, the title page of W. B. Drummond's *The Child: his Nature and Nurture* (1901), which is similarly concerned with a reduction in control and an increase in individualism, is appropriately illustrated by a woodcut of foliage and calligraphy in typical Arts and Crafts style.

Drummond's ideas do not represent a complete revival of Cadogan's, but they do represent the view that children have likes and dislikes, which should be taken into account; a return to the linked values of nature and individualism was becoming manifest.

The childish love of 'goodies' should be met by including a fair amount of sweet things in the diet, especially in the form of cooked fruit such as stewed or roasted apples, or stewed prunes, or ripe fruit such as grapes, oranges or pears. Sweetmeats are best allowed in addition to meals. Chocolate is one of the best forms. The late Dr Milner Fothergill used to recommend toffee when made at home with the best sugar and butter. So made it is not merely a 'goodie' but an excellent article of diet, supplying both sugar and fat.[17]

As for compelling children to eat everything on their plate, as insisted upon by 'the waste-not school', his views were moderate: 'while children should be encouraged to eat the fat with their meat, they should not be compelled to consume greasy articles of diet.'[18] Like Cadogan, however, he too asserts that 'tasty' articles should not be allowed, 'if for no other reason than they are apt to make the children discontented with the plain and wholesome food with which they are perfectly satisfied so long as they have never had anything else.'[19]

Drummond's stricture on the tasty, though at first appearance similar to Cadogan's, has a rationale sustained more by the need to keep children separated from adult diners than with their dietary needs. Although a gentler expression of Chavasse's reasoning that children should find dry bread 'a luxury', he gives no dietetic reason for advocating plain foods.

By the end of the century, tasty food for the dinner-giving classes was dinner party food, though many of them ate plain dinners when not entertaining. Marion Sambourne's diary of the early eighteen-eighties lists her family's plain daily dinners and the elaborate dinner party food they ate at home and at other peoples' dinner parties. These followed a

17. p. 49.   18. p. 49.   19. p. 50.

more elaborate cuisine often supplemented with additions from caterers. Such occasions represented the ultimate exclusion zone for children. To have allowed them 'tasty' food would have accorded them entrance into the adult world. Drummond's views were still in accord with this sense of a need to reinforce the contemporary social hierarchy.

At the beginning of the new century, there was some relaxation in authoritarian attitudes to the young, but nursery children were still separated by rules about food, and rules governing when, where and how it was to be eaten. Writers still opposed the practice of bringing children down from the nursery to join adults for dessert in the dining room. The allegedly harmful effects of sweet-eating were used to justify the exclusion of such unpredictable creatures at the highly structured and constrained Victorian dinner-party. In Ward and Lock's *Home Book*, the author writes:

It is common practice with many parents to give their children permission to ask for and obtain what they like of the dessert from their own table, the children coming down from their nursery for this purpose. This is a cruel kindness. The simple, well-cooked, and much enjoyed dinner they may have had is quite marred by this after loading of rich things. But as children should *not* be called upon to *see* food they cannot help coveting, without being allowed to eat of it, some other time should be chosen for their appearance downstairs than the dessert hour, or else strict supervision as to what they do eat should be exercised.[20]

The Handbook of Carving (1848) is even more emphatic: "If you have children, never introduce them after dinner unless particularly asked for, and then avoid it if possible."[21] Children were considered as out of place at dessert as they were at afternoon calls. Leonore Davidoff, when investigating rules for making afternoon calls as set out in Victorian etiquette manuals, finds that neither dogs nor children were to be taken to call.[22] Dogs and children are classified together – both being regarded as unpredictable. In keeping with an authoritarian view of nature, their living and eating was separated from the rest of the adult family.

After about 1830, plain food was no longer equated with a proximity to nature. Later justifications emphasised instead that children should eat plain food because it was healthier.

20. p. 441.   21. *The Handbook of Carving*, p. 5.   22. p. 44

There were, in any case, many variations in the details of suggested diets. Victorian directions on child-care did not, for the most part, offer a complete diet for children. They were unsystematic in their advice and there were all sorts of variations. Their consistency, however, lay in a universal proscription of well-flavoured foods and elaborate dishes which, in general, followed Cadogan's advice. This list, compiled from a sample of books, shows some of the many variations in the prescription of a suitable diet for children:

Publication	Recommended	Proscribed
Dr Cadogan, 1748	Simplicity	Luxury
The Young Woman's Guide, 1825	Meat in proportion to bread and wholesome vegetables; mellow fruit, raw, stewed or baked; roots of all sorts and all kitchen garden produce; milk.	Spices, seasoning, pastry, butter, unripe fruit, fermented liquors, tea.
Mrs Fry, *The Good Nurse,* 1828	Milk, water, barley water, milk-porridge for breakfast, toast, water, bread, cake with preserved fruit, bread-cake, souchong tea with milk – moderately sweetened.	Bread and butter 'not as good as bread-cake with caraway seeds rather than currants'.
Pye Henry Chavasse, *Advice to Mothers,* 1839	New potatoes, toast, water, home-made bread two to three days old, butter in moderation, grilled mutton chop, lightly boiled egg.	Pork, veal, salt and boiled beef, old potatoes, beer and wine, cakes, sweetened baker's bread.
Mrs Pullan, 1856	Cannot be too simple.	No sudden changes.
Mrs Warren, *How I managed My Children from Infancy to Marriage,* 1865	Rice pudding with nutmeg and milk on the weekly 'diet' day; boiled mutton with gravy; stock, meat, onion and turnips with separate boiled potatoes; boiled onions once	Meat and fish not to be eaten at the same meal; only one relish; chives, fruit etc. with tea-time bread and butter.

a week (to remove worms); chives with bread and butter; roast meat; fish; milk and water flavoured with tea; bread and butter with watercress and chives; fruit; apples raw or roasted.

Minnie Elligot, *A Helping Hand to Mothers*, 1898	Beef tea, milk puddings, eggs, oranges peeled, cocoa essence in water and milk.	No drinking with meals; tea/coffee not good.
W.B. Drummond, *The Child, his Nature and Nurture*, 1901	Diet light, varied and palatable; sweet things – stewed fruit, apples, prunes, grapes, oranges, pears; animal food twice a day; milk; meat once a day; fat, cream, butter, chocolate, home-made toffee.	Jam and Jelly in moderation on bread and butter; all 'tasty' articles.

What emerges here is one overarching theme: the importance for all the authors of plain food. Some allowed sweets but none ever recommended spiced or flavoured food. The justifications varied, as did other rules about eating, but the Victorian child was never to enjoy tasty food, whether in an authoritarian or more naturalistically-orientated household. A diet originally recommended in the middle of the eighteenth century, for its congruity with the child's perceived proximity to nature, was used in an entirely different manner to enforce nursery children's social separation in the strict hierarchy of the Victorian household – and, through their place within it, the household to the world outside.

Bibliography

Armstrong, John, *The Young Woman's Guide to Virtue, Economy and Happiness*, Mackenzie and Dent (Newcastle-upon-Tyne, 1825).
Mrs Beeton's Book of Household Management, S. O. Beeton (London, 1861). This facsimile edition Chancellor Press (London, 1982).

Bowditch, Mrs, *Confidential Chats with Mothers on the Rearing of Children*, Ballière, Tindall and Cox (London, 1890).

Buchan, William, *Advice to Mothers*, T. Cadell Davis (London, 1803).

Cadogan, William, *An Essay upon the Nursing and the Management of Children from their Birth to Three Years of Age*, F. Roberts (London, 1748).

Cassell's Domestic Dictionary, Cassell, Petter, Galpin and Co. (London, probably just after 1875).

Chavasse, Pye Henry, *Advice to Mothers on the Management of their Offspring*, Longman, Orme, Brown, Green & Longmans (London, 1839).

Davidoff, Leonore, *The Best Circles*, Cresset Library, Century Hutchinson (London, 1986).

Douglas, Mary, *Cultural Bias*, Occasional paper No 35, The Royal Anthropological Institute (London, 1978).

Drummond, W. B., *The Child, his Nature and Nurture*, Aldine House, J. M. Dent & Co. (London, 1901).

Durkheim, Emile, *The Elementary Forms of Religious Life*, George, Allen and Unwin (London, 1915).

Elligot, Minnie, *A Helping Hand to Mothers*, James Clarke & Co. (London, 1898).

Fry, Mrs, *The Good Nurse, or Hints on the Management of the Sick and Lying-In Chamber and the Nursery*, Longman, Rees Orme, Brown and Green, (London, 1828).

The Handbook of Carving, George Routledge & Co. (London, 1848).

Mayhew, Henry, *London Labour and the London Poor*, published as 'Mayhew's London', Spring Books (London, 195 –?).

Pullan, Mrs (Matilda Marian), *Children and How to Manage Them*, Darton & Co. (London, 1856).

Pullan, Mrs (Matilda Marian), *The Kindergarten Toys and How to Use Them*, Darton & Co. (London, 1856).

Sambourne, Marion, Unpublished Diaries of Marion Sambourne, wife of Linley Sambourne, *Punch* cartoonist. 1879–1882.

Ward and Lock's Home Book: a Domestic Encyclopaedia, Ward, Lock & Co. (London, 1880).

Warren, Mrs Eliza, *How I Managed My Children from Infancy to Marriage*, Houlston & Wright (London, 1865).

3
Food in Classical cultures

Food and sexuality in classical Athens
The written sources

ANDREW DALBY

How much can be learnt of everyday life from hints and silences in the literature of a long-vanished culture? The question is of primary importance to anthropologists and social historians who study the ancient world. The information they need cannot be observed directly; moreover, the details of everyday life, taken for granted at the time, did not need to be described at length, so that hints and asides are generally the best source material that can be hoped for.

This paper aims to re-examine questions of interaction between the sexes, as exemplified in the beliefs, customs and etiquette that surround food and drink, in Athens, in the fifth, fourth and third centuries B.C.[1] Life in other cities and at other times was not similar in all respects to life in Athens at those times, but the evidence for other classical Greek cities is so slight as hardly to bear interpretation without reference to Athens by way of comparison or contrast. Moreover, the evidence for other cities at this period comes largely from authors who were Athenian, or who adopted an Athenian perspective.

---

1. This paper is partly a revision of one listed in the bibliography, Dalby, 'Men, women and food'. It was presented to the London Food Seminar in 1989, and is printed in the form in which it was presented. If I had now been re-writing it, I would have made an effort to keep the thought in the reader's mind, and in my own, that the literary sources are not transparent; that the pattern of behaviour that is constructed here, a consensus of contemporary literary sources, probably lies distant from what a hypothetical neutral observer would see – and indeed from what many real contemporary observers might have seen.

For details of works by modern authors cited in text and footnotes, see the bibliography.

Sources

Among possible sources for an answer to questions of social behaviour in the ancient world, written evidence is privileged, as compared with that of vase paintings, relief carvings and other iconographic material, because literature offers a narrative, a context. But no evidence of ancient social behaviour is free of bias.

Vase paintings appear to reflect an elegant and expensive way of life enjoyed (or aspired to) by those who bought artistic hand-painted vases. These were surely not the majority, even if it is accepted, as Michael Vickers urges, that earthenware vases were a cheap substitute for gold, silver and bronze.[2] At any rate, vase-paintings – which also come predominantly from Athens – are a rich source of illustrations of social behaviour, and not unnaturally quite a large proportion of them illustrate scenes of eating and (especially) drinking. The most useful ones are of the early fifth century, the beginning of the 'red figure' style. Examples are cited here, when possible, from Boardman's widely available handbook, *Athenian red figure vase painting*.

The principal literary sources[3] for social life at Athens at this period are the comedies of Aristophanes, the legal speeches written by Demosthenes, Lysias and others, and some of the sketches and dialogues by Xenophon and Plato (both cast in the form of reminiscences of Socrates). The brief, impressionistic *Characters* of Theophrastus add useful details. In addition to these there are occasional clues in contemporary historical narratives: and many relevant extracts from lost works of the period are brought together by the antiquarian Athenaeus, an author of the late second century A.D. His long book *The Deipnosophists* is mainly about food, drink and entertainment in classical and Hellenistic times. The extracts quoted by Athenaeus that are cited in this study come from comedies by contemporaries of Aristophanes and from anecdotal social histories and memoirs.

The comedies of Menander, who wrote between 321 and 292 B.C., are

2. Vickers, 'Artful crafts'. The article began a fierce controversy, not relevant here.

3. Greek sources are cited here by standard book and section divisions – in the case of plays and poems, by line numbers –, which will be found in all modern editions and most translations. For more details see the 'Note on ancient sources' at the end of the paper.

also especially important. Until this century they were 'lost', known only from extracts made by later writers, like the plays of all other Athenian comedians except Aristophanes; they were thus not available to the authors of the still standard surveys of ancient Greek private life.[4] Substantial parts of several of Menander's plays are now known from Egyptian papyri. These comedies are quite different from the kind written by Aristophanes a century earlier. Aristophanes' plots are fantasy, generally for the sake of political satire, though in them the patterns and assumptions of everyday life are continually visible. By contrast, the success of Menander's plays (which like so many later comedies turn on misunderstandings, recognitions and reconciliations) depends on the illusion of realism: details must ring true if the audience is to suspend its disbelief. Menander's writings are particularly relevant here because in most of the plays now rediscovered he explores social problems caused by relationships between the sexes.

Xenophon and Plato wrote of life among the wealthy who had the leisure and the money to pursue philosophical enquiry.

Forensic speeches were written for those who became involved in legal action and could afford professional assistance, though they aimed to sway Athenian juries, chosen by lot, in which the lower classes probably predominated. There is only one speech, out of well over a hundred surviving from classical Athens, written on behalf of a petitioner who claims to be so poor he could not have afforded to pay for it:[5] this speech, we must presume, was written for the petitioner out of charity or friendship, or was published as a model for unskilled litigants to follow, as were some others. So, for example, Euphiletus, the defendant for whom Lysias wrote his speech *On the Killing of Eratosthenes*, had a small two-storey house shared by a wife, a child and one slave girl. He had killed his wife's lover, incidentally: his defence relies on the legally defined circumstances in which a husband could justifiably take such a step.

If we are to know anything of the daily life of households poorer than

4. In spite of the huge number of modern specialised studies, reference is still made to Becker's *Charikles* as revised by Göll and to Blümner's *Lehrbuch der griechischen Privataltertümer*. Both must be read in German (though Becker's work in its briefer original form was translated).

5. Lysias, *Appeal against the Withholding of a Disability Allowance*.

that, we must deduce it from archaeology and from Athenian comedies, which were written to attract applause from free Athenian men both rich and poor.

One must say 'men': whether women attended plays remains controversial. The sources are ambiguous. One suspects that a comparison may be appropriate with such august institutions as university libraries: children would never dream of entering them on their own, yet children may be seen in them because they are for the time being part of the impedimenta of an adult. Just so a slave or a woman or a child might have been taken in to the theatre (or even on to the jury benches)[6] by an Athenian man just because he happened to have them with him.

A study which aims to focus on everyday life must ask the question: how 'everyday' is the behaviour described in literary sources? It is important at least to be aware that feasts, dinner parties and drinking parties were (as in most societies) less ubiquitous than their frequent occurrence in memoirs and fiction would suggest;[7] that travellers who cannot call on acquaintances have to eat at inns;[8] that some members of a household spend the whole day away from home, working,[9] taking food with them,[10] or being provided with a communal ration.[11] Supporting evidence from Greek sources can be quoted for all of these statements. The most common cases are likely to have been family meals and working meals – and these are the cases mentioned least in literature. We note, for example, how unusual (and how erotically charged) is the depiction in the *Odyssey* of the meal shared by Odysseus and Calypso on her lonely island:

They came to the hollow cave, the goddess and the man together. Well, he was sitting there on a chair, where Hermes had been, and the *nymphe* put out every

6. Aristophanes, *Wasps* 303–6, quoted below, suggests the possibility of this. I would add now that the difficulty of the question whether women were present at dramatic performances is itself highly instructive. It is a symptom of a pervasive problem of the literary sources. The drama, and nearly all of the rest of Greek literature too, was a discourse between men.

7. They are seldom mentioned in the forensic speeches.   8. Aristophanes, *Frogs* 549–562.

9. Xenophon, *Management* 7.30 observes that it is improper for a man to spend his days at home.

10. Aristophanes, *Wasps* 612–618.

11. Aristophanes, *Assemblywomen* 306–8, *Acharnians* 164–6.

food for him, to eat and drink, that mortal men eat; she was sitting facing godlike Odysseus, and house-girls put out ambrosia and nectar for her; and they set their hands to the food laid out ready. Now when they had enjoyed food and drink, well, Calypso, noble of goddesses, was the one who began with words ...[12]

Calypso is usually described as a goddess, not a nymph. The word *nymphe* more commonly meant a 'young nubile woman' or 'young bride': that is how Calypso is to be seen as she and Odysseus eat in intimate proximity, and naturally the episode ends with them going to bed together.

Men's dinner parties and the separation of the sexes

Athens became stricter, apparently stricter than some other Greek cities, about the seclusion of women.[13] We can take as demonstrated the general fact that contacts in public between the sexes were highly circumscribed, and that women's movements were restricted; this study is limited to food behaviour.

Married women do not go out to dinners with their husbands, nor do they care to dine with men of other families,

so Isaeus observed in the course of a demonstration that a certain Phile, who did these things, was promiscuous.[14] Apparently some women learnt to be still more decorous:

He came to my house one night, drunk, broke open the door and entered the women's quarters; inside were my sister and my nieces, who had had such a modest life that they were shy of being seen even by relations.

– or so the speaker wished the jury to think as they reflected on the incident.[15]

12. *Odyssey* 5.194–201.

13. Athenian women complain that their segregation is becoming stricter in Aristophanes' *Thesmophoriazusae*, especially 414–428, though it may be risky to take the complaint at face value. Walker, 'Women and housing' (p. 88) gives a house plan from the Attic countryside which seems to show less formal separation of men's and women's living space. On women's seclusion in early Greece much has been written. Recently Gould, 'Law, custom and myth' (pp. 40, 46–51) has shown how unrealistic it is to minimise the seclusion of women in classical Athens.

14. Isaeus, *On Pyrrhus's Estate* 14.   15. Lysias, *Against Simon* 6.

By the fourth century the houses of the well-to-do had many rooms, including one set aside for eating and drinking with guests. This room, which an unfamiliar visitor might not be able to find easily,[16] was called *andron*,[17] literally 'men's room', part of the *andronitis*,[18] 'men's quarters'. It will be clear from the two quotations above that women who belonged to such better-off households had no reason to enter the dining room when it was in use, and so did not even observe men's dinner parties (as women had been able to do in Homeric society). This apparently applied both to females of the householder's family and to his female slaves; at any rate, in all the narratives of men's dinners and symposia from the period there is not one certain indication of the presence of a woman of the household. So a privileged guest, wishing to foster serious conversation, could say: 'I think we should tell the flute-girl (who had just arrived) to go away and play to herself, or – if she prefers – to the women inside!'[19]

If confirmation were needed of the general Greek assumption at this period that respectable women ought not to attend dinner parties with men, it comes in a puzzled description of a foreign system of behaviour, that of the Illyrians, by a historian of the fourth century B.C.: 'The Illyrians eat and drink sitting up, and they take their wives to dinner parties; it is even proper for the women to drink toasts to any of the men who are there. They help their husbands home afterwards.'[20]

16. Plato, *Symposium* 174d–e. For a specimen house plan see Walker, 'Women and housing' (pp. 86–7).

17. Xenophon, *Symposium* 1.4 etc.

18. As opposed to gynaikonitis (see below): Xenophon, *Management* 9.6; Lysias, *On the Killing of Eratosthenes* 9. But while 'gynaikonitis' is a common word, and still used in Greece to designate the part of a church that is or was set aside for women, 'andronitis' is rare, used when a balancing term is wanted to designate the part of the house that was not 'gynaikonitis'.

19. Plato, *Symposium* 176e. The speaker is Socrates. They could not simply send the flute-girl home: she had been hired by their host, so must now be given some job to do even if it was only to 'play to herself'.

20. Theopompus quoted by Athenaeus 443a–b. Perhaps this was assumed to be the general custom of 'western barbarians'? Note suspiciously similar statements about the Etruscans made by the same author, quoted by Athenaeus 517d.

Women's meals and entertainments

Let us return for a moment to the suggestion quoted above, that the unwanted flute-girl play 'to the women inside'. If that suggestion was seriously meant, the speaker assumed that the host's womenfolk might welcome entertainment similar to that enjoyed by men. Indeed, it is central to the plot of Menander's *The Arbitration* that the harp-girl Habrotonon (whose usual commissions would be to entertain at men's symposia) attended the Tauropolia, a women's all-night festival, with a party of respectable women, and played to accompany the girls' dancing.[21]

It is further assumed that women would dine and be entertained 'inside' in the *gynaikonitis*, the women's quarters. Separate celebrations (of a betrothal) for men and women are certainly suggested in Menander's *Bad-Tempered Man*:

'There must be a good drinking-party for us now, dad, and an all-night wake[22] for the women.'

'I know better – the women'll drink, and we'll be kept awake all night!'[23]

There are vase-paintings of all-women symposia,[24] though these paintings (in which the women are naked) have been suspected of being male fantasies.

One anecdote depicts two women at a meal together:

Gnathaena was once at dinner at Dexithea's, and Dexithea was putting almost all the dishes aside for her mother. 'By Artemis, woman,' said Gnathaena, 'if I'd known this would happen I'd have had dinner with your mother, not with you!'[25]

21. Menander, Epitrepontes (*The Arbitration*) 451–485.

22. All-night festivals were particularly associated with women: see Gomme and Sandbach, *Menander* (pp. 330, 264).

23. Lines 855–9. I use inverted commas in quotations from plays and dialogues as a reminder that the author is not speaking in his own person.

24. For example Lissarrague, *Flot d'images* figures 41, 69 and 70 (the two latter also to be found in Boardman, *Athenian red figure vases* figures 27 and 38.1).

25. Machon quoted by Athenaeus 580c. The two women were both *hetairai*, see below, active around 330 B.C.; Machon wrote his verse anecdotes at least sixty years later in distant Alexandria. Cf. Diphilus fragment 43 quoted by Athenaeus 291f.

Respectable women certainly did meet for meals, perhaps more often during the day:

'What could have become of her? Has one of your friends' wives invited her round for lunch?'

'So I assume.'[26]

The evidence of that exchange from old comedy seems to be supported by the very title of Menander's lost comedy *Synaristosai*, *Women Lunching Together*, from which several passages survive, including this: 'Somebody give me another drink. That foreign girl took the table away and took the wine as well!'[27] It is not known whether the speaker is a woman, though that seems most likely. But whether the women lunching together in this play were supposed to be 'respectable' women is less clear. From beyond Athens, the early fifth century lyric poet Pindar wrote of a legendary tomboy: 'She did not like the to-and-fro walking at the loom, nor the pleasures of dinners with her housewifely women friends.'[28]

Family feasts

Family parties, in which both women and men were involved, perhaps frequently took the form of visits to shrines, where an animal would be sacrificed and the family would have the luxury of dining off roast meat. One should add that already in the Homeric epics meat was consumed only with religious observances involving sacrifice: wastrels could be criticised for sacrificing too frequently, meaning that they ate too much meat.[29]

Returning to classical Athens, the best description of one of these family parties is in Menander's *Bad-Tempered Man*, a recently rediscovered play which survives practically complete. Different views of the celebration are conveniently contributed by the hero Sostratus:

'I found Getas wasn't at home, because my mother's going to sacrifice to some god, I don't know which, she does it all the time, she goes around the whole area sacrificing – she's sent him out to hire a *mageiros*. I said 'Damn the sacrifice' and came back here;'[30]

26. Aristophanes, *Assemblywomen* 348–9.   27. Menander fragment 385.

28. Pindar, *Pythian Ode* 9.18–19 of Cyrene.   29. *Odyssey* 14.93–5.   30. Lines 259–265.

by the bad-tempered farmer Cnemon:

'The Nymphs are a bad neighbour to me ... The way these vandals sacrifice!
They bring couches, wine-jars – not for the gods, for themselves ... They offer
the gods the tail-end and the gall-bladder, the bits you can't eat, and gobble the
rest themselves;'[31]

by the slave Getas and the *mageiros* 'sacrificer-cook' who was hired to
officiate:

'It's the wrong way round: it's me, the *mageiros*, getting slaughtered [carrying
this sheep]. But luckily here's the Nymphaeum where we're sacrificing. Hail,
Pan! Getas, boy, you're a long way behind.'
   'Those accursed women tied four donkey-loads on to me to carry.'
   'There's a big group coming, then? I can't count the cushions you're carrying
... Take this in. We'll put the mats in place inside and get the other things ready.
Nothing's to hold up the sacrifice once they arrive ... And stop frowning, you
misery! I'll feed you properly today.'[32]

While the plot is played out on stage, the sacrifice and meal are imag-
ined to be taking their leisurely course just outside the audience's vision. First the slave and *mageiros* arrive and make preparations (last
quotation); then Sostratus' mother and some other women of the
household. At this point the sacrifice must be supposed to take place,
though no note is taken of the event on stage. In this story Sostratus
and his father arrive some time after the sacrifice and after the women
have eaten. At that stage Sostratus invites his new friend Gorgias, with
his male slave, to join the meal, but, tellingly, Gorgias's mother cannot
be invited, although leaving her on her own leads to some inconven-
ience.[33] Everything said and implied throughout the play is consistent
with the idea that at family festivities such as this the sexes arranged
themselves in separate groups – separate circles when dining in the
open air, separate rooms, or separate groups in a large dining room,
when indoors. Some shrines certainly provided dining rooms. There is
archaeological evidence of these from various parts of Greece;[34] they
were private rooms, one for each party.
   We may imagine that the men in the *Bad-Tempered Man ought* to

31. Lines 444–453. Cf. Pherecrates fragment 23.   32. Lines 398–424.   33. Lines 616–619.
34. The evidence is conveniently collected by Börker, *Festbankett*. Bergquist,
'Sympotic space' discusses how parties fitted into dining rooms of various sizes.

have arrived in time for the sacrifice, and so that both sexes *ought* to have eaten at the same time; we may on the other hand imagine that roast meat was a man's dish, and that the women could get on and eat while the *mageiros* was still busy with the roasting.

It does at any rate appear, from the cook's remark to Getas, that (as with the English Sunday dinner) a religious timetable provides the occasion, and some special ceremonial may be involved, but one major purpose of the outing is to eat well.[35]

That fashions varied in the number of guests, and in whether women as well as men were involved, at these occasional feasts, is suggested by a further short piece of Menander's *Women Lunching Together*:

'It's fashionable not to gather the women or have a crowd to dinner, but just to have a wedding-meal at home.'[36]

But short fragments, lacking any context, are dangerous. Did the speaker wish to limit expenditure, or to keep the wedding secret? We cannot tell.

Service at dinner parties; eating out

Wherever there is definite evidence about the service of men's formal meals, it suggests that men and not women were the waiters.[37] The occasional vase-painting[38] is not enough to overturn the literary evidence which always refers in the masculine to slaves and hired assistants engaged in these tasks. I must not pass unremarked one definite counter-example, a wine-jug (stamnos) by the Copenhagen painter, Athens, about 480 B.C., which shows a short-haired woman, apparently a

---

35. Compare Menander fragment 264, from the play *Drunkenness*.

36. Fragment 384.

37. See Becker, *Charikles* (vol. 2 pp. 321–4, 354–5). At Naucratis, the Greek trading colony in Egypt, a rule stated: 'no woman shall enter the municipal dining room except the flute-girl alone'. Hermeias, *On the Gryneian Apollo* quoted by Athenaeus 150a.

38. Boardman, *Athenian red figure vases* figure 225 (by Onesimus, Athens, about 490 B.C.), a naked woman 'Doris' mixing wine: no context. For male waiters, usually shown naked, see Boardman, *Athenian red figure vases* figures 76, 253, 248, 376; Lissarrague, *Flot d'images* figure 20, among many other examples; men mixing wine, Lissarrague, *Flot d'images* figure 10.

slave, in a long dress, serving wine to male diners; four couches are shown, two of which are shared by men and (beardless) youths.[39]

A host might hire (or instruct his hired *mageiros* to subcontract)[40] a *trapezopoios*, a 'table-maker' 'who will wash the dishes, prepare the lamps, make libations, and do everything else he should,'[41] including overseeing the service of the meal. This job, unlike that of the *mageiros*, had no religious overtones.[42] The host might on the other hand rely entirely on his slaves:

'Well, boys, bring the rest of us our meal. Set things out entirely as you please, since there is no one supervising you (a thing I have never done): imagine you have invited myself and the others to dinner, and serve so as to win our praise.'[43]

So when Chabrias of Athens gave a celebration dinner at Cape Colias, the waiters were his male slaves.[44] This dinner party and symposium took place, by the way, at a temple (a temple of Aphrodite to be precise),[45] and that really seems to have been the usual Greek location for 'eating out'. Eating at a *kapeleion*, a 'shop' or 'inn', had a very bad name: 'No one, not even a respectable slave, would have dared to eat or drink in a wineshop,'[46] or so Isocrates claimed in a nostalgic speech, and a speech attributed to Hypereides stated that no one who had had lunch in a wineshop would be appointed to the Court of Areopagus.[47] These statements sound exaggerated. On the other side we can find a woman speaker in a comedy by Antiphanes:

'I have a neighbour who keeps a wineshop: whenever I go in there thirsty, he alone knows at once how to mix it for me. I don't know that I ever had it too watery or too strong.'[48]

39. Lissarrague, *Flot d'images* figure 11.

40. Menander, *Samian Woman* 290, quoted below.

41. Antiphanes fragment 152, from his play *The Resident Alien* (quoted by Athenaeus 170d, where there are further relevant quotations). There is no need to discuss here any questions of the status of such hired assistants, whether they were Athenian or of foreign origin, slave or free.

42. Menander, *Bad-Tempered Man* 647.

43. Plato, *Symposium* 175b. I take it that the thing Agathon had never done was to hire a trapezopoios to supervise his slaves when he gave a party.

44. Apollodorus *Against Neaera* 34, quoted below.   45. Pausanias 1.1.5.

46. Isocrates, *Areopagiticus* 49.   47. Hypereides quoted by Athenaeus 566f.

48. Fragment 24, quoted by Athenaeus 441b.

But eating and drinking at a wineshop appears from our meagre sources to have been an unconvivial affair. One did not go there to appreciate good food or wine, or to meet one's friends. Only in Roman imperial times could Cynulcus say to Myrtilus in Athenaeus's fictional dialogue: 'As for you, professor, you wallow in the wineshops with your women-friends, that is ...'[49]

And only much later still, in the late sixth century A.D., do we first have notice of an inn to which people went for the quality of its food. This inn in western Asia Minor, the birthplace of St Theodore of Syceon, marks the real beginning of the history of restaurants.[50]

Everyday meals

Having said something of lunch and dinner parties of the well-to-do, it is necessary to consider ordinary meals without guests, and meals of poorer people. In a town house the women's quarters were often up-stairs,[51] and a man of the house might normally eat there;[52] but the idea of permitting a male dining companion to enter the women's quarters is compared to sacrilege in Menander's *False Heracles*.[53] There a man would expect to be waited on, whether by a slave[54] or by his wife:[55]

'And the little woman says nice things to me, brings me a barley-puff, sits down beside me and goes, "Have some of this! Try a bit of this!" I enjoy all that ...'[56]

She herself, depending on circumstances, may have eaten with him after

49. Athenaeus 567a.

50. *Life of St Theodore of Syceon* 6. For more see: *Three Byzantine saints: contemporary biographies translated from the Greek* by Elizabeth Dawes and Norman H. Baynes (Oxford: Clarendon Press, 1948).

51. Lysias, *On the Killing of Eratosthenes* 9. Ther excavators of the fourth century b.c. new town of Olynthus looked in vain for women's quarters in the uniform rows of houses there – see Robinson and Graham (pp. 167–8): here too, no doubt, the gynaikonitis was typically upstairs.

52. Lysias, *Against Simon* 7.   53. Fragment 452.

54. Aristophanes, *Knights* 42–60, 1164–1220.

55. Just so Calypso in *Odyssey* 5.196–7, quoted above, serves Odysseus with man's food before being served herself by her maids with the nectar and ambrosia appropriate to goddesses.

56. Aristophanes, *Wasps* 610–612. Similarly, men expect to be served breakfast: *Assemblywomen* 468–470.

he had had his choice.[57] It cannot be assumed that this was universal.[58] It is just as likely that she, with any other women and any male slaves of a household, ate first, or ate afterwards whatever was left uneaten, as Gnathaena's mother was to do in the anecdote already quoted.

Hardly ever intruding into literature, scenes such as this are by contrast quite standard on funerary reliefs, on which a reclining man attended by a seated woman may be in turn attended by standing children and slaves. These reliefs – the seated figure is always a man – are to be found in Greece from the seventh century B.C. and so offer a clue to the beginnings (as far as Greece is concerned) of the fashion of reclining at meals: they have antecedents and analogues elsewhere in the eastern Mediterranean.[59]

Food purchase, management and preparation

Certain tasks connected with food were not carried out by women, it seems. They did not deal in meat or fish. 'Again, no-one has ever seen a butcheress, nor yet a fishmongeress!'[60] said a character in an Athenian comedy; the statement seems meant to be obvious and incontrovertible. The normal masculine *mageiros* denoted a tradesman who sold meat and took charge of sacrificing, cooking and serving it, a job with heavy overtones of religion.

It hardly needed to be said, apparently, that women were excluded from this work.[61] A priestess of Artemis says in a passage from Athenian tragedy:

'I sacrifice, for thus is and was the city's law, any Greek man who comes to this land: at least I make a beginning, butchery is work for others.'[62]

57. Aristophanes, *Assemblywomen* 595.   58. Compare the law of Miletus cited below.

59. Dentzer, 'Un nouveau relief du Pirée'; Dentzer, *Le motif du banquet couché*.

60. Pherecrates, fragment 64 from *The Oven*, quoted by Athenaeus 612a–b.

61. See Berthiaume, *Les rôles du mageiros*, especially pp. 30–31 and notes. The exceptions he finds do not come from Athens or cities under its influence. Note for example that at a temple in Sparta, so a second century A.D. antiquarian reported, 'All the ceremonies of sacrifice are performed in secret by women.' (Pausanias 3.20.3; compare his description – which reads as if he were an eye witness – of a ritual at Hermione, 2.35.4.)

62. And the others are masculine. Euripides, *Iphigenia in Tauris* 38–40. Some have thought the passage an interpolation.

Aristophanes makes the comic heroine Lysistrata play the part of a man in many ways, but when she carries out a sacrifice he avoids making her spill blood: instead she 'slaughters' a jar of Thasian wine.[63]

Old women were, however, typical market stallholders dealing in other vegetable food: cabbage,[64] grain, beans, figs, garlic; and in prepared foods such as bread and wine.[65] This goes with other evidence that women over sixty, perhaps seen as no longer at risk, were able to meet men outdoors:[66]

A woman who goes out of the house ought to be at the stage of life at which those who meet her do not ask whose wife but whose mother she is,[67]

said a litigant. One notices that one did not ask what her own name was! As in modern Britain, it was polite to name a woman by reference to her relationship to a man.

It seems quite generally to have been a man's job to do the shopping:

'Out of my jury allowance I've got to get barley and wood and fish for three – and you ask me for figs?'

'Well then, father, if the magistrate doesn't hold a court today, how are we going to buy our next meal?'[68]

Some men thought it proper to delegate to their wives the management of the household stores of food:

'So shall I have to do that?' said my wife.

'Indeed you must stay indoors,' I said ... 'and take charge of what comes in and dispense it when it is to be used, and plan ahead to ensure that the stores intended to last a year are not used up in a month ... and take care that the dried food is ready to eat when needed.'[69]

63. Aristophanes, *Lysistrata* 186–211.

64. Euripides' mother is said to have been a cabbage-seller: on this story see Ruck, 'Euripides' mother'.

65. Aristophanes, *Lysistrata* 457–8, 564, *Thesmophoriazusae* 387, *Wealth* 1120 etc. For a full list see Herfst, *Travail de la femme*.

66. See Lacey, *Family in classical Greece* (pp. 175, 312).

67. Hypereides quoted by Stobaeus, *Florilegium* 74.33.

68. Aristophanes, *Wasps* 303–6, cf. *Wasps* 789, *Frogs* 1068, Theophrastus, *Characters* 9.4 and elsewhere; shopping for medicine, Aristophanes, *Thesmophoriazusae* 504. Of course women did also go shopping, *Assemblywomen* 226; as Aristotle observed of societies which had rules on the seclusion of women, 'the poor use their wives and children as servants, having no slaves' (*Politics* 1323a5–6).

69. Xenophon, *Management* 7.36–7, cf. 10.10–11.

But this was not universal. Note the disagreement in this scrap of comedy:

'I think it's the businesslike man who ought to marry, the one who can manage a big household.'

'No, rather the carefree man who wants his leisure: then he'll have a house-keeper and can roam as he likes.'[70]

Indeed a character in comedy saw reason to say that Athenian men were beginning to watch more closely over their larders.[71]

For a dinner with guests it must have been very common practice to hire the *mageiros*[72] to sacrifice and prepare the meat and take general charge. So the cook in Menander's *Samian Woman* expects to be told

'... how many tables you're going to set, how many women there are, what time dinner will be, if I'm to bring along a *trapezopoios*, if you've enough crockery in the house, if the oven's indoors, if there's everything else ...'[73]

But a *demiourgos* 'pastrycook', literally 'artisan', was sometimes called on to prepare cakes for sacrifice and food (especially at wedding feasts), and this pastrycook was a woman: 'There are four flute-girls to be paid, and twelve *mageiroi*, and pastrycooks demanding pots of honey!'[74] In Menander's *False Heracles* some contemporary laxities were complained of: for example, 'The woman pastrycook roasts thrushes and bits of meat for dessert.'[75] The context suggests that food fashions had changed: the dessert, sometimes entrusted to a *demiourgos*, might now include bits of meat, which it used to be improper for a woman to prepare.

There is less evidence as to who in the household did the cooking day

70. Adespota 119 quoted by Stobaeus, *Florilegium* 67.25.

71. Aristophanes, *Frogs* 980–991; cf. *Thesmophoriazusae* 418–428, 556–7, 812–3; *Assemblywomen* 14–15; Theophrastus, *Characters* 10.13, 18.4, 30.11.

72. The hired cook was a stock character of 4th and 3rd century Athenian comedy: Menander, *Bad-Tempered Man* (extracts above), *The Shield, Samian Woman* etc.; Athenaeus 658e–662e and passim. See Dohm, *Mageiros*; Berthiaume, *Les rôles du mageiros*; Gomme and Sandbach, *Menander* (pp. 431–2).

73. Lines 287–292; cf. Alexis fragment 173 quoted by Athenaeus 386a. Crockery could be hired: Alexis fragment 257, ib. 164f.

74. Antiphanes fragment 225, from *Chrysis*, quoted by Athenaeus 172c.

75. Fragment 451 lines 12–13.

by day. Weaving is stated by our sources to be the woman's task much more often than cooking is; so in Pherecrates' comedy *Doulodidaskalos*, *Servant-trainer*, women weave[76] but a man serves wine.[77] On vases, too, women are often seen weaving but seldom cooking.[78]

But there is a list of women's occupations selected as being of interest to men in Praxagora's speech in Aristophanes' *Assemblywomen*.[79] Here cookery figures prominently and weaving is omitted. In the households sketched in Theophrastus's *Characters* there is one female miller-baker, *sitopoios*: '[The typical rustic] will help the baking-girl to grind enough for everybody in the house including himself.'[80] Sparkes's 'The Greek kitchen' includes photographs of several terracottas showing women making bread, but in his collection of evidence there are few signs of women cooking meat. Still, in the lower middle class divine household of Pluto and Persephone, rulers of the underworld, it was Persephone herself who cooked the dishes for Heracles' return visit (this is in Aristophanes' *Frogs*), except that a *mageiros* was somehow at hand to deal with the fish steaks:

'Darling Heracles, are you back? Come in! As soon as the Goddess knew you were coming she was baking loaves, pounding and boiling up two or three tubs of pea soup, grilling a whole ox for you, making cakes! Come in...'[81]

And on the other hand in Pherecrates' *Deserters* soldiers' wives are pictured by a speaker 'waiting there for us, boiling beans or pea soup, and baking a little fatherless smoked fish.'[82]

What men and women ate

One ought at least to consider to what extent women's typical diet differed from men's.

As to facts, we can really say no more than that women, to the extent that they fed their menfolk before themselves, missed the tastiest *opsa*, 'fish, meat or savouries to accompany bread': 'My husband ate up the

76. Fragment 46.   77. Fragment 41.

78. Guiraud, 'Vie quotidienne des femmes à Athènes' (pp. 48, 56).

79. Lines 214–240.   80. 4.7.

81. Aristophanes, *Frogs* 503–518.

82. Fragment 22 quoted by Athenaeus 119c.

anchovies yesterday evening and was coughing all night.'[83] We may quote a modern parallel relevant to several points made in this paper from J. K. Campbell's observations of the Sarakatsani shepherds of northern Greece:

Even in the extended family household husband and wife do not eat together. The men eat first, the women of the household afterwards. No portion of a cooked dish is set aside for the women, who must satisfy themselves with whatever is left by the men; this is often very little.[84]

But some Athenian wives, it seems, did go shopping and could treat themselves: 'Women buy tasty extras for themselves, just as they always did;'[85] and some might have been able to do so on the basis of a regular allowance: 'He gives her [only] three coppers for *opsa*.'[86]

Tantalising, though difficult to interpret, are the differences between what we see women eating and what we see men eating, where food-stuffs happen to be specified in the sources. A preliminary sample suggests that in the comedians' view (and perhaps in that of their male audience) women drank neat wine when they could get it (see below) and ate salad vegetables, cress,[87] chervil,[88] chick-peas[89] and bread,[90] especially barley rolls or cakes kneaded in what was thought to be an appropriate round shape;[91] and in general, the kinds of food one chewed with wine after meals[92] such as eggs and fruit.[93]

On the whole men were supposed to be the ones who ate meat,[94]

83. Aristophanes, *Assemblywomen* 56.

84. Campbell, *Honour, Family and Patronage* (p. 151).

85. Aristophanes, *Assemblywomen* 226.

86. Theophrastus, *Characters* 28.4. Cf. Thugenides fragment 2.

87. Aristophanes, *Thesmophoriazusae* 616.

88. Telecleides fragment 38 quoted by Athenaeus 56d.

89. *Assemblywomen* 45, 606, *Acharnians* 801: but this is suspect evidence. Erebinthos 'chickpea' is thought by some to have been a euphemism for 'penis' (see especially Aristophanes, *Frogs* 545; so the *Scholia on Aristophanes' Acharnians* 801,802 and the *Suda* s.v. erebinthos) so there may be a double entendre.

90. Aristophanes, *Peace* 853.

91. *Peace* 28, 853, *Acharnians* 732, 835. Cf. Telecleides fragment 38 quoted by Athenaeus 56d.

92. Pherecrates fragment 67 quoted by Athenaeus 159e.

93. Aristophanes, *Lysistrata* 856.   94. *Thesmophoriazusae* 558, *Frogs* 338–9 etc.

garlic preparations,[95] onions,[96] olives,[97] salt fish[98] and *etnos* and *phake* (which were pulse soups).[99] So in a fragment from Pherecrates' comedy *Corianno* it is probably a woman speaker who says: 'No peas for me, by Jove: I don't like them; if you eat them your mouth smells bad.'[100] A male character in Eubulus' *Campylion* liked his women companions to be dainty eaters and was sometimes disappointed:

'How nice she was at dinner, not like the other women who rolled up the leeks into balls and stuffed their cheeks with them, and shamelessly bit off pieces of meat; she just tasted a little of each dish, like a Milesian virgin.'[101]

Why a Milesian virgin? There, it seems, food rules separating the sexes were at their strictest. At Miletus in the fifth century B.C., wives 'are not to share food with their husbands nor to call their own husbands by name';[102] Milesian women, in the late fourth century, were allowed to drink only water, not wine.[103] The result of such rules was to impress men from elsewhere with the abstemiousness and delicacy of Milesian women. Milesian men, by contrast, were seen as rough when drunk,[104] argumentative and not affectionate.[105] Food and drink are

95. *Thesmophoriazusae* 494, *Lysistrata* 690, *Frogs* 549–562, *Wasps* 679, *Assemblywomen* 291, 306–8, *Acharnians* 164–6, 550, *Knights* 494. Garlic and onions were typical accompaniments to bread for soldiers on campaign, who got little meat.

96. *Acharnians* 550, 1099.   97. *Assemblywomen* 306–8, *Acharnians* 550.

98. *Wasps* 679, *Assemblywomen* 56, *Acharnians* 551, 1101.

99. *Wasps* 811–12, *Frogs* 62–3, 503–511: for further references see Ruck, 'Euripides' mother' (pp. 29–30).

100. Fragment 67, probably from the same passage as fragment 69 where the speaker is definitely a woman.

101. Fragment 42, quoted by Athenaeus 571f.

102. We may question exactly what this meant, remembering that Calypso ate at the same time as Odysseus but did not share his food (she was a goddess). To impose that particular rule in a normal small household seems hardly practical: more likely is that women must eat at a different time from men, or in a different part of the house, or from different dishes. The rule was in effect in the 5th century B.C.: Herodotus, *Histories* 1.146.3.

103. Theophrastus fragment 117 cited by Athenaeus 429b.

104. Eubulus fragment 50 cited by Athenaeus 442e.

105. Heracleides Ponticus quoted by Athenaeus 625b. Heracleides was a writer from Heracleia on the Black Sea, Herodotus came from Halicarnassus, Theophrastus from Eresus; all three lived in Athens in the fifth, fourth and third centuries B.C. Eubulus was an Athenian playwright.

such a visible and central part of life that the rules set up around it play a great part in determining the character of each society as observable by others. So it seems to have been from a knowledge of local food customs that other Greeks reached their judgment of the special characteristics of the men and women of Miletus.

Entertainers

There was one class of women at Athens who did eat and drink with men, acting sometimes as hosts[106] and sometimes as guests: these were *hetairai*, 'companions'. Information about the life of *hetairai* comes chiefly from the speech of Apollodorus *Against Neaera* and from anecdotal histories and memoirs quoted by Athenaeus 555a–610b.[107]

It is clear from *Against Neaera*[108] that if a woman went to dinner with men she was assumed by Athenians to be sexually promiscuous – or at least that the deduction might well stand up in court. This explains the innuendo in the bitter exchange in Menander's *Samian Woman* when Demeas throws out his mistress for supposed unfaithfulness:

'All right, I'm going.'

'Good. In town you'll soon know clearly what you are, Chrysis. Don't other girls of your sort simply charge ten drachmas a time and rush off to dinners and drink neat wine till they die? or if they won't or can't do enough of it, starve? You'll be better at it than any of them, you know.'[109]

Demeas is describing professional *hetairai* (he does not use the word) who made a good living while they could: ordinary prostitutes charged their customers a drachma or less.

And, indeed, if dinner for a party of men was followed by a *symposion*, or drinking party, which might go on all night, guests alternately drinking and dozing on their couches,[110] the circumstances did not encourage sexual restraint:

Chionides and Euthetion testify that they were invited by Chabrias to dinner at Cape Colias to celebrate his win in the chariot race, and saw Phrynion (here

106. Machon quoted by Athenaeus 579d–580a etc.
107. For further information see Schneider, 'Hetairai'.
108. 28, 48 etc.; also Isaeus, *On Pyrrhus's Estate* 13–14.
109. Lines 390–396.   110. Plato, *Symposium* 223b–d.

present) at dinner there with the defendant Neaera; they themselves and Phrynion and Neaera fell asleep there, and they observed men getting up during the night to go to Neaera, including some of the waiters, who were Chabrias's slaves.[111]

There are also vase paintings of symposia showing uninhibited sexual activity.[112]

Then there were male and female musicians and acrobats of various kinds, of which the most frequently mentioned is the *auletris* or 'flute-girl'. They arrived at parties, with or without their proprietor, after the eating was over: their entertainment accompanied the *symposion*, which is no doubt one reason why men saw women as typically eating the sort of foods that they themselves ate during the symposium.[113]

Women and wine

At religious festivals, especially all-women festivals, women did a great deal of drinking, if Aristophanes is to be believed.[114] This their menfolk had to pay for, as Smicrines in Menander's *Arbitration* observes of a man who had two women to support: 'Two Thesmophorias, two Scirophorias: you see he'll be ruined!'[115] But Aristophanes, in spite of all his innuendo, once let slip a hint that men did not really know what women did at their festivals,[116] and that may be nearer the truth.

Men's view of the relation of women to wine was in fact somewhat complicated. Comedy authors continually suggest that women, when they could get it, drank wine neat[117] or wanted it mixed strong, as in this three-way conversation between a hostess, a female guest and a slave:

'Undrinkable, Glyce.'
    'Did she mix it too watery for you? – What have you done? How did you mix it, you rascal?'

111. Apollodorus, *Against Neaera* 34.

112. For example, Boardman, *Athenian red figure vases* figure 46; Lissarrague, *Flot d'images* figure 9.

113. For more on flute-girls see Starr, 'Evening with the flute-girls'.

114. Aristophanes, *Thesmophoriazusae* 733–40 etc.

115. Lines 749–50.   116. *Assemblywomen* 442–3.

117. *Thesmophoriazusae* 733–40 etc., *Assemblywomen* 132–146, 1118–24.

'Two of water, mum.'
'And the wine?'
'Four.'
'Go to the [devil]! You should pour wine for frogs.'[118]

Men were quite accustomed to drink a one-quarter or two-fifths wine mixture, not too different from the one-third that the slave girl's first answer lets the audience understand; she is finally cursed for having served a two-thirds wine mixture, already stronger than the half-and-half which was the strongest that Athenian men normally drank.[119] This is a comic caricature of an all-female party. But again Demeas in Menander's *Samian Woman*,[120] in a far from humorous mood, says that *hetairai* at parties drank neat wine and might well die of it, and he would not have been the only one to predict such a fearful outcome. Did not the Spartans say that their King Cleomenes learnt to drink neat wine from associating with Scythians, and went mad?[121]

Yet when *hetairai* and flute-girls are depicted at men's parties in vase paintings, the men are often drunk and the women never. Men are depicted, for example, holding their heads,[122] vomiting,[123] or otherwise behaving boorishly[124] while women assist them, fend them off or attempt to ignore them. And Aristotle in his lost study of *Drunkenness* thought it worth discussing why women are less susceptible to drunkenness. According to the speaker Sulla in Plutarch's dialogue on the subject, Aristotle further observed that those who drink wine off in a quick draught are less affected by it, and, as Aristotle or at least Sulla added, 'We do generally see women drinking in that way.'[125]

118. Pherecrates fragment 70 quoted by Athenaeus 430e. Cf. Pherecrates fragments 69 and 143, Cratinus fragment 273.

119. Evidence collected by Athenaeus 426b–431f.   120. Line 394 (quoted above).

121. Herodotus 6.84. For the three other popular explanations of his insanity, even less likely than this one, see Pausanias 3.4.5. Compare also the epigram quoted by Athenaeus 436d from Polemon's collection.

122. E.g. Boardman, *Athenian red figure vases* figures 32.2, 238; Lissarrague, *Flot d'images* figure 9.

123. E.g. Boardman, *Athenian red figure vases* figure 254; Lissarrague, *Flot d'images* figure 9.

124. E.g. Boardman, *Athenian red figure vases* figures 25, 253.1, 253.3, 265.

125. Aristotle fragments 107–108, cited by Plutarch, *Symposium Questions* 3.3 and by Athenaeus 429c.

Gnathaena, a well-known *hetaira*, was said to have indicated her preference for a generous cupful rather cleverly:

Someone gave Gnathaena a little drop of wine in a tiny cup.
'It's sixteen years old,' he said.
'It's small for its age,' she replied.[126]

This topic – women and wine – demands rather careful deliberation. Let me suggest some possible conclusions. It would be easy to say that men did not often see women drink, except for *hetairai* and entertainers: to these, men for their own amusement provided strong wine, to whose inebriating effects the women needed for professional reasons to become resistant, though they were not immune to its long-term effects on health. From their limited observations men then drew general conclusions. This, as I say, would be an obvious line of argument and I don't say it would be altogether untrue.

But there is more to it than that. Men had a clear sense of the uncontrollable, divine nature of wine, of intoxication,[127] of ecstasy, and indeed of women. I am allowed by the painter Pausias, of the fourth century B.C., to link all these:

[In the Tholos at Epidaurus] there is also a painting of Drunkenness, again the work of Pausias; she is drinking from a glass cup; you can see the glass cup in the picture, and a woman's face through it.[128]

And Dionysus, god of wine, was worshipped not only by the male but non-human satyrs[129] but also by bands of ecstatic women, Maenads, human but uncontrollable.[130]

Men, I would suggest, found it appropriate (though dangerous too) for women to be linked with wine, and in particular neat wine. Men had learnt, moreover, that if the pleasure of inebriation is to continue through a symposium, perhaps lasting all night,[131] alcohol intake had to

126. Lynceus, *Memoirs*, quoted by Athenaeus 584b. The same joke was told of Phryne, Athenaeus 585c, probably from Aristodemus's *Humorous Memoirs*.

127. Plato, *Laws* 672.   128. Pausanias 2.27.3.

129. The choruses of Athenian satyr plays impersonated satyrs. Their revels are often depicted on vases.

130. Pentheus in the plot of Euripides' tragedy *Bacchae* is torn to pieces by Maenads.

131. Lissarrague, *Flot d'images* includes many illustrations from vase paintings of the rowdy later stages of symposia (figures 13, 16, 19, 52, 59–62, 77).

be regulated. Not having available any product as weak as beer, they diluted their wine. This mixing of wine became a central ritual of the symposium: it gave power to the host (perhaps delegated sometimes to a *symposiarchos*, 'ruler of the symposium'[132]) who might determine how strong the wine was mixed and how frequently cups were refilled.

It was observed, too, that excessive alcohol made men (but not women) sexually less capable.[133] All the more reason, I suggest, why the power of mixing wine for men must not fall into the hands of women. Throughout the whole of archaic and classical Greek literature and art no mortal woman is seen to mix wine for a mortal man.

Some conclusions

Let me try to draw conclusions, although tentatively, from the sources I have been quoting. In classical Athens women under sixty were as near as possible invisible to men (outside women's quarters they went veiled and were not spoken to);[134] men did not enter the women's quarters of another household, which were locked against intrusion. Wives and daughters of the well-to-do seldom went out at all.

Athenian men thought it improper for women to sacrifice and to roast meat and also rather disliked seeing them eating it. On the other hand it was appropriate for women to bake and sacrifice barley cakes and it was also quite the proper thing for them to be offered such cakes to eat.

If at home, men without guests ate in the women's quarters and were served by their women, but men with guests ate in the *andron*, 'men's dining room', out of sight of their own women. Women ate before or after their men.

132. The custom of choosing such a figure is first mentioned in passing, as if it were well-known, in a speech in Xenophon's *Anabasis*, written perhaps around 360 B.C., and later in the fourth century by Alexis fragment 21 quoted by Athenaeus 431c. Aristotle, *Politics* 1274b12, uses the word in summarizing Plato's utopian drinking-parties (Plato, *Laws* 671). But the only lengthy discussion of the symposiarchos is in Plutarch's *Symposium Questions* (1.4), five centuries later, and it is hard to know how seriously to take it.

133. *Physical Problems* attributed to Aristotle, quoted by Athenaeus 434f.

134. '[The traveller should never] look too closely at the veiled women ... No allusion must be made to the ladies of the family, who are regarded as under a veil.' Baedeker, *Mediterranean* pp. xxv–xxvi.

Although secluded from contact with men, women mixed with one another: they participated in religious festivals and sometimes invited women guests to meals.

A sacrifice was the accompaniment to or the occasion of important meals, for whole families and for hosts with guests. For celebration, people often held sacrifices and dinner parties away from home, at religious shrines. Sacrifices might be initiated by women,[135] but the act must be performed by the *mageiros*, 'sacrificer-cook'. The entire household might take part in the meal including male and female slaves, though the sexes probably ate in separate rooms or formed separate groups. The hired *mageiros* brought some food and equipment with him, while the family brought the rest. I suspect many such parties took place out of doors.

Hetairai and entertainers were in a special position, mixing freely with men and, in particular, dining and drinking with them. It is worth noting how similar to the ancient *hetaira* is the *geisha* of modern Japan. She also is uniquely privileged to dine with men and to make witty conversation: her work also is linked with sexual promiscuity though she is not a prostitute. Her relative social freedom in itself makes her attractive to men:[136] on this last point compare the remark from a play by Philetaerus:

'No wonder temples to *Hetaira* are everywhere, and there isn't one to Wife in all of Greece.'[137]

A note on ancient sources

Most ancient Greek texts are available in English translation, but most translations suffer from literary pretensions; they tend to be insufficiently reliable in detail for the needs of the social historian. Translations in the *Loeb classical library* series (published by Harvard University Press) are, by contrast, often absolutely free of literary quality.

The only edition of ancient comedy fragments that is accessible to

135. On women's part in the sacrifice see Gomme and Sandbach, *Menander* (pp. 200–202).

136. For information on geisha see Dalby 1983.

137. Fragment 5, quoted by Athenaeus 559a.

the non-specialist is: *The fragments of Attic comedy* edited and translated by J. M. Edmonds, 4 vols (Leiden: Brill, 1957–61). Unfortunately it is far from reliable. The fragment numbering given here is that of the older standard Greek edition, *Comicorum Atticorum fragmenta* edited by T. Kock, 3 vols (Leipzig, 1880–88), which is still widely used: Edmonds' numbering normally agrees with it. Fragmentary plays cited in this paper are by Alexis, Antiphanes, Cratinus, Diphilus, Pherecrates, Telecleides, Thugenides, and from the collection of unattributed fragments ('Adespota').

Notes on some other authors cited here:

APOLLODORUS, *Against Neaera*. This courtroom speech is included in editions of the works of Demosthenes, though it was not written by him.

ATHENAEUS. See Athenaeus, *The Deipnosophists*, edited and translated by C. B. Gulick, 7 vols, Loeb classical library (Cambridge, Mass.: Harvard University Press, 1927–41).

MENANDER's plays are cited here by reference to two editions. *Menandri reliquiae selectae* edited by F. H. Sandbach (Oxford: Clarendon Press, 1972) is most convenient for the papyri. *Menandri quae supersunt*, vol. 2 edited by A. Koerte and revised by A. Thierfelder (Leipzig: Teubner, 1959) is best for fragments surviving in quotations by ancient authors. These editions are in Greek only, but several translations include at least the main fragments. One commentary is particularly valuable: A. W. Gomme and F. W. Sandbach, *Menander: a commentary* (Oxford: Clarendon Press, 1973).

Bibliography

Baedeker, K., *The Mediterranean* (Leipzig: Baedeker, 1911)

Becker, W. A., *Charikles*, new edition by H. Göll (Berlin, 1877–8)

Bergquist, B., 'Sympotic space: a functional aspect of Greek dining–rooms' in *Sympotica: a symposium on the symposion*, edited by Oswyn Murray (London: Oxford University Press, 1990), 37–65

Berthiaume, G., *Les rôles du mageiros: étude sur la boucherie, la cuisine et le sacrifice dans la Grece ancienne* (Leiden: Brill, 1982)

Blümner, H., *Lehrbuch der griechischen Privatalterthümer*, K. F. Hermann's Lehrbuch der griechischen Antiquitäten, 4 (Freiburg im Breisgau, 1882)

Boardman, J., *Athenian red figure vases: the archaic period* (London: Thames and Hudson, 1975)

Börker, C., *Festbankett und griechische Architektur*, Xenia, 4 (Constance, 1983)

Campbell, J. K., *Honour, family and patronage* (Oxford: Clarendon Press, 1964)

Dalby, A., 'Men, women and food in early Athens' in *Ikinci Milleretlerasi Yemek Kongresi = Second International Food Congress, Turkey, 3–10 September 1988*, edited by Feyzi Halici (Konya, 1988), 80–96

Dalby, L. C., *Geisha* (Berkeley: University of California Press, 1983)

Dentzer, J.-M., 'Un nouveau relief du Pirée et le type du banquet attique au Ve siècle avant J.-C.', *Bulletin de correspondance hellénique*, 94 (1970), 67–90

Dentzer, J.-M., *Le motif du banquet couché dans le Proche-Orient et le monde grec* (Rome: Ecole Française de Rome, 1982)

Dohm, H., *Mageiros* (Munich: Beck, 1964)

Gomme, A. W., and F. W. Sandbach, *Menander: a commentary* (Oxford: Clarendon Press, 1973)

Gould, J. P., 'Law, custom and myth: aspects of the social position of women in classical Athens', *Journal of Hellenic studies*, 100 (1980), 38–59

Guiraud, H., 'La vie quotidienne des femmes à Athènes: à propos de vases attiques du Ve siècle', *Pallas*, 32 (1985), 41–57

Herfst, P., *Le travail de la femme dans la Grèce ancienne* (Utrecht, 1922)

Lacey, W. K., *The family in classical Greece* (London: Thames and Hudson, 1968)

Lissarrague, F., *Un flot d'images: une esthétique du banquet grec* (Paris: Biro, 1987)

Robinson, D. M. and J. W. Graham, *Excavations at Olynthus 8: the Hellenic house* (Baltimore: Johns Hopkins University Press, 1938)

Ruck, C., 'Euripides' mother', *Arion*, N. S. 2, No. 1 (1975), 13–58

Schneider, K., 'Hetairai' (1913), in *Paulys Real-Enzyklopädie der classischen Altertumswissenschaft*, new edition by G. Wissowa and others (Stuttgart, 1893–1972)

Sparkes, B. A., 'The Greek kitchen', *Journal of Hellenic studies*, 82 (1962), 121–137

Starr, C. G., 'An evening with the flute-girls', *Parola del passato*, 33 (1978), 401–410

Vickers, M., 'Artful crafts', *Journal of Hellenic studies*, 105 (1985), 108–128

Walker, S., 'Women and housing in classical Greece', in *Images of women in antiquity* edited by A. Cameron and A. Kuhrt (London: Duckworth, 1983), 81–91

Social status and Fish
in Greece and Rome

JOHN WILKINS

THIS paper considers the relationship between the consumption of fish and the social status of the consumer in ancient thought. There is much that could be said on human views of the fish themselves. They were viewed in various ways in the ancient world, but were broadly categorized either as rapacious creatures grouped with animals that are hunted and wild birds – that is, creatures that are inimical to man – or were seen in human terms. So Pliny speaks of the *societas* of fish (9.186), or Oppian of marriage among sargues (4.374ff) or of justice among grey mullet (2.642f).[1] The parrot-wrasse is considered a lascivious fish.[2] In their names for some species, humans assimilate fish to the world they understand: so the Romans called sea-bass *lupus*, the wolf, and in Greek we find the pig, the crowfish, the blackbird and thrush, all as names of fish. Pliny calls attention to the phenomenon (9.2–3), which occurs in English too, with the parrotfish for example. It is, however, the bearing of fish on human social structures that is the subject of this paper.

Fish must first be placed in the general order of things. Living in an element frightening to men, they are often considered man's natural enemies: we eat them whenever we can catch them, and they eat us whenever we fall into the sea.[3] This idea is developed in various ways in

1. On the gentle and amorous grey mullet see also Davidson and Knox p. 78.

2. Greek *skaros*. On the amorous wrasse see Oppian 4.40–126, Thompson pp. 239–40, who also collects ancient evidence on the parrot-wrasse as the only fish to 'chew the cud'.

3. So for example Antiphanes frr. 69.10–14; Kassel-Austin and 127.5–6; and Kassel-Austin; Archestratus fr. 23.13–20 Brandt (on the 'dogfish', a species of shark): 'There are not many mortals who know of this divine food, nor do they desire to eat it, those that is who have the soul of a storm petrel or a locust, and are scared rigid because the creature is a man-eater. But every fish likes human flesh, whenever it can get it. So it is only right that all those who babble on in this way go over to vegetables and join Diodorus the philosopher and with him follow Pythagoras in a strict and severe fashion.'

comic passages, one recurrent suggestion being that large fish are so expensive that they destroy a man's wealth if he develops a taste for them.

Fish are part of the wild, which is distinct from the tame and farmed. The wild is divided into fish, birds and animals for hunting.[4] The division between the farmed and the wild is of great importance for our purposes; particularly so in terms of Greek culture, though the Roman system was similar. Farmed animals were sacrificed; wild animals were not. (There are exceptions but these are few.[5] Very broadly, the sacrifice expressed two ideas, the first being the placing of humans in the universe. In killing an animal in order to honour a god, they were defining their own place in the order of things midway between the bestial and the divine. And in sharing in the guilt of the animal's death and feeding from the equal distribution of the mortal parts of the animal (the meat, as opposed to the marrow and most of the vital organs which were burnt with incense for the gods), they were expressing their sense of community and equality within the civilised world. The animal itself was part of the farmed world, was sprinkled with grains from cultivated cereal crops in a pre-sacrificial ritual, and was sacrificed as a quasi-member of the community or kinship group.[6]

If fish were outside this order and were part of the raw nature with which mankind was always struggling, then there was no need for fish sacrifice, no need for equal distribution of flesh. In other words, fish were part of the secular world. One important consequence of this was that fish were an object of great interest to cooks in a way that meat was not. In the writings of the great cook Archestratus (fourth century B.C.) meat is of little account, and the same holds for the fifteen books of Athenaeus (early third century A.D.), our principal authority on food in

4. This division is articulated for example in Plato, *Sophist* 119e ff.

5. Athenaeus (297c–298b) cites three religious uses of fish: an eel sacrifice for eels of exceptional size in Boeotia, the offering to Poseidon of the first tuna in the Attic fishing village of Halae, and the sacrificial offering of salt fish in a festival celebrating a foundation myth in Phaselis, a town in Asia Minor. These exceptions (and there are some others) may be categorized respectively as the offering of something exceptional and therefore not part of normal human experience to a god or king (compare p.X), as an equivalent of a farmer's first-fruit offering, and as the perpetuation of a city's foundation myth (such myths often incorporate distinctive or bizarre features).

6. For this structural interpretation of sacrifice see Detienne and Vernant pp. 1–86.

antiquity. Meat is for equal distribution and definitions of identity (belonging and not belonging to the group, for example); fish is for eating, whether for gourmet or peasant eating being determined principally by price. This holds good for mainland Greece and the Greek Mediterranean, including southern Italy.

There is a great variety of fish in the Mediterranean; it is a ready source of protein and an important part of the economy and diet of communities by the sea. It is also pleasing to the palate. People want to eat it. Large fish tend to be more expensive than small fish. Richer people therefore are more likely to eat the larger fish. Price is a clear determinant, and is affected by weather, season and the migration patterns of the fish. Freshness will command a premium. Fish not destined for fresh consumption could be smoked or salted. This was a widespread practice which I discuss later. Fish will tend to be more expensive inland and is often unavailable except in the form of the fermented fish sauce, known in Greek as *garos* (Latin *garum*).

In ancient perceptions it is possible to draw a distinction between the diets of Greeks and Romans. The diet of the Greeks, it appears, depended heavily on fish; in the case of the Romans, meat, especially pork was more important. This distinction may be illustrated in two ways. As early as the fifth century B.C. a Greek historian gave the etymology of the name 'Italy' as derivative of Latin *vitulus*, calf: Italy was in Greek perception the Texas of the Mediterranean. Secondly, moralizing authors, both Green and Roman, praised the old-fashioned diet: for the Greeks, barley cake and gathered green leaves were the primitive diet; in the case of the Romans a form of preserved pork was added to the idealized frugal dish. The distinction is important for our purposes – which concern the impact of ideas about fish on human society – but is a distortion of what actually happened in the ancient world. People ate fish when it was available, and it was as available in Italian as in Greek waters. Romans may have considered themselves inland people, but other Italians living by the sea ate much fish. We are especially well-informed about the southern Italians in this respect.[7] River and lake fish were also eaten. Bass in the Tiber is praised by Pliny (9.169), for example. In general, though, river fish (with the exception of those of the

7. We may add that in many archaeological sites in the Roman Empire, the Roman presence is marked by the heavy consumption of shellfish, oysters in particular.

Nile) were then, as now, considered inferior to sea fish. (See Athenaeus 120f (quoting Diphilus of Siphnos), 306e (quoting Dorion *On Fishes*), 355f.)

We may be fairly certain that the majority of the populations of ancient Greece and Italy ate very little meat or fish, and that they subsisted on a diet of cereal porridges (*maza* in Greece, based on barley; *puls* in Rome, based on spelt and other cereals, wheats and millets) and pulses made palatable by strong-tasting vegetables – garlic, onion, wild herbs – and cheese, with meat only on some festival days. Small fish – sardines, anchovies, sprats – were available in fishing communities. Richer people could afford to be more ambitious at fish markets; richer peasants made their own hams and bacon. Richer families could afford to choose wheat rather than barley, bread rather than porridge, meat and fish rather than vegetables. The choice marked a basic social distinction.

The fish element in the diet depended upon location. A comic poet makes the point:

A: This dinner is a reception for a stranger.

CHEF: Who? Where's he from? This makes a big difference to a chef. Those little strangers from the islands, brought up on freshly-caught little fish of every species, are not tempted by salt fish and only take to it as an afterthought. They would rather have something stuffed with meat or a dish of rich Lydian meat sauces. Arcadians on the other hand are remote from the sea and are tempted by little oysters, while your plutocratic Ionian goes for a main dish of rich meat sauces, sexy food[8] in fact.

Menander, *Trophonius* fr. 462.

From the perspectives of cooking and eating fish, size was only one criterion. Also to be considered were flavour and texture, availability, and the preferred parts of the fish. The head was often singled out as a delicacy,[9] as in Spain and the Far East, though I have not found clear

8. Mainland Greeks associated the luxurious lifestyle of the Persian-dominated Greek cities on the west coast of Asia Minor (Ionia) with rich eating (meat-based sauces in particular) and immorality. Luxurious eating and sex were closely associated in Greek thought.

9. For the head as a delicacy see for example Athenaeus 293f (conger eel, quoting Archestratus), 295c–f ('grey fish' (*glaukos*) quoting Archestratus and others), 326b (a species of tuna (*aulopias*), quoting Archestratus).

evidence of different people taking different cuts, for example of an eel, as has been reported to me of Hong Kong,[10] where greatest prestige goes to the person who buys the head and thereby sets the date for the killing of the fish. In the case of the tuna, some of the lower belly section was especially prized and presumably was bought at a premium. So, too, in the salting industry, *horaia* was tuna caught and salted at its best, hence especially prized.

So, if we are looking at the social categories of people who have access to fish, price is determined by all these things. Expense itself may also be important. A person who wishes to pay a large sum (more on this below) is not necessarily interested in the succulence or other excellence of the fish.

What of the fishmongers? The status of the buyer is not the same as that of the seller. There are details of this in Athenaeus (224c-228c) taken, as is much of his evidence, from comedy. The fishmongers overcharge, they are more difficult to get a straight answer from than the politicians, they glare at their customers, they charge in foreign currencies, they illegally water their stock to make it look fresh, and much more. They are a stock bad element of Athenian life, and this is confirmed by non-comic sources, Plato (*Charmides* 163b) for example, or Plutarch (*Table-Talk* 631d). Fish is a very desirable product in Athens, and this desire is manipulated for all it is worth by these allegedly rascally vendors. It is a feature of Athenian invective that people who interfere in any way with a citizen's supposedly legitimate desire are dishonest and of low status. Dealers in grain and politicians also fall into this category.

We may also consider fishermen. In contrast to their valuable and desirable catch, fishermen were of low status in antiquity. This is brought out in the numerous stories expressing the social distance between fishermen and kings. An early example of this is to be found in Herodotus 3.41-3, the story of Polycrates (tyrant of Samos, sixth century B.C.) and the fisherman. This is part of the pattern of thought which held that fortune smiled on a monarch and when something extraordinary was found, it was to be offered to the monarch. The fisherman says to Polycrates: 'O king, I caught this fish and did not

10. By Shaun Hill.

195

think it right to take it to market, even though I am a man who lives by the work of my hands. It seemed to me to be a fish worthy of you and your authority. So I have brought it to you as a gift.'[11] Similar stories, with different endings, were told of the emperors Tiberius and Domitian; comparable was the presentation to Nero of one of the last stalks of silphium, a herb often used to flavour fish and, in an earlier period, part of a flourishing industry in Cyrene in North Africa.

There were different communities living by the sea. Although the Piraeus was famous for its *aphuai*, or small fish of various species (including sprats and anchovies), Aristotle (*Politics* 1291b22–24) singles out Tarentum and Byzantium as ports with an important fishing population. Piraeus is seen as a military base, Aegina as a trading base, Tenedos as a ferry base. Fishermen clearly operated out of all these harbours, but, as far as Aristotle's neat categories were concerned, were politically significant in those two, Tarentum and Byzantium.

To summarize so far: meat defines the eater as a mortal. Fish defines the quality of the palate and purse. Both are highly desirable as foods, meat for its rarity, fish for its strong flavours, variety and a ready supply.

What was the availability of fish in the Greek world, though? A somewhat disputatious work appeared in 1985, *A Fisherman's Tale*, by Tom Gallant. This attacks the belief among a number of ancient historians that an extensive fishing industry at Byzantium and in the Black Sea supplied Greece with so much salted fish (largely tuna) that this was a staple of the Greek diet. He makes much of the variations in quantity and location of fish shoals, and of the limited supplies of salt; he reconsiders the nutritional and calorific values of fish. He tries to show that notions of the fish 'industry' and of fish as a 'dietary staple' are exaggerated. The point is an important one, but Gallant goes much too far. The ancient evidence refers often to Black Sea salted fish, in addition to products from Cadiz, Egypt, Sicily and Sardinia.[12] It was transported to Greece in comparatively large quantities, but was still more expensive than small fish caught locally. So on a price scale starting from the cheapest we would expect to find local small fry and small fish, *garum*, imported salt fish, larger fresh fish. And above all this, quality com-

11. This phenomenon has been discussed by Braund.

12. See Pollux *Onomasticon* 6.48, edited by E. Bethe (1931), second edition (Stuttgart, 1967).

manded a high price. Best salted fish was very expensive; the inferior or damaged product was cheaper.[13] Fish that was fresh came at a premium; that is no surprise. Nor would we wish to push this idea of an industry feeding Greece very far. The people eating imported salt fish were those living near the sea, and especially those with important port and trading facilities, such as Athens.

Romans were rather different. In the early period they did not see themselves as fish-eating people at all. Fish, when it came, came from elsewhere and was therefore not Roman. But when the desire for fish (and fowl) did come, assuming that it really was new, it was strong (Athenaeus 274d–e) and clearly coincided with the expansion of Roman power. Foreign birds and fish from all quarters of the world were eaten to express – consciously or unconsciously – Roman domination over the human and natural world.[14]

Another place where fish seems insignificant is in the literary artefact known to us as the works of Homer. In Homer no one eats fish. This is discussed by Athenaeus at some length (8f–19a). The epic heroes Achilles, Ajax and Agamemnon feast on endless oxen and some smaller animals, roasted, offered in sacrifice and eaten in equal portions. The very name for the feast, *dais*, expresses this equal division. The heroes are given meat because, in the later society that recited the poems, they are seen as semi-divine, related to gods; greater and braver and stronger than were contemporary men. So they ate this expensive and, says Athenaeus, tedious diet. They were close to the gods, but a mortal version of them, and so expressed this in their sacrificing and feasting. They were not given the natural protein of Greece – fish – even though they were fighting beside the rich fishing grounds of the Hellespont, as Homer himself acknowledges in some epic epithets, because they were special and extraordinary. In status they were second only to gods.

In the Greek world everyday eating, as opposed to banqueting was composed of *sitos* and *opson*, the cereal base and the accompanying strong flavour, which was frequently provided by proteins as men-

13. Details may be found at Athenaeus 116a–121e.

14. The most striking examples of this display of domination are the use of exotic birds – flamingos, parrots, ostriches – in Roman cookery and the importing of granite from Mons Claudianus, a remote site in the Eastern desert of Egypt, with which to adorn public buildings in Rome.

tioned above. *Opson* often simply meant fish. Consider Plutarch *Table-Talk* 667f8a:

First let us consider word usage There are many delicacies (*opsa*), but fish has won the title of delicacy more or less because it is far the superior in quality. And when we talk of 'eaters of delicacies' (*opsophagoi*) and 'lovers of delicacies' (*philopsoi*) we do not mean those who enjoy their beef like Heracles who 'ate green figs to follow his meat', nor fig-lovers like Plato, nor grape lovers like Arcesilaus, but those who show up when the selling of fish commences at the sound of the bell.

Athenaeus (276e–277a) has a similar passage: 'of all the so-called side dishes which are delicacies (*opsa*), fish has carried the title because of its special eating quality and people's mania for it I am well aware that *opson* properly refers to everything that is prepared for eating with heat, either from *hepson* (something boiling), or from *optesthai* (to be roasted).'

In apparent contradiction of this, in Plato's *Republic* (372b–373a) *opsa* are set out that do not include fish and do not require cooking:

SOCRATES: They will eat barley cakes and wheat loaves 'and wine.' Glaucon interrupted: 'You seem to be forcing these people to feast without *opson*..' Socrates: 'I forgot that. They will have salt and olives and cheese and hyacinth bulbs and green salads And for second courses we will set out for them figs and chickpeas and broad beans and myrtleberries and beechnuts ' Glaucon complains that this is food fit for pigs and that the usual *opsa* are needed. Socrates' reply is: 'I see. We seem to be considering how to set up not so much a city as a city based on luxury If we consider this we will quickly see how justice and injustice come into being in a city. In this style of life there will be dining couches in addition and tables and all the other furniture and utensils and indeed *opsa* and perfume and incense and party girls and cakes and all of that.'

Opsa then could be any strong flavour, but the preference was for flavours based on fish. There is much evidence for this clear preference of fish over radishes or capers[15] or other vegetables. We may conclude that wherever possible, *opsa* were based on fish, if only on *garum* sauce. Luxury versions of *garum* were available in the Roman period, one – attributed to Apicius – based on mullet livers, but in general *garum*,

15. See for example Amphis fr. 26 Kassel-Austin: 'Whoever goes to the market for flavourings and wishes to buy radishes when real fish are available is mad'; also Plutarch, *Table-talk* 668a, quoted above.

fermented and salted, was the best-preserved, most easily transported, and most concentrated essence of fish. It could be used by peasants as a strong flavour on breads and porridges, or at the other extreme by gourmets as the basis of a fish or meat stock.

Whenever a larger fish is at issue, pretention and political ambition are in close attendance. Consider Aristophanes, *Wasps* 488–499:

It's all tyranny and conspiracy with you these days, accusations on any matter, great or small. These are words I haven't heard for fifty years, and now they're worth much more than salted fish, and so the terms bob up and down in the market. If someone buys sea-perch and doesn't want sprats, the man nearby selling sprats immediately says 'this man is buying fish to set up a tyranny'. And if he asks for a horn onion to season his anchovies, the woman selling vegetables squints at him with one eye and says: 'Tell me. You want this horn onion. Is it for setting up a tyranny? Or do you think Athens should pay you a tribute of seasonings?'

Or take Plutarch, *Table-Talk* 668a: Demosthenes makes abusive allegations of *opson*-eating and depravity against Philokrates, buying prostitutes and fish with gold he had received for treason. These passages, starting with that from Plato, make a clear connection between luxurious living, political ambition, sexual depravity and fish. In these cases the fish are generally large fish.

When political status is not at issue, then enjoyment of fish which money can buy is important. Athens was considered eccentric. The Athenians were enthusiastic fish eaters, but not in great quantities or of great size. Consider the following comic passage: 'There is something unpleasant about eating in Athens. The cook sets before you a large tray with five little dishes on it, one with garlic, one with two sea urchins, one with bread in sweet wine, one with ten cockles, one with a slice of sturgeon' (Lynceus, *Centaur* fr. 1). This may show a liking for fish, akin to that seen in the gourmet Archestratus, but there is also a simplicity of presentation. This is upmarket eating, of a high social status but unpretentious and with no trace of gluttony. On the contrary.

This brings us to Archestratus, an important figure and Europe's earliest surviving food writer. And he comes from Sicily, which was the France of the Greek world; that is, the region with the best products, a sufficient level of wealth, a certain interest in luxury (condemned by Plato in his seventh epistle: compare the proverbial luxury of Sybaris and Croton), and chefs who knew how to be inventive with food. It is this area that influenced both Athens and the Italian mainland. There is a similarity between the claims to simple Athenian eating above, and comments about the simplicity of the Roman diet. The eating that Archestratus prescribes is practical, based on taste, availability, texture (all, surprisingly perhaps to us, expressed in the literary style of the mock epic). How is social status evident here? Ability to pay is evident, together with the desire to have all the corners of the Mediterranean fished. This is elegant, gourmet enjoyment of social status, based on quality rather than display. It appears to be without political connotation as far as we can tell. As far as I have seen, this is the highest quality produce and cooking known in the ancient world. It is rather different from the complex flavours of Apicius.

Having 'noticed' the Greek cities in southern Italy, Rome began both to control them politically and to be enchanted with them culturally. So when moralists speak of an unacceptable wave of oriental Greeks sweeping into Rome, they are speaking in fact of their southern neighbours in cities established by Greeks in the eighth and subsequent centuries.

Certain Romans embraced the new influences with enthusiasm, expressing high social status by importing foreign foods, including fish. This had several interesting consequences. Firstly, inflation in the prices of luxury goods took place to the extent that the cost and, in the case of fish, the size of the beast became an end in itself. Secondly, by way of reaction in some quarters, the rejection of this path led to the high status assertion of other values; in particular, tradition, religion and the home-grown. A notable example is Cato the censor (234–139 B.C.) as reported by Plutarch (*Table-Talk* 668b–c) and Athenaeus (274f–275a): 'Certain people had imported into Rome foreign luxuries: they had bought a jar of salt fish from the Black Sea for 300 drachmae and beautiful boys for more than the cost of land' (note fish and sex in association as in the case of Philocrates above). These high prices recur: by Pliny (9.67) we are told of 'a challenge to all spendthrifts by giving 8,000 sesterces for a mullet' and a particularly large mullet would be an added advantage (Pliny speaks of a Red Sea mullet weighing 80lb in the same chapter). Seneca (*Epistles* 95.42) reports a four and a half pound mullet being sold for 5,000 sesterces. High social status here is conveyed by price and size but, contrary to what we find in Archestratus, not by taste. That is of no interest with these giant fish, as Alan Davidson remarks in this context.[16] Fish again represents something beyond eating and taste. What is important for our purposes is that some acquire status in this way, while others deny it.

The assertion of tradition may be seen in later mythologies of the early history of Rome. consider Poseidonius, as preserved by Athenaeus (274b–c):

What we say in prayers or do in the sacred offices is plain and frugal; again, we do not overstep nature either in our dress or in the care of our bodies or in the offering of first-fruits; and as we wear clothes and shoes which are cheap, on our heads we put hats made of rough sheepskins; the utensils which we bring are of earthenware or bronze, and in them are the simplest foods and drinks in the world, because we think it absurd that while we bring to the gods offerings ordained by ancestral custom, we should indulge ourselves in exotic luxuries.

Similar sentiments are expressed by Ovid (*Fasti* 6. 169–84).

The Romans knew of course that certain fish were better in certain places, as Archestratus had set out (Pliny says as much at 9.168). But if the fish came from abroad they were associated with the unacceptable status group who had somehow sold out on true Romanness, even though eating foreign food was a demonstration of Roman power and domination. There are many variations on this theme. Even Pliny, with his scientific credentials as something of a natural historian, complains of the introduction of the 'foreign' parrot-wrasse into Italian waters.

The poor true Roman of the satirist Juvenal is a victim of class distinctions (5.99ff): 'Before Virro is set an enormous moray-eel which came from Sicily For you an eel, relative of the water snake, or a Tiber bass bloated with sewage.' Difference in status is expressed by fish, irrespective of questions about the taste or quality of the fish. The origin of the fish expresses status; the qualities of the fish for eating are buried beneath other significances. For Pliny, Tiber bass is good (see above); for Archestratus, bass and eels (albeit sea varieties) are good (Athenaeus 298e–f, 311a–b); for Juvenal, whose priorities are elsewhere, they are very bad. Horace (*Satires* 2.2.33–8) points out similar absurdities: 'You idiot! You praise a three-pound mullet, which you are

16. Davidson pp. 92–3.

forced to cut up into smaller portions Why then do you hate a long bass? It is, of course, because nature made the bass large and mullet light in weight. Only a stomach that is rarely hungry scorns things that are common.'

There were no fish at all in early Rome according to Ovid in the *Fasti* passage mentioned above: 'At that time fish swam round with no traps set for them by humans, and oysters were safe in their shells.' The moralist is trying to impose his strictures on the historically more likely truth that the early inhabitants of Rome ate whatever came most cheaply and conveniently to hand. It is, though, Ovid's desire for proof that is important. As social historians we are quite happy to accept that people living away from the sea eat a little fish. This even happened in Sparta (whether river or sea fish is not known) where the standard issue of barley with an *opson* of a little pork in black gruel was supplemented with a treat from the wild, a hare, a dove, or fish. If fish was found in the gastronomic desert of Sparta, it was found everywhere.

In Roman authors, much is made of enormous fish, the most notable being the fish for the emperor in Juvenal's fourth *Satire*. It is striking, then, that in the *Satyricon* of Petronius, which is sometimes considered a benchmark of Roman gastronomy, Trimalchio knows nothing of fish: almost every course of his banquet is based on pork. He is not even aware of the argument. This in fact, like his colloquial Latin and his artistic judgements, is a sign of his status. His is not luxury food, any more than his friends are of high status. This is ignorant aping of sophisticated snobbery. Endless pork is for poorer people, like these ex-slaves, after they have struck it rich. Aristocrats mark their exclusivity either by eating rare foreign fish or birds, or by farming their own exotic produce in fish ponds and aviaries.

What has all this done to fish? It has taken them out of the sea and put them in artificial lakes (Varro, *De agri cultura* 3.17; Pliny 9.168–72). We began with the categories of the wild being hunting, fowling and fishing. The first of these has great prestige for aristocrats, the second less, the latter little at all. But these latter two are completely changed by the Romans for whom fish live in ponds and birds in aviaries. The wild has been tamed and farmed both for the bourgeois masses (Varro) and the very rich. Why have they done this? Because of the status that fish has in diet, either for marketing or prestige. Does it affect the taste and quality of the fish? We are not told, because that is irrelevant to the function that fish has in human society.

Bibliography

Braund, D.C., 'Treasure-trove and Nero', in *Greece and Rome*, 30 (1983)

Davidson, Alan, *Mediterranean Seafood* (Harmondsworth: Penguin, 1981)

Davidson, Alan, and Charlotte Know, *Seafood* (London: Mitchell Beazley, 1989)

Detienne, M. and J-P. Vernant, *The Cuisine of Sacrifice among the Greeks* (Chicago: University of Chicago Press, 1989)

Gallant, T., *A Fisherman's Tale* (Gent: Miscellanea Graeca, 1985)

Gulick, C. B., ed., *Athenaeus* (Cambridge, Massachusetts and London: Harvard University Press and Heinemann, 1927–41)

Oppian, *Halieutica*, ed. by A.W. Mair (Cambridge, Massachusetts and London: Harvard University Press and Heinemann, 1928)

Pliny, *Natural History*, ed. by H. Rackham et al (Cambridge, Massachusetts and London: Harvard University Press and Heinemann, 1938–62)

Plutarch, 'Table-Talk', in *Moralia*, ed. by F.C. Babbit et al (Cambridge, Massachusetts and London: Harvard University Press and Heinemann, 1927–69)

Thompson D'Arcy, W, *A Glossary of Greek Fishes*, (London: Oxford University Press, 1947)

The Beast at the Feast
Food in Roman verse satire

NICOLA HUDSON

187 B.C., Asia, the Roman army had just pulled off a magnificent victory. Little did the triumphant troops realise that the spoils of war contained the germs of a virulent and chronic disease:

These soldiers were responsible for the first importation of…what was at home recognised as sumptuous furniture – pedestal tables and sideboards. Banquets began to be laid on with great elaboration and at greater expense. It was then that the cook, who had to the ancient Romans been the least valuable of slaves, and had been priced accordingly, began to be highly valued, and what had been a mere service began to be an art.[1]

That was the opinion at least of the Roman historian Livy who was writing with the benefit of a sizeable chunk of hindsight (about a century and a half of it).[2] From him we learn a couple of things about Roman attitudes to food. First, that conspicuous consumption, especially as it related to food and its accoutrements, could be treated as a moral issue; second, that as far as cookery went, there existed a nostalgia for the simple ways of the past. The two elements resonate with his audience in combination. In this case he enlists a version of the past to provide explanation for – and therefore protection against – present 'interesting' times: in late first century B.C. Rome, an era of diversification, expansion and importation.

At about the same time, the late 30s B.C., the poet Horace was constructing his verse satires.[3] These were poems of about two to three

1. Livy, *History of Rome* 39.6.3–9. For similar sentiments see also Sallust *Catiline* 13.3.

2. Livy –Titus Livius, 59B.C.–A.D.17. Author of a History 'from the foundation of Rome'. Only 35 out of 142 books survive.

3. Horace – Quintus Horatius Flaccus, 65–8B.C. He also wrote verse *Epistles*, an *Art of Poetry*, *Odes* and *Epodes*.

hundred lines dealing entertainingly with the moral issues of everyday life. Sex, money, social climbing, and literature came under the scrutiny of the keen-eyed satirist. But it might be said that he was disproportionately interested in the ethics of eating. Out of a total output of eighteen satires written by Horace, four dwelt exclusively on the subject of food. A century or so later, his most famous antecedent in the genre, Juvenal, devoted a quarter of his sixteen satires to the subject.[4] The food themes they addressed were restricted. They concentrated on those areas in which the 'show-off' role of food in society could be exposed: the *cena* (dinner party), the intellectualisation of food (gastronomy), and the contrast of town food with city food. On the surface they shared Livy's view of past and present. But they elaborated and embellished the contrast, suggesting that in contemporary Rome certain people took food too seriously and, worse still, used their knowledge about so-called elegant dining to get ahead.

Roman verse satire was a home-grown literary genre with a strong sense of its humble relationship to other sorts of literature.[5] The satirist's idea was to criticise society's foibles by the dual process of denunciation, presenting his own ideas as common sense. He usually, however, ended up assuming an extreme position. The satirist could be ironic, vicious, angry, self-mocking, two-faced and sardonic. He used everyday language, juxtaposed with epic or other elevated styles, and he worked within a tight framework to achieve his aim: broadly speaking, a complete denunciation of a chosen type of human failing. It helped the satirist enormously if he could delineate or draw upon a clear set of norms from which misguided behaviour is seen to deviate. It also helped that he painstakingly created victims for his attack; stereotypes who were the product of some acute observation, but were not traceable to named individuals. In the case of each food satire, for example,

4. Juvenal – Decimus Junius Juvenalis, *c*.60–*c*.A.D.130. Few details of his life survive. His literary output comprises sixteen satires, the last of these unfinished.

5. The conversational style and apparently mundane subject matter of Roman verse satire might, for example, be contrasted with the big themes and lofty language of epic poetry. As Horace says in his Satire 2.1.13–15, 'not everyone, after all, can portray/ lines of battle bristling with lances, Gauls dying/ with their spears splintered, or the wounded Parthian slipping from his steed'. We should not imagine from this that the satirist necessarily considers epic poetry and its writers to be superior.

the satirist presents for our inspection the 'perfect' food criminal committing the 'perfect' food crime.[6]

Roman poets were extremely talkative about the subject of food in Rome, as eaten and discussed by a well-connected, urban elite. Nonetheless, since Roman verse satire dealt with the paradigm, with stereotypes and well-worn images, there is no good reason to look for verifiable fact, precise social observation, or accuracy of culinary detail in the satirists' treatment of food. Enormous care has to be taken in trying to discern the image of food as reflected in the distorting mirror of satire.

The fat of the land

Horace's satirist (it is important to dissociate the man from the voice he adopts in his poems) lets the reader know that he feels immense self-satisfaction at having found favour with the intellectual arm of the Augustan elite, through the good offices of his patron Maecenas, a supremely wealthy man with impeccable contacts and dubious artistic tendencies.[7] From this elevated and protected position the satirist proclaims the ancient rustic values of self-sufficiency, piety and bravery. Forget the inherent irony. This is the same innate moral probity mourned by Livy. According to the satirist, a pure distillation of these ancient virtues could be found in the everyday meals that the humble tenant farmer eats, or so he would have us believe:

As a rule ... on a working day I would never eat
any more than a shank of smoked ham and a plate of greens.
But if friends arrived whom I hadn't seen for a long time,
or a neighbour dropped in for a friendly visit on a wet day
when there was nothing to do, we used to celebrate, not with fish
sent out from the town, but a chicken or kid, followed by dessert –
raisins taken down from the rafters with nuts and figs.[8]

6. An excellent discussion of the role of the satirist's persona can be found in W.S. Anderson, 'Roman satirists and Literary Criticism' in *Essays on Roman Satire*, (1982), pp. 3–10.

7. Gaius Maecenas, *c*.70–8B.C. He was patron to a number of poets, including Virgil and Propertius, and a close friend of the Emperor Augustus.

8. Horace, *Satire* 2.2.166–22.

In this deceptively simple passage, the satirist has achieved a complex set of objectives. He emphasises that country life, as embodied in diet, is governed by necessity and fellow-feeling. Hence he illustrates the distinction between the everyday (regularity of nature and habit), and the celebratory (the extraordinary contexualised by the ordinary). Before we are seduced by the idyll, however, what is a satirist doing in this territory, whom is he trying to seduce, and why does he want to make the seduction in the first place?

We can look for answers in the foods described by the farmer, the aptly named Ofellus.[9] Of course, everything is home-grown, even the celebratory stuff. In fact Ofellus goes out of his way to tell us there won't be fish. What, after all, could be less rural; first because it comes from the sea, but second, and more importantly, because fish are more often caught in the urban fish market. Thus we might deduce that his comments are aimed directly at a city-dwelling reader who has the freedom, and money, to take his urban eating habits to the country.

As food writing goes, this is not particularly rousing stuff. The country menu is no gastronomic evocation of the rural idyll. There's not a great deal of detail, and questions of preparation, seasoning and serving, for example, are not at the top of the agenda.[10] Instead our orientation comes from the literary context of the poem, rather than the culinary. This means that we should not imagine that Ofellus's meals as described by the satirist are accurate representations of what Roman country people ate. Where, for example, are the diverse vegetables, herbs, baked goods, grains and dairy products found in both the archaeological and literary record?[11] Where are the traces of regional Italian products and cookery? They aren't here because the satirist's

9. Ofellus, possibly from 'ofella' meaning 'mouthful', 'morsel', 'meatball'.

10. The same is true of the delicacies rejected by Ofellus in the earlier part of the poem. He talks rather blandly of 'delicious savours' and 'fine appearance', giving examples but not going into culinary detail. This does not, however, suggest a paucity of ingredients available to the Roman cook, or a restricted gastronomic vocabulary. See Andre, passim, and Flower and Rosenbaum, p. 19 on favourite Roman flavours.

11. The agricultural writers Varro and Columella, for example, list numerous crops and products cultivated and manufactured in Italy. These range from grains to vegetables and fruit, livestock and dairy products. The writers even provide some recipes, see Columella, for example on a range of home-produced cheeses, including varieties flavoured with pine kernals, applewood smoke, and thyme.

purposes are best served by a homogeneous, antiseptic view of the rustic idyll. For that reason food is chosen and moulded to evoke the harsh, but convivial and spiritually uplifting qualities of life away from the city (Rome). So, when the satirist says 'country', he means 'not city', and more specifically, 'not Rome'. And, when he describes country food and eating habits, he really means 'not dinner parties in Rome'.

Ofellus's meals therefore inhabit a place in the satirist's world of moral extremes. As constructed by the satirist, they provide one form of extremely partial exemplary material. Juvenal recognised the value of contrasting city and country eating habits and injected new life into the antithesis. In his eleventh satire he describes the perfect meal which he would like to serve up to his 'city-traumatised' friend Persicus.[12] The menu includes tender lamb 'innocent of grass' (unweaned), whose veins 'hold more milk than blood'. This will be accompanied by mountain asparagus and straw-packed eggs (in other words, eggs still warm from the hen), followed by Syrian pears and fragrant apples. Who's to say that such a meal could never have been put together? But to approach the satire in this way would be missing the point entirely. The really important thing is that all items on the menu are guaranteed to be gastronomically seductive, yet morally safe. The kid, the mother hen, even the serving boy fresh from the country evoke innocence and family virtue. The whole menu is set against the debauchery and loose morals of the public parts of the city but, cleverer still, this country meal, this emotional therapy, will be eaten in the heart of the city, within earshot of the Circus in Rome.[13]

So we see the country and city meal as concentrated metaphor. The country meal contains everything that is lacking in Rome: a sense of proportion about what really matters in life; a proper understanding of the physical and emotional necessities; dare one say it, the holistic approach. Of course this does not mean that Horace and Juvenal wanted to live like an Ofellus. Far from it, satire simply provides a license to be unrealistically idealistic, sanctimonious, bigoted even. First and foremost, the satirists like to show off to their audience; they like to entertain with a carefully managed display of exaggeration and righteous indignation.

12. Juvenal, *Satire* 11.65–76.   13. Ibid., 197–8.

Punishment for gluttons

If, as the satirists would have us believe, moral probity lives in a farm-house, depravity has to be found lurking in the city. This will come as no surprise to the modern reader. Today, ancient Rome is synonymous with the orgy and the banquet. 'Everyone knows' that Romans threw up at dinner so that they could increase their intake, or that emperors ate larks' tongues. Common sense alone suggests that most people couldn't afford to eat like that, nor could the market sustain those kinds of habits, yet the *Quo Vadis* version of Rome persists, and the satirists have had their fair share of complicity in developing that particular myth. Their accounts of city dinner parties are designed to epitomise everything that is misguided about the conspicuous consumption of food.[14] They illustrate through carefully contrived paradigms the cock-eyed rationales and systems of etiquette of so-called elegant dining. The point is that while the satirists are telling their audience that all Rome dines off seven courses a night, any reader worth his or her salt knows full well that it does not.

The satirist, however, is probably writing for an audience that has firsthand and not unfavourable experience of the good things of city life, including the pleasures of the table. How else would they get his gastro-jokes? This means that he has to focus his criticism carefully, laying into those who love to intellectualize food, and who seek to elevate themselves socially through what they serve at table – when, of course, they should be making their mark in literature or public service, or through plain good breeding. The upshot is that the idea of dining well is left unchallenged. In fact if good (not elegant) food is left to those who deserve it, it will help to maintain the *status quo* and control the flow of upwardly mobile individuals. The satirists therefore get a lot of mileage out of constructing disastrous dinner parties and gastro-nomic 'events' in their poems. In each case the gastronome, host or guest labours under a (socially) fatal misapprehension: food is impor-tant in its own right.

---

14. Not half as much, however, as the description of a massive banquet thrown by Trimalchio to be found in Petronius's *Satyricon*. This piece belongs to the imported prose genre Menippean satire, not to be confused with home-grown Roman verse satire.

Horace's makes particularly ingenious use of this device. The two gastronomes he describes are figures of fun. The first is Catius, whose words of gastronomic 'wisdom' form the body of *Satire* 2.4 as he recounts to the satirist the contents of a lecture he has just heard. The subject is the proper way to dine, from eggs to apples, from hors d'oeuvres to 'After Eights', as it were. After promising life-changing philosophy to rival the Greeks he manages to deliver drivel. He shows that he is neither coherent on gastronomy nor able to discern the differences between the culinary, the gastronomic and the dietary. He isn't helped by the fact that he is brimming with self-congratulation and the consciousness of his own place in the gastronomic scene. Catius's subject may be the art of elegant dining but he is described in terms that for a Roman reader would be reminiscent of the philosopher, the comedy cook, and the doctor. This underscores the satirist's point about the over-intellectualisation of food.

A neat dramatic twist comes in the gradual revelation of the depths of Catius's gaucherie. At first the signs are that he is the genuine article, an expert. That is until he gets into the swing of his subject:

When serving eggs remember to serve the long variety,
for they are superior in flavour to the round, and their whites are whiter;
(the shells, you see, are harder, and contain a male yolk).[15]

Any well-read Roman reader knows that this is Aristotle on natural history, but lifted and skewed.[16] Moreover, where Aristotle was concerned with natural observation as a means to enlightenment, Catius uses 'science-speak' to validate his bizarre culinary ideas. Through the satire, he publicly proclaims himself an innovator, as if he had given the original lecture. While he may value life on the cutting edge of culinary research, the satirist makes it clear that his innovatory fervour is quite beyond the pale in the context of deeply traditional and hierarchical Roman society.[17] Innovation, it seems, has to be tried and tested by the rigorous standards of those who understand the proper set of values.

15. Horace, *Satire* 2.4.12–14.   16. Aristotle, *Natural Histories* 6.2.559a.

17. Compare Brillat-Savarin on the influence of the 'gastronomized' middle classes, 'Cooks did battle with genealogists, and although the Dukes did not wait to take their leave before they made fun of their hosts, they had come as guests, and their presence was proof of their defeat.' *The Philosopher in the Kitchen.* (Harmondsworth: Penguin, 1970), p.145.

Horace's second and final book of satires climaxes with the story of another character mined from the same vein as Catius: Nasidienus. The satirist bumps into his friend, the comic poet Fundanius. 'How did you enjoy your swell party chez Nasidienus?', he asks. 'I've never had such a swell time in all my life', comes the reply, an ambiguous one as it turns out. What follows is Fundanius's description of the outrageous dinner served up by Nasidienus to a collection of cultural bigwigs, including Horace's patron Maecenas.[18]

The key to the satire is the characterisation of the nouveau riche host through the food that he chooses. In his supposedly elegant fare we see an eloquent depiction of his mores:

'First there was boar from Lucania, which our gracious host kept telling us was caught in a soft, Southerly breeze'.

This opening onslaught is ripe with meaning for the Roman reader of Horace's satire. Boar had a special place at the *cena*. It should have been a *pièce de résistance*, served as the high point of the meal, certainly not as an appetiser. By putting the boar first, Nasidienus is not only making an innovation, he is turning his back on the traditional meaning of the meal. He is also rejecting the idea of the convivial centre-piece,[19] and declaring that his dinner will start where normal, elegant meals leave off. 'Whatever next?', the guests are supposed to wonder admiringly.

At this point Ofellus's words should be ringing in our ears:

Our ancestors used to say that boar should be eaten high,
not that they had no noses; they meant, I assume,
that it should be kept for a guest who was late, though it might go off.[20]

In Nasidienus's case, we see that the important issues are not taste *per se*, but non-gustatory qualities, such as provenance (Lucanian) and questions of pseudo-science ('caught in a Southerly breeze').[21] From this outrageous start, the satirist uses the poem to give substance to the full range of horrors committed in the name of gastronomy (not, one

18. The other guests include Viscus, and Varius, a writer of epic poetry. Horace has already told the reader in an earlier satire (1.10) that he holds these two, together with Fundanius, in high esteem.

19. Juvenal, *Satire* 1.140-1, boar as an animal designed for conviviality.

20. Horace, *Satire* 2.289-91.   21. Horace, *Satire* 2.8.6-7.

should add, gluttony). He describes a nightmare host giving a night-mare meal to some of Rome's celebrated intellectuals. We see the conflict of the 'cookish' versus the 'bookish' drawn up, literally on op-posite sides of the dinner table. The satirist describes a meal with nine diners, three per couch. He 'reports' in minute detail their conversa-tion, their actions, and even at times, their facial expressions. In short, he brings the dinner party dramatically and dynamically to life.

The condemnation of Nasidienus accumulates with every dish and every comment. The structural pattern of the meal is used to increase narrative tension. Each break in the dinner, for example, gives the guests a chance to goad their host and enhance the atmosphere of dysfunction. The crowning moment, gastronomically and dramati-cally speaking, comes when Nasidienus uses his power as host to di-vulge a secret: his recipe for sauce:

> 'Venafran oil (the first
> pressing of course), liquamen (from the guts of the Spanish mackerel),
> wine that is five years old, but from this side of the sea (this
> is to be added in the course of boiling; after boiling, Chian
> is better than anything else), white pepper, and one mustn't
> forget the vinegar, made from the fermented Methymnaeum grape.
> I pioneered the practice of boiling sharp elecampane
> and green rockets with the sauce. Curtillus uses sea urchins
> unwashed, for the liquor provided by the shellfish is better than brine'.
> As he spoke, the awning suspended above collapsed on the dish.[22]

Little wonder that the meal ends in disaster. Nasidienus has man-aged to break just about every guideline for proper dining laid down in the earlier satires. He is clearly more interested in the look, cost and curiosity value of his food, than in anything so mundane as nutrition or taste. Like Catius, he is designed to fail when assessed by reference to the standards explicitly laid out by the satirist. More than that, failure is the sole reason for the existence of the gastronome. His self-belief adds piquancy to his downfall, especially when described in terms of mock intellectual behaviour. But in Nasidienus's case there is an extra dimen-sion. Dining for him is a kind of performance. He needs the applause of the audience for what he considers a serious drama about profound

22. Ibid., 45–54.

questions. The satirist, of course, sees the meal rather as slapstick, or farce, in which the threat to the *status quo* (the upstart Nasidienus) is given enough rope to hang himself. Thus normality is first challenged, and then re-affirmed.

About a century later, the poet Juvenal was giving a new twist to the satirical depiction of eating matters. Not only did he follow the Horatian example in contrasting town with country, he carried on the tradition of discussing in narrative and discursive form fancy food in Rome, the elegant dinner, and the relationship of host and guest. In Juvenal, however, we do not hear the smug tones of the Horatian satirist. Instead he depicts wealthy hosts who do genuinely hold the social initiative.

One of the best examples is the ghastly Virro, a wealthy patron who uses what he serves as a means to widen the gulf that exists between him and his poor client guests. Juvenal's fifth satire sees the satirist reprimanding the wretched client Trebius for putting up with the indignities of a meal chez Virro. If Rome is a gastrocracy, Virro is right at the top of the heap. His wealth demands that he dole out favours in the form of a *cena*. At the meal the patron enjoys delicacies from exotic locations, served up to enhance their 'show-off' potential. Meanwhile the guests have to make do with foods that perfectly express what the patron thinks of them.[23]

Given the thesis, and the satirist's overheated imagination, the scope for the evocative description of food and dining is enormous. This does not, however, mean a bumper harvest of culinary or gastronomic detail. The boar, for example, served up by Virro is 'worthy of Meleager's sword'[24] rather than gamey, pungent, spicy, marinated in pineapple juice, or served with a loganberry *coulis*. Moreover, if a culinary term does arrive, it has to squeeze in amongst a barrage of allusions and indirect references:

The wine's so rough sheep-clippings wouldn't absorb it,
and turns the guests into raving madmen. At first

23. For example, 'Just get the size of that crayfish: it marks out a platter/ reserved for my lord. See the asparagus garnish/ heaped high around it, the peacocking tail that looks down/ on the other guests as it's brought in, borne aloft.' (80–3) and 'Virro is served with a lamprey: no finer specimen/ ever came from Sicilian waters' (101–2).

24. Juvenal, *Satire* 5.116–7.

it's only insults – but soon a regular battle
breaks out between you and the freedmen, cheap crockery flies
in all directions, you're slinging cups yourself
and mopping blood off with a crimsoned table napkin.[25]

The reference to sheep clippings first luridly dramatizes the wine and then takes it out of the gastronomic field altogether. The reader initially imagines qualities of viscosity, gaining some idea of what it might be like to drink this stuff. But then there is the reference to sheep clippings. Are we being transported to the shepherd's hut, or even into the doctor's surgery?[26] Then there is the battle that ensues. Thick red wine becomes blood. A dinner which is designed to delineate the gulf between rich and poor degenerates into a battle between the clients. Trebius, freeborn, would imagine that he is a rung higher up on the social ladder. Not so, however, in Virro's world, where his type will have to slug it out with former slaves. Meanwhile, Virro presides serenely over the chaos, quaffing a vintage that perfectly, albeit ironically, befits his position:

The wine that Virro, your host, is drinking has lain in its bottle
since the Consuls wore long hair: those grapes were trodden
during the Social Wars – yet never a glassful
will he send to a friend with heartburn. Tomorrow he'll choose
some other vintage, the best, a jar so blackened with smoke,
so ancient, that its source and date are illegible:
Such wine our Stoic martyrs would toss down, garlanded
on the birthday of Brutus or Cassius'.[27]

This description of wine tells us rather more about Virro than it does about top-quality wines. Of course we see that vintage is an issue. That is as far as it goes however. The wines date to the Social Wars[28] and the heroes of Republicanism, not for specific qualitative reasons, but in order to underline the raging social inequalities evident at Virro's table.

25. Ibid., 24–9.

26. Wool had a variety of medicinal uses, including plugging wounds. Given the context here, a fight, we are given an advance warning that it would be useful for staunching the flow of blood.

27. Juvenal, *Satire* 5.30–7.

28. 91–88B.C., Rome's Italian allies rose up against her to achieve enfranchisement.

Time after time the poem tells us that Virro can be likened to a king. But, for the Roman reader kingship has all sorts of negative connotations: despotism and corruption, to name two of them. True, his menu is fit for a king, but an imaginary menu for an imaginary king.[29]

Redefining dining

As we have already seen, the satirists draw for us a simplified moral and cultural map of the Roman view of the world. This is used to plot and explain the state of, for example, eating habits as they fit into a rigidly hierarchical and structured society. They give us a moral compass aligned to the moral superiority of Rome's rural past. Our key shows that foods can be good or bad, both nutritionally and in the wider ethical sense. More specifically, they can be shaded as being ancient or modern, rural or urban, Roman or foreign, natural or unnatural, simple or complex, sufficient or excessive (the list goes on). The destination is a point-blank rejection of gastronomy and culinary sophistication.

Food is clearly a gift to the genre. The satirists embraced the subject, and mined it for imagery, resonance, and allusion. The resulting satires about food in Horace and Juvenal are very different in tone and style, reflecting two very individual literary voices. Some shared features can be discerned, however, and some of these derive from what might be considered certain objective 'truths' of dining in the Roman world. For example, both satirists seem to share a belief that eating habits and food matters are schematised and defined by codes of practice and behaviour. They use these codes to provide a ready-made framework for the inversion and perversion which characterises the behaviour of the misguided gastronomes described by them. It seems that the more rulebound the subject, and the more aware the reader is of the proprieties, the more tempting it is to create anarchy. Therefore we see dinner party satires in which dysfunction is translated into farce; as in the case of the collapsing awning at Nasidienus's dinner, and the fight that breaks out between the guests when Virro entertains.

29. In the years immediately after its foundation (believed by the ancients to be in 753B.C.) Rome was supposed to have had seven kings. This period ended with the expulsion of Tarquinius Superbus in 510B.C. There followed the Republic which lasted until 27B.C. when Octavian became the Emperor Augustus.

The satirists also detect a fertile area of extra-gastronomic significance in the field of eating and dining. For example, they pack an enormous amount of allusion into their descriptions of the simplest foodstuff, making the satires vibrant and evocative. The accretion of this kind of information helps them in their biased exploration of the wider world of motives and behaviour. Thus we see the satirists looking at food and eating habits as an expression of group identity and organisation, and exploring these areas through schemes of images inspired by food, but relating to the larger social order. So, we see them building a complex and subtle characterisation of the individual (the satirist, Ofellus, Catius, Nasidienus, Trebius, Virro, Persicus etc.) as the microcosm of the group.

This aspect of satire enables the reader to consider the wider ramifications of food, eating and dining in the Rome at a certain period. However, the same proviso is necessary for dealing with the group, as with drawing conclusions about the individual. That is, Ofellus and Nasidienus did not exist. Nor should they be seen as fully paid-up members of major identifiable groups. However their behaviour is suggestive of a broad conflict, based on aspirations and reflected in attitudes to food.

The clearest area of conflict is that of the established hierarchical approach to entertaining and dining (the satirists, Maecenas, the past, Ofellus), versus the destabilizing food innovator (city, Catius, Nasidienus). Of course, it is the satirists' job to delineate and firm up the lines of conflict, but, in doing so they cover up the grey areas of overlap between the protagonists. The modern reader, of course, wants to examine the unwritten (the 'reality' which is common knowledge to the ancient reader).

One grey area suggested but glossed over by the satirists is the apparent paradox that elegant eating habits, and a broadening of the range of foodstuffs available, were part and parcel of the notion of civilisation and empire. But they do not fit in with those very qualities upon which, according to the myth, the Empire was founded: austerity and self-control. Livy had already said as much when he depicted luxurious habits as one of the nasty by-products of conquest. He has also implied that contemporary Rome was at the top of a luxury curve which started with the victory in Asia.

We get a hint of the dynamics of the paradox when the satirist confronts the gastronome. When we see the likes of Catius and Nasidienus, the importance of socializing as a means to participation in society becomes clear. These are people who want to make useful social contacts, but who misinterpret where the *status quo* resides. Thus Catius, who assigns to food (and to himself) an importance it does not deserve, is marginalized, rather than integrated, for being interested in innovation. Much of the same could be said about Nasidienus, who believes that he is at the centre of affairs in general by being a gastronomic innovator, and having the clout to invite influential guests. The reader knows that he is in fact a complete outsider for that very reason. The message seems to be leave innovation on the margins. The channels through which new ideas are integrated into the orthodoxy are opened only from the inside.

The satirist therefore seems to be describing his gastronome in a kind of 'Catch 22'. Nasidienus fails to break into society because the more he tries, the worse he becomes; Trebius wants to make an impression on the patron Virro, but is separated from him by the socially divisive possibilities of gastronomy in a plutocratic society. The satirist therefore seems to be using the *cena* as a model for participation in society. In the food poems, he presents us with the ideal and the corrupt version. This explains why the apparently isolated rustic life is in fact to be recommended for its commensality and conviviality:

When shall I see that place in the country, when shall I be free
to browse among the writers of old, to sleep or idle,
drinking in a blissful oblivion of life's troubles?
When shall I sit down to a plate of beans, Pythagoras' kinsmen,
and cabbage with just some fat bacon to make it tasty?
Ah, those evenings and dinners. What heaven! My friends and I
have our meal at my own fireside. Then, after making an offering,
I hand the rest to the cheeky servants. Every guest
drinks from whatever glass he likes, big or small.[30]

Similarly, Juvenal's satirist, while advocating the quiet life in the heart of the city, nonetheless measures modern dysfunctional Rome against the city as it was before the foreigners got to it, that is, a highly participative society:

30. Horace, *Satire* 2.6.65–8.

Once as a special treat on feast-days, they'd bring down
a side of salt-pork from its rack, or a flitch of bacon
for some relative's birthday, and maybe a little fresh meat
if they'd run to a sacrifice. You'd find some kinsman who'd been
three times consul, perhaps who'd commanded armies or held
the Dictatorship, knocking off work an hour or two early
on such an occasion, trudged down from the hillside
with his mattock over his shoulder.[31]

This is what might be called having one's bacon and eating it. Almost perversely, this escapist rustic fantasy is one of the luxuries of belonging to a rigidly organised urban society. The satirists are therefore using their poetry to bring about a confrontation between the values of a hierarchical society (validated by tradition) and those of an innovatory society based on plutocratic values. While the latter may have the vestiges of a hierarchy, it is by the satirists' standards inherently fragmentary and potentially destabilising. The only 'solution' is to ignore the fact of gastronomic integration (your audience already knows how that works) and offer an alternative participative society of fake 'isolationists'. Therefore each model of society, the corrupt and the ideal, is precisely the opposite of what it seems, especially in terms of participation. High fashion and urban habits bring isolation and rejection to the gastronome host. Self-imposed 'exile', however, brings conviviality and a confirmation of one's place in the orthodox hierarchy.

Finally, then, Roman verse satire's pool of material seems to be firmly based in the 'real' world of acting, re-acting, interacting, and sensing. Subjects like eating are its bread and butter, as it were. Yet, on closer inspection, we see that the satirist really operates in the realm of ideas. He deliberately creates confrontation in order to see what happens when black meets white. For that reason, in some eyes his poetry may even have a cathartic function. The result is a concentrated mix of polarised images and examples, with little grey between. For anyone trying to deduce what Romans really thought of food, and did with it, this is an obstacle. Could the satirists really have been happy with eking out a frugal living from the earth? Did elegant hosts really care whether their boar was caught in a soft southerly breeze? These are questions which have dogged the analysis of Roman verse satire. In asking them

31. Juvenal, *Satire* 11.83–90.

we fail to grasp what satire really can tell us. It is worth closing with Horace on Horace. Should we be thinking of taking his austere intentions, and any of his other opinions about food seriously, there's no evidence that he did:

'And when you feel
like having a laugh, call on me, I'm fat, I'm fine!
one of Epicurus' sleek, well-cared for swine'.[32]

Notes

This article has only been able to touch on some of the major themes in the food satires of Horace and Juvenal, and as such has not been able to convey much of the wit, irony and poetic intelligence of the satirists. A reading of the following should redress the balance:

Horace, *Satires* 2.2; 2.4; 2.6; and 2.8. (*Satires* 1.6, 1.10 and 2.1 will give a better idea of the satirist's feelings about the genre, and of the literary and historical context).

Juvenal, *Satires* 4, 5, 11 (and 15 for those with strong stomachs. *Satire* 1 gives the satirist's explanation of why he has chosen the genre).

I have made no reference to other Roman satirists, notably Lucilius and Persius. They both deal with the imagery of eating, and the role of dining in their work. The former survives only in frustrating, fragmentary form. The latter has a vivid imagination when it comes to the physical process of eating and digestion, and his six satires are well worth a trawl (see Rudd in Bibliography).

Bibliography

For ease of reference all quotations from the satirists have been drawn from the Penguin translations (except where marked):

N. Rudd, *Horace: Satires and Epistles. Persius: Satires* (1979)
P. Green, *Juvenal: the Sixteen Satires* (1974)

32. Horace, *Epistles* 1.17

Also quoted:

S. P. Bovie, *Satires and Epistles of Horace* (Chicago, 1959)

The following verse translation is also recommended for combining accuracy with exuberance:

S. Robinson, *Sixteen Satires Upon the Ancient Harlot* (Manchester, 1983)

There are no really good general introductions to Roman food in English. There is, however, one very thorough French treatment of the subject:

J. Andre, *L'alimentation et la cuisine a Rome* (Paris, 1981)

The following might provide some helpful background to the culinary and social aspects of cooking and dining:

J. H. D'Arms, 'Control, Clientship and Clientela' in *Echos du monde classique* 28 (1984), pp.327–38
– 'The Roman Convivium and the Idea of Equality' in O. Murray, ed., *Sympotica. A Symposium on the Symposium* (Oxford, 1990)
B. Flower and E. Rosenbaum, *The Roman Cookery Book. A Critical Translation of the Art of Cooking by Apicius* (London, 1958)